The Wine Lover's Guide to France

The Wine Lover's
— Guide to —
FRANCE

MICHAEL BUSSELLE

Contents

Author's Introduction

Over the past two years I have spent five months in and driven almost 50,000 kilometres through the vineyards of France, taking photographs and collecting information for this book. The experience has provided me with some of the most enjoyable and exciting times in my life. On my travels I have felt – although on a more modest and less exotic level – a little how I imagine a real explorer might feel in the more far-flung places of the globe. Even for those intrepid beings there are increasingly fewer places left to explore as the world of the Macdonald's burger takes over. But rural France remains as unselfconscious as ever; for me the yellow Michelin map is as exciting and inviting as a chart of the South Sea islands.

In many countries, the tourist is regarded as a necessary intruder, at best tolerated but more likely resented and exploited. Travelling through the French vineyards, however, you are less a tourist and more a fellow-enthusiast, sharing the locals' interest and pleasure in the wines they make with such skill. Wherever I have travelled in the wine regions my interest has prompted a genuinely friendly and helpful response. Busy *vignerons* have struggled patiently with my inadequate grasp of their language to explain which grape types are used, how long a wine takes to mature, or simply how to get to the next village.

You do not need to be a wine lover to enjoy the countryside which produces it, but it is a simple fact that the wine-growing regions of France are among the most beautiful in the country, and the Routes des Vins are often the most scenic roads. Even at the height of the holiday season they are often deserted, with only the occasional *vigneron* driving a tractor or a battered Renault to his vineyard. The pleasures of this countryside satisfy many different interests. It is certainly a photographer's paradise – a recommendation which, over the years, I admit I've learned to treat with scepticism. But the plains and hillsides patterned with vines are a delight for those with an eye for landscape, the villagers and *vignerons* are sometimes so archetypal that you might think they were bit-players in a film and the villages and châteaux are a treasure-trove of architectural gems. And it includes perfect country for walking and cycling, while, for those with a love of nature, there is a fascinating variety of wildlife and plantlife to observe. Last, and certainly not least, there is no better place to enjoy good food and wine.

To the casual traveller driving through, perhaps *en route* to a holiday resort, one vineyard or wine-growing region may seem much like another. In fact the opposite is true: each region has its own quite unique character and atmosphere. Even adjacent regions can be markedly different: the Chalonnais has little in common with the Côte d'Or on its north edge or with the Maconnais to the south.

Friends often ask me which regions and villages I have enjoyed most. This is very difficult to answer objectively since the pleasure I derive from a place is often partly the result of having taken a photograph I'm particularly pleased with, having met some agreeable people or, I must admit, having had a particularly good meal or bottle of wine. However although it would be a hard choice to make, if I were going purely for a holiday I think that I would choose Alsace, Beaujolais, Roussillon and Languedoc. Villages which I have found particularly charming include some of the obvious places like Riquewihr, St Emilion, Sancerre and Roussillon, but also a host of less well-known places, such as St Guilhem-le-Désert in the Languedoc, Caromb in the Vaucluse, Entrecasteaux in Provence and Arbois in the Jura.

My travels have also resulted in a much greater enjoyment of wine. When I choose a bottle of wine now I can visualize the vineyards and villages it came from and often my experiences and pleasure in a particular region are recalled quite vividly by simply reading a label. I also have to admit that I have become something of a wine snob and have become quite possessive about the bottles I have brought home from my travels, opening them only on special occasions with someone who I feel will really appreciate them. I say something of a snob because my 'cellar' does not contain prized vintages of Château Lafite-Rothschild but little-known wines from even less-known villages and vineyards, usually quite inexpensive. Much of the pleasure of drinking these wines is gained because I have actually discovered them myself and because the fun of tasting and buying wine from the *vigneron* who produced it seems somehow to make it taste even better.

This book reflects the extreme enjoyment I've experienced in compiling it. I hope it will stimulate others to follow at least some of my footsteps.

Michael Busselle

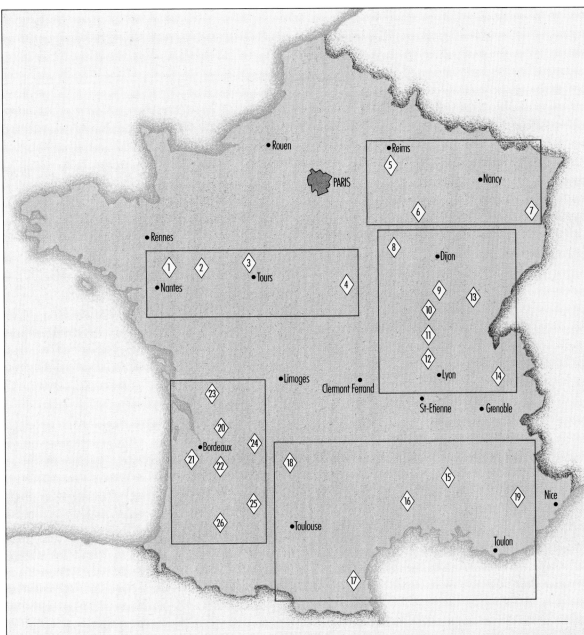

Map of France with town labels: Rouen, PARIS, Reims, Nancy, Rennes, Nantes, Tours, Dijon, Limoges, Clermont Ferrand, St-Etienne, Grenoble, Lyon, Bordeaux, Toulouse, Toulon, Nice

Tour numbers shown on map: 1, 2, 3, 4, 5, 6, 7, 8, 9, 10, 11, 12, 13, 14, 15, 16, 17, 18, 19, 20, 21, 22, 23, 24, 25, 26

Notes on using the maps

Each of the five regions (shown above) is also located on a small map at the beginning of each section. In addition, each wine tour has its own map – taken from the Michelin 1:200 000 series – on which the scale is 1 centimetre to 2 kilometres. All the towns and villages mentioned in the *routes des vins* are indicated by a small blue square – unless the village is too small to appear on the map. Long tours are shown on a series of maps, and the point at which the tour continues on to the next map is indicated by a yellow arrow.

KEY TO MAP SYMBOLS

Secluded hotel or restaurant	▣	Communications tower or mast	
Campsite	▲	Church or chapel	
Petrol station	⚠	Cemetery or wayside cross	
Quarry or mine		Castle or ruins	
Factory or waterworks		Statue or building	
Fort or lighthouse		Windmill	
Hospital	✚	Forester's lodge	M F
Emergency telephone		Forest or wood	

Tourist attractions

Scenic route	
Viewing table	
Panoramic view	
View point	
Château	
Church or chapel	
Ruins	
Other place of interest	▲

Tour number

Tour number — Map number

Tour continues on next map

Tour continued from previous map

7

About Wine

For anyone with a love of France or the countryside exploring the vineyards and wine villages of France is a wonderful way to spend a holiday. For the wine lover it is even more so as it involves the discovery of new and interesting wines and provides a look behind the scenes which, in turn, can enhance the enjoyment of wine even further. Travelling in wine country can be even more rewarding if your knowledge of wine goes beyond simply reading labels, pulling corks and drinking it, wonderful as that is.

The making of wine is a fascinating combination of tradition, technology, craft, art, patience and a little magic. It is a natural process. The grape contains the means for fermentation, the transformation of sugar into alcohol: the juice contains sugar and acid, the skin contains tannin, and the bloom upon the skin provides the yeasts enzymes that trigger the change. The only outside help that is needed is for the grape to be crushed and left to ferment in a suitable atmosphere and at the right temperature.

Of course, it is not quite as simple as this when wine is made 'to order' in vast commercial quantities. Then, every stage of the wine-making is very carefully controlled, from the type of vines that are planted to the length of time the wine matures in the bottle. Some help, such as temperature control and additives, is given to aid fermentation and to guarantee the quality of the final product. With the cheaper, more anonymous wines, this can happen to such a degree that technology almost takes over from the natural process.

In the huge Caves Co-opératives the fermentation processes take place in enormous steel or concrete tanks and the resulting wine is filtered and blended to make a standard product and to reduce the length of time between the harvest and sale of the wine. However, in the best vineyards, where the finest wines are made, interference is kept to an absolute minimum. The grapes are crushed and the must fermented in wooden casks, then the wine is left in a cellar, where the ambient temperature controls the speed of the process, and allowed to clear in its own good time, with only minimal help. It is then racked off into other wooden casks, leaving the lees behind, to age for a period of years before being bottled, then left to age even further before it is mature enough to drink.

When you consider that the time-span between

Above: Poppies sprinkling a vineyard in Sauternes
Left: Harvesting in Fronsac in the Northern Bordelais

manicured vines, pruning, weeding, spraying and finally harvesting, with a dedication that owes more to love and pride than to purely commercial considerations.

The wine-buying guides at the end of each section of this book are categorized by designation so it is useful to understand this system of classification when comparing wines. The designations follow an ascending order of importance and can be used as a rough rule for price and quality, although there is considerable overlap in both these factors between the designations.

Vin de Table
This is the most basic wine type within the European Economic Community. It invariably comes from the bulk wine-producing co-operatives and is allowed to be a blend of any wine from any year, region, grape-type, or country within the EEC. Blends from more than one country of the EEC are required to state this on the label. The Vin de Table label may not indicate any specific geographical region, grape type or vintage.

Vin de Pays
These are superior, promoted Vins de Table from specified districts and may show grape-type (if one single variety is used) and vintage on the label.

VDQS
This is the standard abbreviation for Vin Délimité de Qualité Supérieure, the designation given to wines produced in specified districts from approved grape types. Each wine must pass a tasting panel test each year to qualify for the designation. VDQS wines may show a vintage and a grape-type on the label.

planting a vine and having a fine wine ready for the table can be as much as twenty years it is no wonder that good wines tend to be expensive. A vine is capable of production about three years after planting but it will not begin to give its best until it is about ten years old. It can go on improving in quality for up to eighty years, although the quantity of wine produced diminishes as it ages. In every area of France, vine growers have to take into account, the climate, the soil and even, ultimately, the wine-buying public, before choosing and planting their vines, so it is hardly surprising that in the best vineyards the vines are given more attention and care than prize blooms in a flower garden: all through the year the *vignerons* can be seen out in the regimented rows of pampered and

Appellation Contrôlée
This designation, usually abbreviated as AC and sometimes known as *Appellation d'Origine Contrôlée* (or AOC), accounts for the top 20 per cent of French wine. The wines have to come from designated vineyard areas, from permitted grape varieties, and be vinified in a specified manner. The basic or generic ACs cover wide areas (eg Bordeaux), but smaller more specific ACs may exist within them. The AC system is controlled by the Institut National des Appellations d'Origine (INAO).

Wines are promoted up the scale from Vin de Pays to Appellation Contrôlée after a period of many years of continuous merit and successful parliamentary lobbying.

NORTH–WEST FRANCE

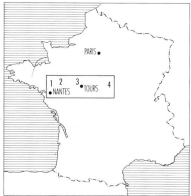

Set in lush meadows, beside ancient châteaux, there is some justification to the claim that the vineyards of North-West France are among the most beautiful in the world. There are four distinctive wine regions. The Pays Nantais, near the sea, produces Muscadet, a classic white wine. In Anjou-Saumur (left, the Château of Saumur) there are an abundance of flowery rosés and sparkling whites. In adjacent Touraine, there are no fewer than eleven Appellation Contrôlée wines, while the villages of Pouilly and Sancerre produce two of France's greatest white wines. The sea and the river dominate the cuisine of the region, and wine, food and scenery harmonize to perfection.

Wine Tour Nº 1
THE PAYS NANTAIS

The medieval keep of Oudon overlooking vineyards by the Loire

The most westerly vineyards of the Loire lie to the south of the city of Nantes, quite close to where the great river begins to widen into the estuary before it flows out into the Atlantic. The vine has been cultivated here since the time of the Roman occupation. The area's proximity to river and sea transport meant that a thriving wine trade grew up over the centuries. During the seventeenth century the Dutch were enthusiastic customers; they were exacting too, always wanting more and better quality wines. Much of the wine made here was red and it was not until a catastrophic winter in 1709, when the sea itself froze and most of the vines were destroyed, that white wine began to be made in any quantity.

The wines
The disaster was a blessing in disguise. The *vignerons* decided to replant their vineyards with a white grape that was more frost resistant than the black they had been using. The grape, Melon de Bourgogne, became known locally as the Muscadet; the wine made from it, although generally inexpensive, is recognized as one of the classic whites of France. *Muscadet de Sèvre-et-Maine* was awarded an Appellation Contrôlée in 1926. It is a crisp, dry wine, and is the perfect accompaniment to the seafood and shellfish found in the region.

The vineyards of Muscadet extend south and east of Nantes, but the most highly acclaimed wines are made around the villages to the south-east of the city. They take their name from the two rivers that traverse this countryside – the Sèvre and the Maine. The best Muscadet de Sèvre-et-Maine comes from the regions of the towns of Vallet and St Fiacre. *Muscadet des Coteaux de la Loire* is produced in vineyards on both banks of the Loire. Much of the Muscadet you will see is called *Muscadet-sur-Lie;* this is very slightly *pétillant*, a mere tingle on the palate. The term *'sur lie'* means that the wine is left to drain naturally after fermentation while still in contact with the lees (the sediment of the must), rather than being racked off and filtered into a fresh cask or container; this causes a small amount of carbon dioxide to be retained after bottling, creating the very slight fizziness.

Another notable dry white wine is produced in the Pays Nantais region. *Gros Plant*, which has the designation VDQS, is made from the Folle Blanche grape and the area of production is much wider than the Muscadet region, extending from the Atlantic coast to the south of the Loire estuary. It is also made *'sur lie'. Coteaux d'Ancenis* wines are produced in the vineyards around the town of Ancenis, on the north bank of the Loire. They are mainly red or rosé, with some white, and are also classified VDQS. In addition, some Vins de Pays are made in the region: *Vin de Pays des Marches de Bretagne, Vin de Pays de Rètz* and *Vin de Pays des Fiefs Vendéens*.

The cuisine

The sea is a strong influence on the cuisine of the Pays Nantais. The most spectacular dish that you will see – and one on most menus in the area – is *plateau de fruits de mer*, a tempting selection of shellfish fresh from the sea – winkles, mussels, crab, langoustines, tiny brown shrimps and clams – served on ice with wedges of lemon and freshly ground black pepper. All you need to complete the feast is a glass of Muscadet or Gros Plant. At Sunday lunchtimes, you'll often see restaurants full of French families consuming dishes of *fruits de mer*. It is quite a sight, and usually it will be well into the afternoon before they are ready for the next course.

Coquilles St Jacques, the plump scallops that come from the deep, cold waters of the Atlantic, are often served *gratinéed* in a local white wine and cream sauce;

they are also delicious served as a *brochette* in which halved or quartered scallops are threaded on to a skewer with tiny mushrooms and pieces of bacon and grilled. *Palourdes farcies* are freshly opened clams on the half shell, which have been stuffed with shallots, parsley, chives, butter and breadcrumbs, then grilled – a marine version of *escargots*. Grilled or poached fish is often served with *beurre blanc à la Nantaise*, a frothy sauce made from shallots, butter and Muscadet.

The Route des Vins *Michelin maps 63 and 67*
Ancenis, situated on the north bank of the Loire, and boasting a tenth-century château which was partly destroyed in 1624, is a good place to start exploring the Pays Nantais vineyards. The town was a busy port during the eighteenth century but is now known for its pig market and its wine trade. It is worth visiting the large Cave Co-opérative situated on the main road just to the east of Ancenis.

You can set off along the Route des Vins by crossing the suspension bridge to the village of Liré, where there is a museum dedicated to Joachim du Bellay, the

Flourishing vineyards at the village of La Varenne

sixteenth-century poet who was born here. Continue westwards along the D 751 to the small wine village of Drain and then to Champtoceaux, an attractive town set high up on the hillside above the Loire. Along the edge of the hill behind the church, there is a small park with lovely views over the river below. From Champtoceaux the road winds down to the riverside, a pleasant spot for a picnic or a stroll. The road climbs again, providing some sweeping views over the vineyards to the Loire and the northern bank of the river, and then continues to the village of la Varenne. The Château de la Varenne, a large elegant mansion set in a wooded park, has a *caveau* where visitors are welcome to taste the wine.

The route continues through the village of la Chapelle-Basse-Mer, notable for its lofty church spire, to the important wine town of le Loroux-Bottereau. From here the wine route continues along a very pleasant road, the D 307, past Moulin-du-Pré, where a number of ancient windmills are to be seen on top of the vine-clad hill. Drive up to the oldest one – which has a cross mounted on it – where the views over the vineyards are quite breathtaking. The route continues through the small wine villages of le Landreau and la Chapelle-Heulin to Vallet, which is known for its wine market, held each year in March. There is a Maison du Vin here where you can taste and buy wines from 40 different *vignerons* and a lively market takes place in the church square on Sundays. The Route des Vins follows the D 763 to the small but important wine village of Mouzillon, distinguished by its Gallo-Roman bridge, and then on to Clisson, a very picturesque small town with a ruined château, an ancient covered market that is still in use, narrow streets lined with old houses, a fourteenth-century church and an impressive viaduct spanning the river Maine. There is a tasting cellar next to the covered market.

A few kilometres north of Clisson, on the N 149, is Pallet, an important wine town where a number of *vignerons* and *négociants* invite visitors to sample their wines. There was a fortress erected by the dukes of Brittany here once; now you will have to content yourself with a picnic on the gentle banks of the river Sèvre. Crossing the river just beyond Pallet you come to the village of Monnières. Nearby is the old mill of la Minière, surrounded by vineyards. The view is superb – it is claimed that ten church steeples can be seen from here. One of these is in the next small

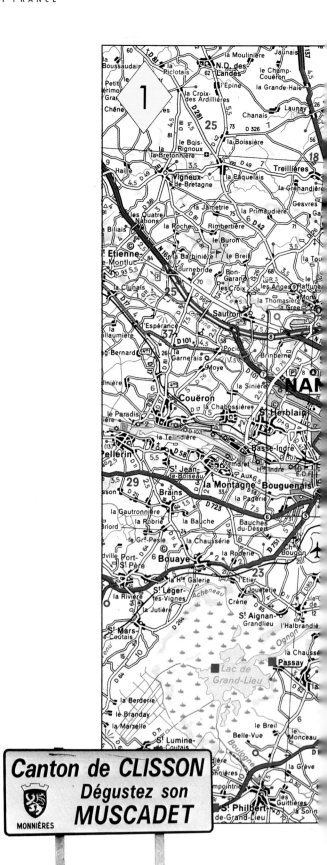

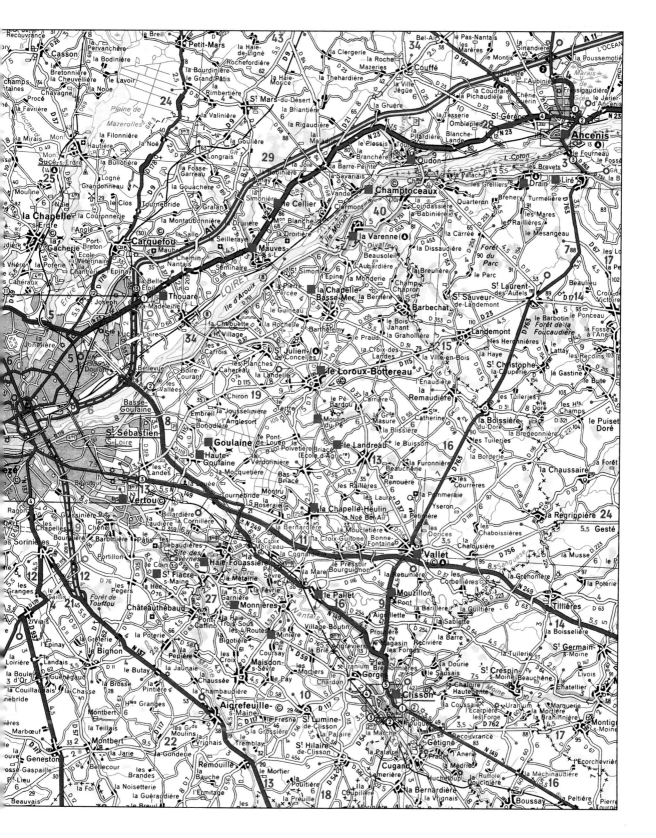

village, St Fiacre-sur-Maine, where the Byzantine-style church tower soars up high above the vineyards. This is one of the most highly reputed wine communities in the Pays Nantais, and there is a greater proportion of land given over to vines than anywhere else in France. If you are in the area at the end of September it is worth taking a short detour to la Haie-Fouassière, which holds a convivial wine fair at this time every year.

The next wine town, Vertou, on the outskirts of Nantes, is a lively, medium-sized place; there is an attractive riverside promenade and plenty of opportunities to taste and buy the wines of the region. Vertou is to the east of the Lac de Grand-Lieu – you can reach its shore through the village of Passay. It is a large and remote lake fringed with reeds and willowy trees; a small fleet of curious black-tarred, flat-bottomed boats fish the lake for *sandre* (like a large perch), pike, bream and eels. I watched a fisherman unload two enormous *sandres*, 10 or 12 kilos each, and a basket of plump bream into a perforated keeping-box half-submerged in the water before punting his small

The wine Château de Goulain (top) near the Lac de Grand Lieu (above left) where there is an abundant supply of sandre and bream. Eels, too, are caught in practical but oddly shaped nets (above). They are considered a great delicacy in the region

craft out to the lake for another sortie. The nearby town of St Philbert-de-Grand-Lieu is an important production area for Gros Plant and there is a tasting kiosk on the edge of the town.

Returning to Vertou you take the D 74 towards the village of Haute-Goulaine. On the outskirts is the magnificent Château de Goulaine, which dates from the fifteenth century. You can taste the château's own wine and take a guided tour of the building. From here, cross over the Loire to Thouaré-sur-Loire and continue through the wine villages of Mauves and le

Cellier (which has an annual wine fair at the end of September too) to the riverside town of Oudon, dominated by an enormous medieval keep – if you brave the climb to the top you'll be rewarded with a panoramic view of the Loire valley. The wine villages of Couffé and St Géréon complete the circuit back to Ancenis.

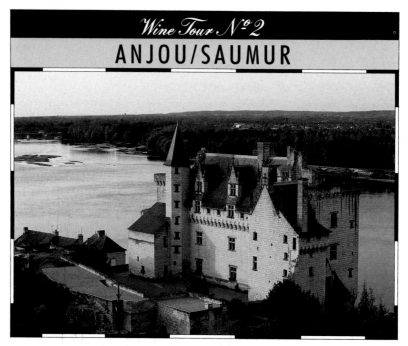

Wine Tour Nº 2
ANJOU/SAUMUR

The dominating Château de Montsoreau on the banks of the Loire

A little further along the Loire to the east are the towns of Saumur and Anjou. The main wine-growing region here is situated to the south of the river between the two towns. Vines have been grown here for well over 1,000 years and the wine was widely exported, much of it to London, especially after Henry Plantagenet, Count of Anjou, succeeded to the English throne in 1154. From the Middle Ages right up until last century, the Loire was an important waterway and the export trade continued to flourish; the Dutch, as in the Pays Nantais were major wine customers and to a certain degree exercized control over its production.

The wines

This relatively small area produces a considerable variety of wines. The most widely known are the rosés, most particularly the sweetish *Rosé d'Anjou*, made mainly from the Groslot grape variety; its popularity has declined somewhat recently because of the general trend away from rosés and to dry wines. *Cabernet d'Anjou*, another rosé made here, is generally considered to be superior; it can be either semi-sweet or dry. *Rosé de Loire* is quite a dry wine; Gamay and Pinot Noir grapes are used in its production. Finally, there is *Cabernet de Saumur*, a rosé similar to Cabernet d'Anjou but a little drier and paler in colour.

Méthode champenoise wines – *Saumur Mousseux* or *Saumur d'Origine* and *Anjou Mousseux* – are also made in this region, those of Saumur being particularly well known. Much of the wine is stored in vast caverns and tunnels carved into the tufa (coarse rock) cliffs near Saumur, very much like those of Champagne itself. These wines are made from a variety of grapes, including the Chenin Blanc, Chardonnay, Sauvignon, Groslot, Pinot Noir and Gamay. Another sparkling wine found in the region is *Crémant de Loire*, and *pétillant* wines are also made.

The region's white wines also offer some very interesting varieties, those from *Savennières* for example, produced in a few vineyards on the north bank of the Loire just to the west of Angers. Highly alcoholic, the wines are dry and fresh with a lovely bouquet reminiscent of honeysuckle. There are two additional separate appellations within this tiny region: *Coulée de Serrant* and *La Roche-aux-Moines*, both capable of considerable ageing. White wines are also made in the Layon valley, south of the Loire. The appellation is *Coteaux du Layon*; it is a sweet wine made from the Chenin Blanc grape, capable of considerable ageing, and often served chilled as an aperitif. Within this region are two individual appellations, *Quarts de Chaume* and *Bonnezeaux*, both sweet, fruity, white wines. An appellation from the region around the small river Aubance is *Coteaux de l'Aubance*; these wines are mainly white, but red and rosé wines are also made here. *Anjou-Coteaux de la Loire*, from vineyards to the north of the river, is a white wine, either dry or semi-dry. There are also dry white wines produced under the appellations *Anjou Blanc* and *Saumur Blanc*.

Red wines are also made in the region of both Anjou and Saumur from the Cabernet Franc, Cabernet Sauvignon and Pineau d'Aunis grapes. The appellations are *Saumur Rouge, Anjou Rouge* and *Saumur-Champigny*, the latter being a particularly appealing wine of rich ruby colour reminiscent of violets.

The cuisine

The cusine of Anjou-Saumur is very similar to that of other regions of the Loire. Freshwater fish is abundant; *alose* (shad), trout, salmon, *brochet* (pike), *sandre* and *anguilles* (eels) are found on most menus in the region, usually grilled or poached with a white wine and cream sauce or a *beurre blanc* (which is a local recipe), or made into a *bouilleture*, a stew with eels. Eels are also used to make pâtés and *terrines*. *Ecrevisses à la nage* are freshwater crayfish in the shell cooked in a *court-bouillon* flavoured with tarragon and usually served cold with mayonnaise. I have also tasted a wonderful light, creamy soup called *veloutée d'écrevisses* delicately flavoured with *écrevisses* and saffron in one of the many riverside restaurants to be found along the banks of the Loire. The area is renowned for its excellent poultry, beef and, most notably, pork, which is made into *charcuterie* such as *rillettes* and *andouilles*. Familiar recipes are frequently given a local flavour – *fricassée de volaille au vin d'Anjou*, sautéed chicken simmered in dry white Anjou wine, for instance. The most famous cheeses from the region are the *crémets* (soft fresh cream cheeses) made in Saumur and Angers.

The Route des Vins *Michelin maps 63, 64 and 67*

The vineyards of Anjou-Saumur are separated from those of Touraine by only a few kilometres. The wine route is signposted, but it is fairly convoluted and I have suggested a simplified circuit, which you can extend or modify as you wish.

The little village of Montsoreau is the starting place; it lies beside the Loire, and has an imposing fifteenth-century château with a fortress-like exterior looming

high above the houses. There are hotels and restaurants, and a well-positioned camp-site by the riverside. It is also a good spot for angling. A small road climbs the hill behind the village and you can follow a track up through the vineyards for a magnificent panorama of the château and river.

A short detour to the south along the D 147 leads to Fontevraud l'Abbaye with its famous abbey founded in the eleventh century and containing the bones of four, possibly eight, Plantagenet kings and queens. This was no ordinary abbey – it was made up of communities of monks, nuns, repentant prostitutes and lepers, under the control of a woman. Fontevraud is particularly fine architecturally, because the complete medieval monastery buildings survive. The kitchens are especially interesting; set in a huge octagonal tower, they have an ingenious ventilation system, the smoke from the five fireplaces being removed by a cluster of twenty chimneys.

Returning to the D 751 (which becomes the D 947 after Fontevraud), continue towards Saumur. The road runs between the tufa cliffs and the river bank, passing the small wine villages of Turquant, Parnay and Souzay-Champigny. It is well worth while taking some of the small roads which wind up into the vineyards behind these villages, as the countryside is both pleasing and peaceful. Take a detour to the nearby town of St Cyr-en-Bourg, which has an excellent Cave Co-opérative where you can buy a good Saumur-Champigny.

The town of Saumur is about 5 kilometres north. This was a Huguenot stronghold in the sixteenth and seventeenth centuries. Like every self-respecting town in the Loire region, it has a spectacular château; here, it is perched high up above the town over the blue-grey slate roofs of the houses. The Château de Saumur was built by Louis X at the end of the fourteenth century and in its time has been a prison and a barracks as well as a fort. It now houses two museums, including one of the history of the horse – Saumur is now famed for the Cadre Noir, the national riding school.

A kilometre or so west are the twin towns of St Hilaire and St Florent, where most of the sparkling Saumur wines are made and stored in huge tufa caves; here the *vignerons* vie for space with the flourishing mushroom-growing trade, and you can sample the wines and visit a mushroom museum.

A short drive to the south of Saumur along the N 147 leads to the hilly town of Montreuil-Bellay, set

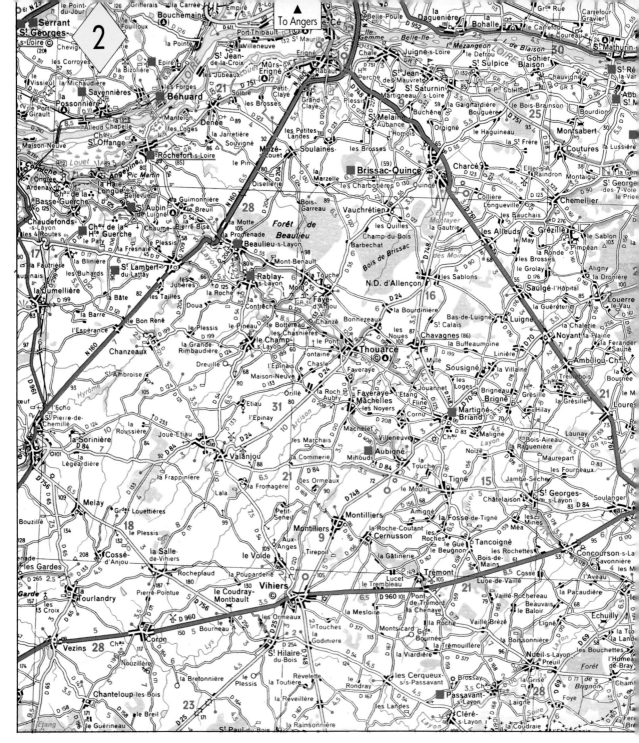

on the left bank of the river Thouet. From here you take the D 88 and the D 31 to the village of Bouillé-Loretz and from here follow the D 159 to the village of Passavant-sur-Layon, where there is a serene, ruined château overlooking a small peaceful lake. The Layon valley leads northwards through a succession of quiet and pretty small villages set in the midst of gently undulating countryside where the vineyards that pro-

duce the wonderful sweet white wines of the Coteaux du Layon are mingled with meadows and vast fields of sunflowers and maize. The wine village of Martigné-Briand is doninated by the ruins of a château destroyed in the war between the republicans and royalists in 1793. Continuing through the villages of Aubigné and Rablay-sur-Layon, you come to Beaulieu-sur-Layon. Here there is a Cave des Vignerons, where you can

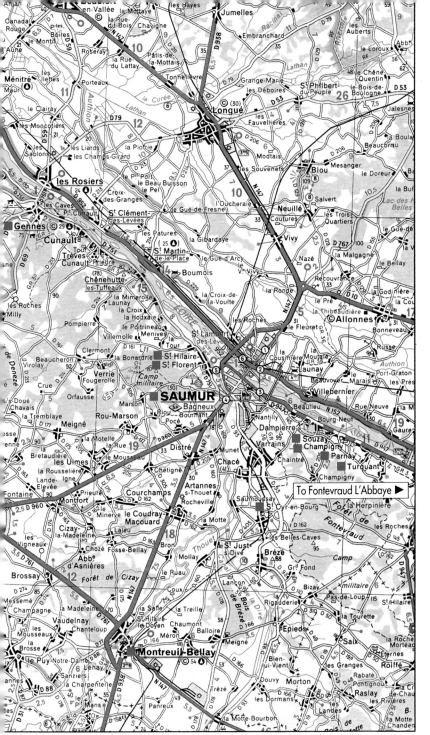

Top: The hill town of Montreuil Bellay. Its ancient ramparts encircle its château and its church.
Above: A much overgrown *caveau* in the village of St Aubin-de-Luigné near Rochefort-de-Loire, a self-styled 'capital of wine' attractively situated on the banks of the Loire

sample and buy the local wines, and there is an impressive collection of ancient Angevin wine bottles and glasses.

A little to the south along the N 160, cross the Layon to the wine village of St Lambert-du-Lattay. From here a small road, the D 17, winds through the hillsides where the *Quarts de Chaumes* grapes are grown to the village of St Aubin-de-Luigné; nearby is the ruined Château de la Haute Guerche. Drive down to the riverside town of Rochefort-sur-Loire, which declares itself a capital of wine; it has a tasting chalet just outside the town. Rochefort also boasts a Romanesque church built of granite and a fine campsite. Crossing the Loire, or rather its several 'arms', you come to Savennières, famed for its dry white wine. As you cross the river a road on the right leads to the

island of Béhuard, where there is an ancient village of stone houses; in the centre is a tiny chapel built on a rock. From Savennières, it is only a short detour to St Georges-sur-Loire, where there is the remains of an ancient priory, part of which is used as the town hall. Close by is the grandiose, moated Château de Serrant, which was designed by Philibert Delorme, the architect of the Tuileries (the chapel is by Jules Hardouin-Mansart, whose most famous works are the Invalides Chapel and the Place Vendôme in Paris). The château is surrounded by a well-tended park and is magnificently furnished.

Returning to Savennières and taking the riverside road, the D 111, turn right into a small lane about 1 kilometre before Epiré and you will come to the Château de la Roche-aux-Moines, where the famous Coulée de Serrant wine is produced from the vineyards high on the hill above the river; visitors are welcome both to taste the wine and to visit the château and gardens. The neighbouring village of Epiré is the home of a number of growers producing Savennières wines as well as Coulée de Serrant and la Roche-aux-Moines. It was in these prize vineyards that I saw a machine being used to harvest the grapes. No, this wasn't mechanization at the cost of quality, I was told. On the contrary, the machines allow the grapes to be harvested in a fraction of the time taken by hand picking and therefore the level of ripeness is more constant – which must improve quality. Another advantage is that harvesting can be continued at night.

Along this riverside road to the east is the town of Angers, which has a fine medieval château with no fewer than seventeen bastion towers; it houses a superb collection of tapestries, including the famous Tenture de l'Apocalypse. Recross the Loire here and follow the D 761 south for about 12 kilometres to the town of Brissac-Quincé, with its elegant, seven-storey château dating from the seventeenth century; it was built by the second Duc de Brissac and, uniquely, was returned to the family after the Revolution.

You can complete the wine circuit by going back to the Loire along the D 55 to St Rémy-la-Varenne, with the nearby ruined Abbaye de Sainte Maure, and then following the very attractive riverside road through the villages of le Thoureil and Gennes back to Saumur.

A glorious sweep of flowers near the village of Coutures, and (overleaf) sunflowers ready for harvesting. Nursery gardening is an important part of agriculture here

Wine Tour Nº 3
TOURAINE

The highly individual chateau of le Gué-Péan, displaying
its towers – one pointed and one bell-shaped

Some of the grandest châteaux are in Touraine, which is the real heart of the Loire Valley and the region where Rabelais set his satirical work *Gargantua* and where Balzac was born. It is the 'garden of France', said Rabelais. The vineyards of Touraine extend from near Vierzon in the east to the confluence of the Loire and the Vienne rivers about 50 kilometres west of the city of Tours. Here, there are very few vineyards on the banks of the Loire; instead, the 6,000 hectares of vines are found on the shallow hills that define the valley and along the valleys of a number of the Loire's tributaries, such as the Cher, the Indre and the Loir, which wind their way through the countryside.

The wines
The wines of Touraine are wonderfully varied: red, white and rosé wines are all made here, from a variety of grape types. Excellent red wines, such as those from Saint-Nicolas-de-Bourgueil and Bourgueil, are made from the Breton, a variety of the Cabernet Franc. The Gamay and Pinot Noir are also used to produce both red and rosé wines. The Chenin Blanc or Pineau de la Loire is the classic white grape of Touraine, used to produce Vouvray and Montlouis; white wines are also made from the Sauvignon Blanc and the Chardonnay.

Both *méthode Champenoise* and *pétillant* wines are also made in the region.

The Appellation Contrôlée wines of the region are: *Vouvray* (white; *pétillant* and *mousseux* as well as still wines); *Montlouis* (white; *pétillant* and *mousseux* as well as still); *Vin de Touraine* (red, white and rosé; *pétillant* and *mousseux* as well as still); *Saint-Nicolas-de-Bourgueil* (red); *Bourgueil* (red); *Chinon* (red, white and rosé); *Touraine-Amboise* (red, white and rosé); *Touraine-Mesland* (red, white and rosé); *Touraine-Azay-le-Rideau* (red, white and rosé); *Jasnières* (white); *Coteaux du Loir* (red, white and rosé). VDQS wines are also produced in Cheverny and Valençay.

The cuisine
The menus in Touraine, as in other regions along the Loire, feature freshwater fish extensively, often with subtle local variations such as *truite au Vouvray*, trout cooked in white wine. One famous speciality is *rillettes de Tours*, pâté made from slowly cooked, finely shredded pork; they are found on every menu and in every *charcuterie* and *épicerie* in the region. *Rillons* are small cubes of pork cooked until golden brown but left whole and preserved in pork fat; they are usually served as part of a *salade composée*.

An antique shop, in every sense, in the market town of St Aignan

Goat cheeses tend to predominate on the cheese-board and there are many to choose from: *Chabie* and *Selles*, small round discs from the town of Selles-sur-Cher, which declares itself to be the capital of goat cheeses; *Sainte-Maure*, like little ingots of creamy, tangy cheese, and *Coeur*, a quaint heart-shaped cheese. (Cows'-milk cheeses to look out for are those of *Vendôme* and *Ligueil*.)

The Route des Vins *Michelin map 64*

The wine route is well signposted in Touraine; however, it seems to have been designed by an over-zealous wine enthusiast since the signs indicate every single village of any interest – and it's not uncommon to be pointed in two or three directions at once. So I have suggested a rather more selective – and more rational – route, from which you can be distracted at will. My route starts at Selles-sur-Cher, about 48 kilometres from the Blois exit of the Autoroute A 10. There are two other small circuits which can be explored in the vicinity of Blois if you have the time.

One is the region of Mesland; for this the Route des Vins is signposted from the N 152 near Onzain. The other is around the charming small town of Cheverny, with its still lived-in château; this is on the D 765 a dozen or so kilometres south-east of Blois.

Selles-sur-Cher is a delightful village built around a steep curve in the river Cher. There are ruins of a fortress dating from the thirteenth century nearby, and the Château de Selles, which is set in a small park on the riverside. From here the wine route starts along the D 17 through the small villages of Meusnes and Couffi, detouring through Châteauvieux and Seigy, towards St Aignan. All along this route you will see Route des Vins signs – the work of our enthusiastic designer! – leading away from the river, up into the vine-covered hillsides and the peaceful countryside of the *vignerons*. This is the time to follow the local signs: you won't see most of the vineyards from the roads that run close to the riverbank, and driving along these quiet lanes you will come across farms and houses where you can sample the wines.

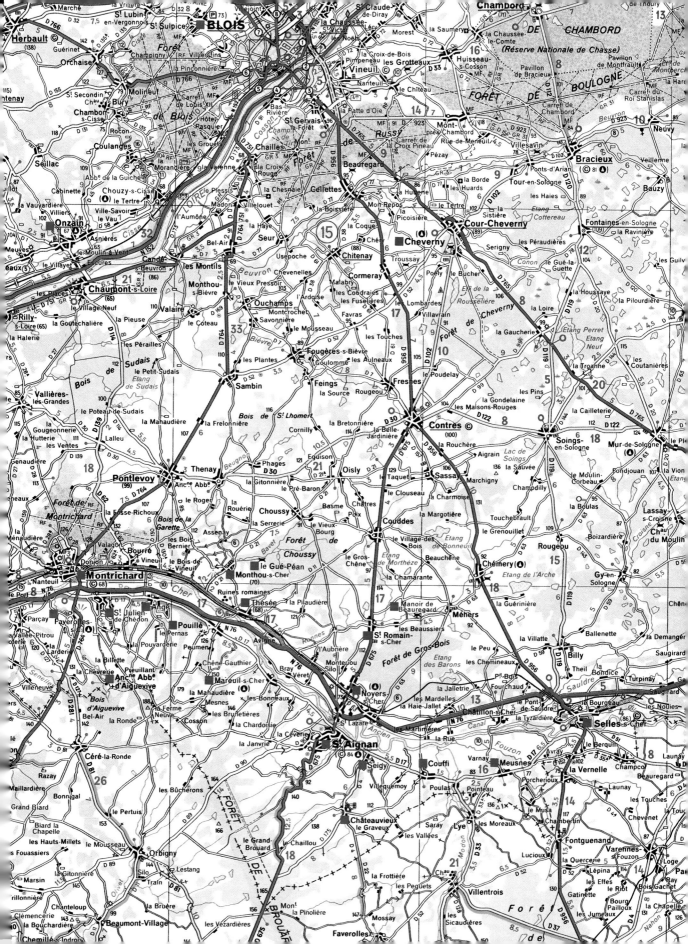

A little to the south of the village of Reugny, stands the Château La Côte, romantically reflected in its own lake

St Aignan, with its narrow cobbled streets, medieval houses, Romanesque church and imposing Renaissance château, is a very appealing town. Just across the river are the small wine villages of Noyers-sur-Cher and St Romain-sur-Cher. The Route des Vins continues along the riverside on the D17 through Mareuil-sur-Cher and Pouillé. Just across the river from Pouillé are the wine villages of Thésée and Monthou-sur-Cher. On the north side of Monthou is the château of le Gué-Péan, built in the late fifteenth century by the Italian, Nicolas Alaman, who was *valet de chambre* to both Louis XII and François I; his blue and white building displays a quirky individuality, notably in its one pointed and one bell-shaped towers. The château is open to visitors and also offers *chambre d'hôte* accommodation and a riding stable. Follow the route to Angé, St Julien-de-Chédon and Faverolles-sur-Cher; there are many diversions along the tiny *vignerons'* roads amongst the vines, and it is worth

going a few kilometres out of your way to see the ruined Abbaye d'Aiguevive set amongst remote fields and woods, just south of St Julien-de-Chédon.

Montrichard, on the north bank of the Cher, is the next town on the wine route. About all that is left of its medieval castle is the great square ruined keep; Richard Lionheart was besieged in the castle by Philip of France in 1188. From here the Route des Vins continues along the north bank on the N76 towards Tours, passing through Chissay-en-Touraine and Chisseaux, where you can try *Fraise d'Or*, the local strawberry liqueur. Just across the river a small detour takes in the wine villages of St Georges-sur-Cher, la Chaise and Durdon. Now take the D40 to Chenonceaux. This is the site of one of the most popular and grandiose châteaux in the whole of the Loire region. Henri II gave the unfinished Château de Chenonceaux to his lover Diane de Poitiers; on the king's death, his widow, Catherine de Médici, reclaimed it. Nearly two centuries later, Jean-Jacques Rousseau spent several years there as the then owner's secretary. It is a magnificent Renaissance building of epic proportions, with an extraordinary three-storey classical arched bridge spanning the Cher. The château contains some fine paintings, including works by Rubens, del Sarto, Correggio and Murillo.

The wine road continues towards Tours along the N76 on the south bank of the Cher, passing through the towns of Bléré and Véretz. From here the D85 heads north for a few kilometres, across the now narrow strip of countryside which separates the converging Loire and Cher rivers, to the town of Montlouis-sur-Loire, known for its subtle, dry white wine, meant for early drinking.

The drive on the D751 to Amboise is a worthwhile diversion – the road runs along the riverside, and there are a number of small wine villages up on the hillside where you can try the local wine. The chalk tufa cliffs here are seen in many parts of this region: the deep caves that have been cut into the soft chalk of the cliff were troglodyte dwellings originally – indeed some are still used as homes; now they are used mainly as wine cellars and for cultivating mushrooms. The town of Amboise seems untouched by time; in fact, in 1560 it was the scene of one of the bloodiest episodes in French history when 1200 Protestant plotters against François II were captured and strung up from the château, the town walls and every available tree. The château was a favourite of Charles VIII, who brought craftsmen back from Italy to work on it. Leonardo da Vinci spent the last few years of his life at Amboise at the invitation of François I, and is reputedly buried in the chapel of the château.

Follow the N 152 along the north bank of the river towards Tours to Vouvray, known for its white wine, which is made both dry and sweet, as well as still, *pétillant* and sparkling. This small region has its own wine circuit which leads into a succession of small valleys and villages, first along the river Brenne to Vernou-sur-Brenne, Chançay-la-Vallée and Reugny, then to la Vallée-de-Cousse and the villages of Vaugondy and Jallanges. Just to the west of Vouvray are the villages of Parçay-Meslay, where there is a medieval fortified farm, and Rochecorbon, famous for its plums. Then there is Vallée Coquette, where the

Cave Co-opérative of Vouvray is situated, and where you can eat grilled goats cheese dusted with herbs in a troglodyte cave, at a restaurant called Saint Martin.

Tours is a large, bustling city, with much to offer: broad tree-lined avenues, pavement cafés and superb restaurants as well as theatres, museums and elegant shops. This would be a good place to stop for the night; you could spend the next morning at the Musée des Vins de Touraine, which is housed in cellars under the Church of Saint Julien and contains a rich assortment of things to do with wine, including the cultivation of grapes, wine-making processes, legends, archaeology and social customs.

The Route des Vins continues to the west, along the south bank of the Loire, through the village of Savonnières to Villandry, which has a château sur-

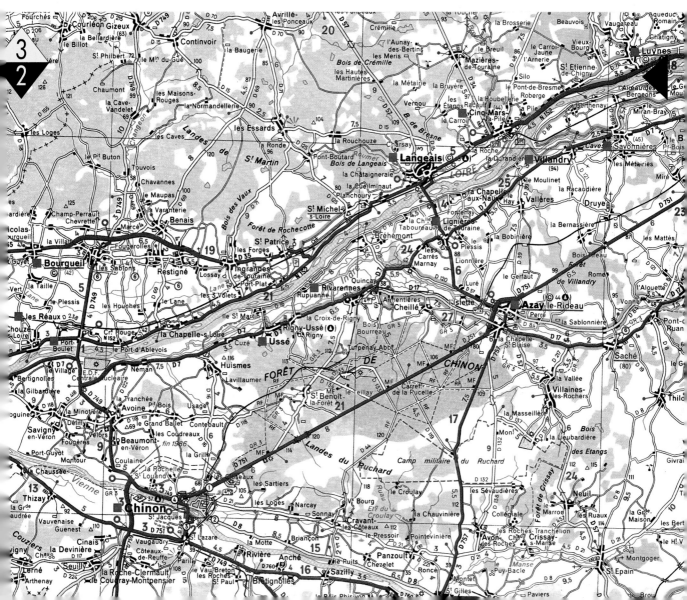

In this region, flowers, and particularly sunflowers (top and right) are as abundant as vines in the summer. The pruning of the vines (above) is a very necessary task at this time of year to train the branches to the optimum height

rounded by a superb formal garden in the Italian style. The route continues along the D 7 through Lignières-de-Touraine and Rivarennes to Ussé. Here, there is an enchanting château with towers and gables built high above the banks of the river Indre. It is particularly beautiful from the bridge opposite, with its terraces descending steeply to the riverside; Charles Perrault is supposed to have been inspired by it when he wrote *Sleeping Beauty*. A little to the south is the town of Azay-le-Rideau. Its château was Honoré de Balzac's favourite (he called it 'a diamond cut in facets') and today it is one of the most visited in the Loire.

Chinon marks the western limit of the wine route and it is a delight, set beside the broad, lazy waters of the river Vienne. The village is renowned for its excellent red wines. It is built on a hill, the top of which is ringed by the remains of ramparts and

fortifications. In Vieux Chinon, the old town that dates from the fifteenth century, the streets are lined with lovely old timbered and gabled houses.

From Chinon take the D 749, which crosses the Loire at Port-Boulet. Nearby is the small but charming château of Les Réaux, which offers *chambre d'hôte* accommodation. A little further north are the villages of Bourgueil and St Nicolas-de-Bourgueil, famed for their red wines. Just north of Bourgueil is a Cave Touristique where you can taste the wines and visit the small museum which has a number of ancient presses.

To complete the wine circuit drive along the riverside road, the N 152, towards Tours, which passes the attractive towns of Langeais, Cinq-Mars and Luynes. All three have interesting châteaux; the first was built by Louis XI and has not been altered since, the second was owned by a favourite of Louis XIII's and was largely destroyed on the orders of his neighbour at the third château, Luynes, the king's chief minister, Cardinal Richelieu.

At Cinq-Mars there is also an oddly shaped square tower, with four of its five pinnacles remaining.

Wine Tour Nº 4
THE EASTERN LOIRE

The hilltop town of Sancerre (above) with the famous Sauvignon
Blanc vines growing in the foreground. Right: Château de Boucard
and a house in the village of St Andelain

The rolling hills overlooking the upper reaches of the Loire are planted with the Sauvignon Blanc grape. From it are produced two of France's greatest wines: Pouilly-Fumé and Sancerre. The two towns around which the wines are produced are separated by the river; why Sancerre and Pouilly-Fumé are so different is a matter of endless debate. There are certainly differences in the soil; Sancerre's is composed of clay and limestone, and the best of its wine is produced where there is most limestone. Which is the better of the two wines is also hotly disputed – one expert will describe Pouilly-Fumé as more complex and flowery, while to another Sancerre is fuller and rounder.

The wines
The wines of this region are predominantly white and are made from the Sauvignon Blanc grape: *Sancerre* and *Pouilly-Fumé* are famous examples. The term *fumé* refers to the smoky bloom that forms on the grapes as they ripen, and not to the flavour of the wine. A lesser wine, *Pouilly-sur-Loire,* is made here from the Chasselas grape and some red and rosé is also made in Sancerre and other outlying villages from Pinot Noir, Pinot Gris and Meunier grapes.

In addition to the wines of Pouilly and Sancerre, interesting wines of all three colours are produced in the villages of *Ménétou-Salon, Quincy* and *Reuilly,* which are situated further to the west, away from the river. Reuilly is known for its white wine made from the Sauvignon grape and also for a rosé made from the Pinot Gris. Quincy has its appellation for white wine, also made from the Sauvignon, while Ménétou-Salon, like Sancerre, makes all three types.

Some VDQS wines are also produced in regions to the north of Pouilly and Sancerre: *Coteaux du Giennois* wines in the vineyards around Cosne sur Loire and Gien and *Vin de l'Orléanais* around Orléans. Much further to the south you will find *Côte Roannaise* around Roanne, and *Côte du Forez* in the region of St Etienne, and to the north of Tours is *Jasnières.*

The cuisine
Good food abounds in this region, and freshwater fish from the Loire appear on most menus. *Friture de la Loire* is a dish of tiny fish quickly sautéed in butter or oil. Salmon from the Loire is highly regarded; it is often served with *beurre blanc,* the rich and creamy sauce borrowed from the cuisine of the nearby Anjou

◀ To Quincy, Reuilly and Bourges

In early spring, these pruned vines (top) near the village of Veauges look very bleak, in sharp contrast to this luxuriant growth (above) in a vineyard near Chavignol later in the year

region. *Sandre*, like a large perch, is another delicious freshwater fish of the region and *alose* (shad) is also caught in the river; it is usually served with a sorrel sauce, *à l'oseille*. *Anguilles* (eels) are a regular feature on most menus either grilled, sautéed or more often served as a *matelote*, stewed in wine with onions and mushrooms.

The hillsides of the eastern Loire region are not only covered with vines, they are also quite often dotted with herds of delightful, rusty brown goats which actually get equal billing on the Sancerre wine route. *Crottin de Chavignol*, a goats'-milk cheese for which the region is famous, starts life as a small flat cylinder of soft creamy curd, quite mild in taste, about 10 to 12 centimetres in diameter; as it ages it shrinks and forms

a crust, becoming firmer and stronger in flavour. In addition to being served as part of the cheese-board, the cheeses are often sprinkled with herbs and toasted under the grill; served on a croûton with a garnish of green salad they are a delicious variation on the cheese course. For those with a sweet tooth there is a local speciality, *croquets de Sancerre*, a crunchy, nougat-based confection.

The Route des Vins *Michelin map 65*

Although Pouilly and Sancerre are only about 8 kilometres apart, each has its own well-signposted wine route. In each case it is best to start the circuit in the town itself. Sancerre is one of the prettiest of all the wine towns. It has a dramatic setting on a hill which is itself surrounded by other hills; the effect is rather like an amphitheatre. There are beautiful, sweeping views of the vineyards on all sides and of the Loire valley, and when you drive around the surrounding hills you

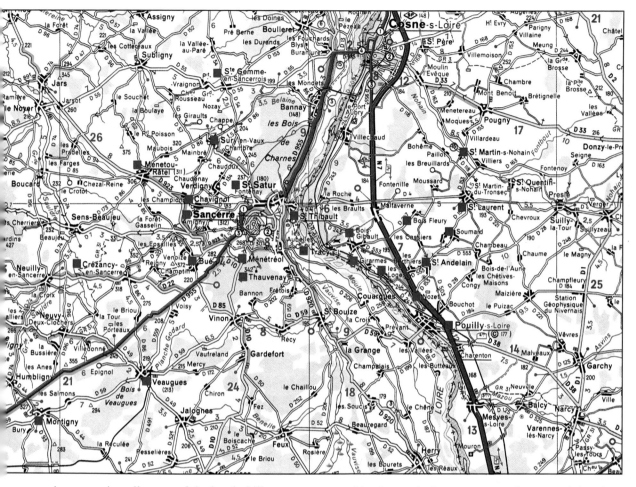

are always getting glimpses of the lovely hilltop town. Sancerre's history is an interesting one: in the ninth century a colony of Saxons, banished by Charlemagne, settled in the area, and a fort was erected to keep them in order. It was occupied by Huguenots during the religious wars of the sixteenth century; they lost it after a siege lasting 220 days, and it was finally destroyed in 1621, leaving only the twelfth-century Tour des Fiefs. Later, in 1745, a group of Bonnie Prince Charlie's Scottish followers settled at Sancerre and one of their descendants became a marshal under Napoleon. The village is a web of steep, winding, narrow streets lined with crumbling stone houses. There are some wonderful restaurants and tempting food shops as well as numerous places where you can sample and buy the wines.

The wine route, not a true circuit, goes off in several directions, involving a little to-ing and fro-ing; but the distances involved are very small, and the roads quiet –

making it a real pleasure to meander around the vine-clad hills and valleys.

Just north of Sancerre is the beautifully situated village of Chavignol, which produces some of the best Sancerre wine and a famous goats'-milk cheese, *crottin de Chavignol*. The vineyards rise up steeply all around the cluster of houses and the village church, and there are many places where you can try the local wines. The communes of Sury-en-Vaux and Ste Gemme are north of Chavignol. Here the countryside is much more open, with rolling hills covered in meadows and a variety of crops as well as the vineyards. The villages of Crézancy and Ménétou-Râtel mark the limit of the Sancerre vineyards to the west. Close by is the sixteenth-century château of Boucard; it is surrounded by meadows, woodland and ancient farm outhouses. This is one of the buildings included in a very interesting château route called the Route Jacques Coeur.

In the open, rolling countryside near Sury-en-Vaux, the vineyards are intermingled with meadows and fields of grain

In the foothills a few kilometres east of Sancerre are two adjoining villages on the Canal Latéral, which runs parallel to the Loire. St Satur is a canal port and boasts a Gothic church which was based on the designs for Bourges Cathedral but was never completed. It was built by Augustinian monks who were also responsible for introducing grapes to the area in the twelfth century. St Thibault, between the Loire and the canal, was a thriving port at one time; the river is

village of Thauvenay.

Bué, a few kilometres south of Sancerre (take the D 955 and turn off at the sign), is a delightful small village of stone houses with brown tiled roofs nestling in a steep-sided valley. It is an important wine centre, selling the excellent wines from the surrounding vineyards. There is a popular small restaurant here, Le Caveau des Vignerons, which is owned and run by a co-operative of *vignerons*, and serves very good, simple country food. It is particularly busy at Sunday lunchtimes when its long wooden tables are full of noisy local families. There are fewer vineyards to the southwest, but it is worth visiting the communes of Veaugues and Montigny just off the D 955, and then taking a detour to the vineyards of Ménétou-Salon, 10 kilometres away.

Continue on to Quincy and Reuilly. Both towns have a rather tired and run-down atmosphere and offer little of interest apart from their wines. However, the surrounding countryside is delightful, the journey through the ancient city of Bourges will be rewarding, and the Sauvignon Blanc wines are pleasantly fruity.

The second Route des Vins centres around Pouilly-sur-Loire, on the eastern bank of the Loire. It is a tranquil, one-street town, and a good place to stop overnight; there are several hotels, a campsite by the river, a number of good restaurants and places to taste the local wines. The small wine circuit takes you into gentle countryside which is flatter and has less immediate appeal than that of Sancerre, but which has a rural appeal all its own. A few kilometres to the north is the village of les Loges, its old stone houses lining a steep street that rises away from the river; there are a number of *vignerons* here who welcome visitors. The route then continues through the communes of les Girarmes and Bois-Gibault to the village of Tracy, which has an impressive fourteenth-century château.

The Route des Vins continues away from the river through a number of small hamlets such as Bois Fleury, St Laurent, Soumand and St Martin-sur-Nohain. The largest community, and the most important Pouilly-Fumé wine village, is St Andelain, set on a hill; its slender-spired church is visible from miles around. Close by is the largest and undoubtedly best-known estate of Pouilly-Fumé, Château du Nozet. Returning towards Pouilly you arrive at the hamlet of les Berthiers, where there are a number of signs inviting visitors to taste and buy wine.

wide and shallow at this point, with large sandy beaches. You'll find good camp-sites here as well as waterside restaurants, one on a moored barge. The village of Ménétréol, also on the Canal Latéral, is shaded by tall, slender green trees and is a lovely place to linger, and there is a château nearby in the little

NORTH–WEST FRANCE
Wine-buying Guide

THE PAYS NANTAIS

A region of few wines, of which none are acknowledged as great but all go well with the seafood for which the area is famous.

Appellations Contrôlées

Muscadet, within which there are two other appellations, *Muscadet des Coteaux de la Loire* and *Muscadet de Sèvre-et-Maine*. All are dry white wines with a maximum alcohol content of 12°. (This is the only appellation to specify a maximum alcohol level.) The best is the Muscadet de Sèvre-et-Maine, which accounts for about 75% of the Muscadet exported. Drink them as young as possible to savour their freshness, but be prepared to be unexcited by these wines. The additional qualification of *sur lie* (straight from the cask) is widely used and enhances the flavour.

VDQS

Coteaux d'Ancenis Little known red, dry white and rosé. The grape name must be stated on the label.

Gros Plant du Pays Nantais Thin and very acidic white wine in the Muscadet style. You will probably not enjoy this wine if you take it home.

Addresses

Maison Drouet
Les Vins Drouet Frères
6 rue Emile Gabory
44550 Vallet

ANJOU/SAUMUR

This is a region that provides many types of wine to satisfy, very adequately, most tastes for uncomplicated drinking. Although the wines of Saumur have a reputation as old as those of the ancient royal province of Anjou, and are still officially classified as Anjou, they have more in common with the region of Touraine. As in Touraine, there is no Cru classification system in Anjou/Saumur, but there are superior sub-appellations within more general appellations.

Appellations Contrôlées

Coteaux du Layon This appellation covers sweet and semi-sweet white wines from Chenin Blanc grapes affected by Botrytis fungus. The Layon river has cut a deep enough gully in the tufa chalky-clay rock to provide several sheltered vineyard sites. All Coteaux du Layon benefits from ageing, especially in those years with a long, hot summer in which Botrytis has been really active. The best way to enjoy it is either fairly cold as an apéritif or less cold after a meal.

Quarts de Chaume and *Bonnezeaux* These are two Layon vineyards which are outstanding enough to have their own appellation, like the Grands Crus of Burgundy. The Quarts de Chaume production is tiny (there are only 40 hectares of vineyards), and its richness and finesse can be spectacular. Bonnezeaux has about twice the vineyard area, just south of Rochefort-sur-Loire, and is also well worth a visit. The two appellations produce essentially the same style of wine, Quarts de Chaume being marginally the finer.

Coteaux du Layon-Chaume This is a rarely used appellation for wines of similar style to Coteaux du Layon but coming exclusively from the commune of Rochefort-sur-Loire.

Savennières This is a dry to semi-sweet white wine produced from Chenin Blanc grapes on the north bank of the Loire, west of Angers. There is only a small production of this delicious wine which happily is not well known and is therefore excellent value. Two communes within Savennières are sufficiently outstanding to be allowed to add their names to the appellation: *Coulée de Serrant* and *La Roche-aux-Moines*.

Coteaux de l'Aubance Produces wines similar to, but less rich than, Coteaux du Layon.

Saumur This is a blanket appellation for white wines, both dry and sweet, produced from the Chenin Blanc grape, with a maximum addition of up to 20 per cent Chardonnay or Sauvignon Blanc; some red wine, mainly from the Cabernet Sauvignon and Cabernet Franc; and some rosé, from Gamay grapes and several other local varieties, including the Groslot. The wines of Saumur are more weighty than their Anjou counterparts. Saumur white and rosé can be made *pétillant* or *mousseux* by the *méthode champenoise*, although their lightness and fragrance bear no resemblance to true Champagne.

Saumur-Champigny This is red wine only, the best red of the Anjou/Saumur region. The appellation covers wines similar to,

but sturdier than, the Touraine appellations of Chinon and Bourgueil.

Anjou Produces red, white and rosé wines from the same grapes as Saumur. The wines are usually lighter and more delicate than those of Saumur. This blanket appellation contains many superior sub-appellations, a selection of which are listed below.

Anjou Coteaux de la Loire Making only white wines of dry to semi-sweet style, around the town of Angers.

Anjou Gamay A light red wine made from Gamay grapes, less interesting than the red Anjou made from Cabernet Franc.

Rosé d' Anjou A very well known sweetish rosé made from a mixture of grapes including the Cabernets, Gamay and Groslot. *Pétillant* also exists.

Cabernet d' Anjou Slightly drier and better than Rosé d'Anjou, made exclusively from the Cabernet Sauvignon and Cabernet Franc grapes.

Anjou-mousseux White and rosé exist but are less good than sparkling Saumur.

Other Appellations Contrôlées

Cabernet de Saumur A semi-sweet rosé.

Coteaux de Saumur A tiny production of demi-sec white.

Rosé de la Loire A dry rosé made in Anjou, Saumur and Touraine.

Crémant de Loire Another blanket appellation for sparkling rosé and white wines of two-thirds of the sparkling pressure produced by the *méthode champenoise* in Anjou, Saumur and Touraine.

VDQS

Vin de Thouarsais Making red, dry white and rosé wines around Thouars, to the south of the region.

Vins de Pays

There exists a blanket Vin de Pays designation covering most of the Loire Valley called *Vin de Pays du Jardin de la France*. If the wine is made from a single grape variety this may appear on the label.

Addresses

To find these gems of the Anjou try the following addresses:

Quarts de Chaume
Domaine Baumard
49190 Rochefort-sur-Loire

Bonnezeaux
M Joliette
Domaine des Pierres Blanches
49190 Rochefort-sur-Loire

TOURAINE

The Touraine region produces a wide range of wine types. The white may be sparkling (*mousseux*), semi-sparkling (*pétillant*) or still, and range from fully dry (*brut*) to very sweet (*liquoreux*), with medium-dry (*demi-sec*) and fairly sweet (*moëlleux*) in between. Sparkling and still rosés are produced as well as still red wines.

There are five important Appellation Contrôlée wines, with a succession of lessers ACs and a few Vins Délimités de Qualité

Crumbling château steps in St Aignan in Touraine

Supérieure. All sparkling wines made in ACs have to be made by the *méthode champenoise*.

Appellations Contrôlées

Bourgueil and *St Nicolas-de-Bourgueil* These are reds only, made principally from the Cabernet Franc grape grown on the north bank of the Loire, west of Tours. Some rosé does exist but it is extremely rare. The more noble grape, Cabernet Sauvignon, is allowed to be grown, but this too is fairly rare. Some claim that St Nicolas-de-Bourgueil is slightly better than Bourgueil.

Chinon Although white Chinon from Chenin Blanc grapes does exist, as does rosé, it is the red for which Chinon is famous. Here on the south bank of the Loire the Cabernet Franc makes a wine marginally softer than the Bourgueils, but essentially very similar in style. You are doing well if you can spot the difference between the hint of violet in the Chinon and the hint of raspberries in the Bourgueil.

The red wines from Chinon and Bourgueil can be drunk cool when young but in good years age well in bottle, preserved by the natural acidity and tannin of the Cabernet Franc. The best can last 10 to 15 years if kept in optimum conditions. If you wish to lay down these wines, buy a *Vin de Garde*, literally a keeping wine, preferably from a *vigneron* with old vines in his vineyard.

Vouvray White wines only, all made from Chenin Blanc grapes on the north bank of the Loire, to the east of Tours. The style can be sweet to dry, with the above-mentioned designations of which *brut* and *liquoreux* are the best, and still to fully sparkling. The sweetness is caused by varying degrees of Botrytis fungus which is also responsible for

the famous sweet wines of Barsac and Sauternes.

The sweeter styles of the still wine age very well preserved by the natural acidity of the Chenin Blanc grape. Outstanding vintages such as 1976, 1971, 1969, 1964, 1955, 1953, 1949, 1947, 1945, 1934, and back to the legendary 1921, are excellent and still found in small quantities. However, do not expect to purchase these wines, much less to obtain a tasting, unless you are a substantial purchaser of the young wines. The 1982 vintage was very good, so don't be in a hurry to consume these wines.

Montlouis Until 1938, when a separate appellation for Montlouis was fully implemented, these wines were sold as Vouvray. Therefore Montlouis offers the same range of styles as Vouvray, but is a little softer and always less intense in flavour, and is often marginally cheaper.

Other Appellations Contrôlées

Jasnières White wine only, which can become rich with age. This wine is very rare and worth finding.

Coteaux du Loir Making red, dry white and rosé. Nowadays there are only 20 hectares in production.

Touraine Red, white and rosé wine, sweet to dry, and still to sparkling. This is a blanket appellation with many individual sub-appellations, the best of which are listed below:

Touraine-Amboise Again red, white and rosé wines, grown around Amboise. These wines have to be one degree higher in alcohol than straight Touraine.

Touraine-Azay-le-Rideau Visitors to Azay-le-Rideau are advised to call in at the Château de l'Aulée, situated just outside Azay on the right-hand side of the road to Tours. The Château de l'Aulée produces a still white wine from the Chenin Blanc grape and a *mousseux* by the *méthode champenoise* called Jockey Club. This estate is owned and run by the Champagne house Deutz of Ay, and so produces really excellent quality wines.

Touraine Mesland Red, white and rosé wines, one degree higher in alcohol than straight Touraine.

VDQS

Cheverny, Coteaux du Vendômois and *Valençay.*

Addresses

Chinon
Domaine Olga Raffault
Savigny-en-Veron
37500 Chinon

Bourgueil
Domaine Pierre-Jacques Druet
La Croix Benais
37140 Bourgueil

Vouvray
Domaine Huet
Domaine du Haut-Lieu
37120 Vouvray

Domaine Prince Poniatowsky
Le Clos Baudoin
37210 Vouvray

Montlouis
Jean et Michel Berger
St Martin-le-Beau
37270 Montlouis-sur-Loire

Azay-le-Rideau
Château de l'Aulée
BP13
37190 Azay-le-Rideau

THE EASTERN LOIRE

This is perhaps the most interesting and exciting part of the Loire valley. It has two well-known appellations as well as several others hardly seen outside their own areas.

Appellations Contrôlées

Sancerre A well-known appellation, producing mostly white wines although red and rosé do exist and have become fashionable in recent years. Many small growers scattered round outlying villages around the town of Sancerre on the west bank of the Loire make most of the wine. Some wine, such as Sancerre Comte Lafond, however, is bought in from a number of growers and marketed by a local *négociant*, Ladoucette, who owns no vineyards in the area. The best wine is found around some of the smaller villages of which Bué, Chavignol, Ménétréol and Fontenay are the most worthy. Sancerre should be drunk young when its fresh spicyness is most attractive. The Pinot Noir grape, indigenous to Burgundy, makes the red and rosé. The red is only good in years when there is enough sunshine to ripen the grapes, and then it is worthy of attention and its price.

Pouilly-Fumé (Also called *Blanc Fumé de Pouilly*) Over the river on the east bank is this appellation, producing less wine than Sancerre from the same Sauvignon grape. It is white only and usually fetches a few francs more per bottle than Sancerre. The best estate is Château du Nozet, owned by Patric de Ladoucette. This should not be missed as it sets a standard by which the other growers can be judged. Less easy to visit, but well worth it, is the Château de Tracy. For reasons perhaps best attributed to the soil, the best Pouilly Fumés take longer to develop than Sancerre. Leave them for 18 months to 2 years for your first try, and then for another year if all the harmonies have not come together. Pouilly Fumé is less aggressive, but with a richer, longer taste in the mouth, and has more finesse than Sancerre.

Pouilly-sur-Loire A light dry white from the less noble Chasselas grape, from the same delimited district as Pouilly-Fumé. This needs to be drunk young and has nothing like the finesse of Pouilly-Fumé.

Quincy A dry white wine that is slightly softer than Sancerre and can be delightful in good years.

Reuilly This produces dry white, red, and rosé wines that are slightly more austere than Quincy and less exciting.

Menetou-Salon Again white, red, and rosé wines. The whites are akin to a mini-Sancerre with less pronounced character despite being grown on the same chalky soil.

VDQS

Chateaumeillant Red and rosé wine only, of which the rosé is the better.

Coteaux du Giennois Quite rare red, dry white, and rosé.

Côte Roannaise A small production of red and rosé wine only from the Gamay and Pinot Noir grapes.

Côtes d'Auvergne Red and rosé, similar to Côte Roannaise, but also occasionally some white wine. Most of the production is drunk locally.

St Pourçain-sur-Siole Red, dry white and rosé wines. Most of the production is by the local co-operative.

Côtes du Forez Red and rosé only.

Vins de l'Orléannais Again red, dry white and rosé.

Haut Poitou Single co-operative producing well-made ordinary wines either from a single grape variety or a blend of varieties.

Addresses

Sancerre
M. Archambault
Clos la Perrière
Verdigny
18300 Sancerre

M. Baily Reverdy
Bué
18300 Sancerre

M. Vincent Delaporte
Chavignol
18300 Sancerre

Pouilly Blanc Fumé
Château de Nozet
58150 Pouilly-sur-Loire

Château de Tracy
58150 Pouilly-sur-Loire

Jean-Claude Dageneau
Les Berthiers
58150 Pouilly-sur-Loire

Quincy
Pierre Mardon
18120 Quincy

St Pourçain
Union des Vignerons
03500 St Pourçain-sur-Sioule

NORTH–EAST FRANCE

Whenever there's an excuse for a celebration, people bring out Champagne. All the great Champagne houses have their headquarters in this area, in the cities of Reims, Epernay and Ay. But although Champagne dominates the North East, the distinctive Rosé des Riceys from the nearby Aube region and the fresh white wines of Alsace are also outstanding. The character of the countryside varies greatly, from the flat plains and far horizons of Champagne (left, near Bergères-lès-Vertus) to the Germanic and dramatic, wooded slopes of the Vosges mountains of Alsace. Indeed, the North East is a feast of contrasts both for the eye and for the palate.

Wine Tour Nº 5

CHAMPAGNE

The Canal de la Marne near the village of Mareuil-sur-Ay

The Champagne vineyards, the most northerly in France, are less than two hours' drive from Paris and only slightly further from the ports of Calais and Boulogne. The city of Reims is the centre of the Champagne industry, although Epernay closely rivals it and the nearby town of Ay is also important. Most of the major Champagne houses have their headquarters in one of these three towns and each would make an ideal base from which to explore the vineyards. You must visit one of the Champagne houses. They are built in the vast caverns and miles of tunnels, many dating back to Roman times, carved out of the chalky hills. Here millions of bottles of Champagne are stored – an awe-inspiring sight. Most of the major houses actively welcome guests, often without formal appointments, and will take you on a guided tour showing you how the wine is made, and you can also taste and buy some Champagne. The cellars of Pommery & Greno in the historic city of Reims are particularly impressive: they have 17 kilometres of tunnels and caverns cut into the chalk up to 30 metres below the surface.

The wines
Originally the wines of the Champagne region were still rather than sparkling. In the seventeenth century

it was discovered that if – instead of being left to ferment completely in wooden casks – the wine was bottled at an early stage, the fermentation would continue inside the bottle and, since the air was trapped, the gas given off by the process would dissolve in the wine. The result was that when the pressure was released by removing the cork, the wine was found to be full of bubbles.

Demand for this sparkling wine, particularly by the English, led to the perfection of the technique known as the *méthode champenoise* (which is used to make some other wines too). The grapes are picked, pressed and begin their fermentation in casks in the usual way. But here the work of the *vigneron* stops and the shipper takes over. The wine is taken to one of the Champagne towns – Reims, Epernay or Ay – to the shipper's 'maison'. Here a small amount of sugar is added to stimulate the continuing fermentation, then it is bottled and stored in the enormous underground cellars cut into the chalk. To keep the wine clear of the sediment that would otherwise accumulate, the bottles are stored pointing head down in special racks (*pupitres*) so that the sediment drops towards the cork. Every day over a period of several months the bottles are given a little twist to encourage this (a procedure known as *remuage*). When all the sediment has settled the cork is removed, the small amount of wine containing it is released (a process called *dégorgement*), the bottle is topped up with more of the same wine, and a new cork put in. The bottles need to be especially strong and the corks wired down to contain the pressure of the gas within.

The bubbles created by this natural process (as opposed to the artificially injected gas which makes soft drinks, and even some wine, fizzy) are small and gentle, spread evenly throughout the wine and last for a long time. *Crémant* is the term used for a wine with a gentler, more subdued sparkle.

During the re-fermentation in the bottle all the sugar in the wine is used up. The resulting very dry Champagne is called *Brut*. If sweeter Champagnes are required a little sweetened wine is added at the *dégorgement* stage, in varying quantities: the results are dry (*extra sec* or *extra dry*); slightly sweet (*sec*); sweeter (*demi-sec*) or sweet (*doux*).

Champagne is made from a blend of different sorts of grapes; the blend is called the *cuvée*. In the seventeenth century, the famous cellar master of the Abbey of Hautvillers, Dom Pierre Pérignon, was the first to perfect the technique of blending to improve the quality and balance of Champagne. The balance of the wine is adjusted by both the selection of the grape types and by the combination of wine from different vineyards and, in some cases, from different years. (Vintage or *millésimé* is Champagne made from the grapes of one year only). The grapes used are the white Chardonnay, grown in the Epernay region, the Pinot Noir (Montagne de Reims and Vallée de la Marne), and Pinot Meunier.

White Champagne is produced from these last two black grapes by extracting the juice rapidly in shallow presses and removing the skins quickly to prevent them from giving their red colour to the wine (to make red wine the skins are left in for longer). *Blanc de blancs* is white wine made exclusively from white grapes. Some rosé champagne is made by mixing a little red wine in with the white, a practice not permitted in other regions. The traditional way to make rosé is to allow the skins of the black grapes to colour and impart flavour to the juice, as in *Mailly-Champagne*.

There is also the usual distinction of *crus*, the wines from the best vineyards. Those with the most favourable siting and soil are designated Grand Crus. There are twelve of these: *Ambonnay, Avize, Ay, Bouzy, Cramant, Louvois, Mailly, Puisieux, Sillery, Tours-sur-Marne, Verzenay* and *Beaumont-sur-Vesle*; there are a further forty-eight communes which qualify as Premier Crus, a slightly lower quality.

Champagne, however, is not the only wine made in this region. Still red and white wines, and a little rosé, are produced under the appellation *Coteaux Champenois*. These wines are made from the same three grape types used for Champagne, they are bottled in the same elegantly distinctive bottles and sealed with the same cork. The best known of these wines has a

The orangery of Moët et Chandon in the town of Epernay

name that appeals to English wits – *Bouzy Rouge*. *Ratafia* is another regional wine. It is sweetish and fortified, rather similar to Pineau des Charentes, and is usually drunk chilled as an apéritif. *Marc de Champagne* is a distilled wine made from the *marc* (the mud-like residue of grape skins, pips and stems left after pressing the grape juice for the Champagne).

The cuisine

The cuisine of the Champagne region, although excellent, is not as distinctive as in some other areas of France. Champagne is featured in a variety of dishes. In *poulet au Champagne*, for example, the chicken is simmered in Champagne. Freshwater fish are often served in Champagne-based sauces, such as *écrevisses au Champagne* (freshwater crayfish poached in a *court-bouillon* containing Champagne). A sorbet made from Marc de Champagne is often served as palate freshener between courses.

The great French cheese *Brie* comes from here; a slice from a large flat, creamy Brie de Meaux is a revelation if you have only experienced the bland, plastic versions so often found in supermarkets; Brie de Melun and Brie de Coulommiers are two other types worth looking out for. *Maroilles* is a creamy cows'-milk cheese with a rust-coloured crust and a rich smell and flavour. The fruit is also excellent in this region. The *rousselet* pear of Reims is highly prized, as are the cherries from Dormans.

The Routes des Vins *Michelin map 56*

There are three sections in the Champagne Route des Vins: the Montagne de Reims, which lies between Reims and Epernay; the Vallée de la Marne, and the Côte des Blancs, the most southerly vineyards of the region. There are additional areas of vineyards entitled to the Champagne appellation still further to the south in the valley of the Aube (see Wine Tour No 6). I have suggested that you start the route from the direction of Reims but it would be a simple matter to join the circuit at any convenient point.

The only reason the Montagne de Reims is clearly visible from the city – 'mountain' is a slight exaggeration since it is only a few hundred metres high – is because of the unrelieved flatness of the surrounding plain. There are vines on the slopes of the hill; on its northern side the vineyards and fields of corn and other crops extend on to the plain below.

Take the Château-Thierry road from the city, the RD 380; you will soon be climbing the gentle but persistent slope of the Montagne towards the wine village of Jouy-lès-Reims. The wine route turns to the east now, along the D 26. At the small wine village of Ville-Dommange, there is a lovely twelfth-century church, and the pretty hilltop chapel of Saint Lie hidden in a copse on the slopes above the vineyards; from the narrow lane which climbs up behind the village to the chapel you will get some beautiful sweeping views north and west.

The route continues through the village of Sacy, which has a fine Romanesque church, to Sermiers, on the main road between Epernay and Reims, the N 51. Cross this and continue along the D 26 to a succession of small villages close to the top of the Montagne: Rilly-la-Montagne, from where there are superb views of the plain below and distant Reims; Ludes, a tiny village virtually taken over by the establishment of Canard-Duchêne; and Mailly-Champagne, a Grand Cru commune famous for its rosé. Verzenay also has Grand Cru vineyards overlooked by its distinctive windmill, a feature that can be seen from far away.

The next stop is Verzy, and from here you can make

An autumnal view of the wine village of Oger, surrounded by the vineyards of the Côte des Blancs

a detour to Mont Sinai, the highest point of the Montagne, and also to the Faux de Verzy, an extraordinary forest of gnarled and mis-shapen trees that look like giant bonsais. The wine route continues around the side of the Montagne, now providing vast panoramas to the east with the fields of corn stretching away into the distance – in summertime, the lush green vineyards are in vivid contrast to the golden fields below. This was where I watched a young helicopter pilot spraying the vines; he made his craft duck, weave and bob among them, often disappearing into a hollow below the tops of the vines to reappear in a completely unexpected place.

As the wine route continues through the village of Trépail towards Ambonnay and Bouzy, it begins to descend from the Montagne. The village of Bouzy, famed for its still red Coteaux Champenois wine, marks the point where the vines give way to other crops. You begin turning westwards towards the valley of the Marne. Tours-sur-Marne is set beside the canal that runs parallel to the river and houses the headquarters of Laurent-Perrier. Mareuil-sur-Aÿ is also by the canal; you should walk up the narrow vineyard roads in the hill above the village and look out over the Marne Valley.

Aÿ is a much larger town and is the base of a number of important Champagne houses, including Deutz & Geldermann, Ayala and Bollinger; it is one of the Grand Cru communes. There is a Musée Champenois here which displays ancient tools and implements used in vine cultivation and wine-making. From here a brief detour can be made through the Val d'Or to the villages of Avenay-Val-d'Or and Louvois, which has a twelfth-century church and a privately owned château. From Aÿ, the wine road joins the main N 51 on the outskirts of Epernay. However, drive back towards Reims up the winding hairpin bends to the village of Champillon, then to the Royal Champagne Hotel further up the hill at Bellevue; its rooms border the vineyards, and it has an excellent restaurant which serves a special marc de Champagne sorbet.

Returning to Dizy along the main road you can continue westward along the Marne Valley, taking the D 1 towards Château-Thierry; the road runs alongside the river for most of the journey. You must take a short detour to the village of Hautvillers, high up on the slopes. Dom Pérignon was cellar master to the Benedictine abbey here which is now owned by Moët & Chandon and can be visited. The road continues

The isolated, hilltop church of Chavot, beseiged by a sea of vines and (overleaf) the plain near the village of Cuis

through a succession of wine villages such as Cumières (a Grand Cru commune), Damery and Venteuil to Châtillon-sur-Marne, where the vast, monolithic statue of its most famous son, Pope Urban II, dominates the town from high on the hill above. At Verneuil the road rejoins the main RD 380. You can return directly to Reims; alternatively, continue to Dormans, where you can cross the river and start the route through the Côte des Blancs.

Instead of taking the main road, the N 3, direct to Epernay, a quieter and more interesting route follows the D 222 through the small wine villages of Oeuilly, Boursault and Vauciennes towards St Martin-d'Ablois, Vinay and Moussy. As the road climbs up out of the valley there are some fine views of the Montagne on the other side of the river. Here the vines are almost exclusively Chardonnay and the landscape is generally flatter, with gentle hills creating slight contours.

This part of the tour is quite short and meanders through a sequence of small villages, including Monthelon, Chavot, which has a hilltop church set among the vines, Courcourt, from where there are lovely views, Grauves, Cramant and Avize – the latter two are Grand Cru communes.

The southern limit of the tour is reached along the D 9 through the villages of le Mesnil-sur-Oger and Vertus to Bergères-lès-Vertus. Here there is quite a different atmosphere and character from the countryside nearer the Marne; the land is very flat, with only occasional hilly outcrops, and the sky appears to be endless. Climb to the top of Mont Aimé to the south of Bergères-lès-Vertus; there is a Table d'Orientation here which is a perfect place to open a bottle of Champagne and drink to the fruitful land below.

Wine Tour Nº 6
THE AUBE

The endless horizons, typical of the Aube region, near
the village of Bergères

The vineyards of the Aube are cultivated mainly between the towns of Bar-sur-Seine and Bar-sur-Aube, about 40 kilometres east of the medieval city of Troyes and about 100 kilometres south of the Marne vineyards. The Aube vineyards are in fact part of Champagne, entitled to the same appellations, made from the same grapes and in the same way. However the region is very much the poor relation, and the most famous and respected Champagne houses are all based around Reims in the more northerly vineyards of the Marne.

The wines
It is generally accepted that the wines produced in the Aube are of a lesser quality than those of its more illustrious neighbour, Champagne. At the end of the nineteenth century the vineyards of the Aube were badly affected by Phylloxera, and the depleted vineyards became separated from those of the northern Champagne and excluded from the appellation. A succession of bad harvests and problems experienced in selling and transporting the Aube wines led many thousands of *vignerons* and their supporters to descend upon the city of Troyes in the spring of 1911 to protest at their exclusion. As a result the government re-

defined the limits of the appellation and gave them back their earlier status.

To some extent this reunion has not been entirely successful because the wines from the Reims region have retained their reputation for superiority and are much more widely exported. However there is much of interest here for the wine lover, including some excellent Champagne as well as interesting Coteaux Champenois wines. *Rosé des Riceys*, for example, which Louix XIV was fond of, is a delightful deep pink, full-bodied rosé which is quite unusual and rarely found outside the region.

The cuisine
The food of the Aube is very similar to that of the Marne. The *charcuterie* is outstanding, particularly the *andouillettes* of Bar-sur-Aube and Bar-sur-Seine and the Troyes version which are made of mutton. There are some interesting local cheeses from the villages of *Chaource* (a light, creamy, cows'-milk cheese with an almost soufflé-like texture) and its neighbour *Mussy* (a cheese of similar appearance but with a firmer texture and slightly stronger flavour). Another cows'-milk cheese is produced in the village of *Les Riceys* and goes perfectly with a glass of Rosé des

Riceys. *Fromage blanc*, a creamy mould of fresh cheese curd, is commonly served in many parts of France with sugar and cream as a dessert; I was given it in a small restaurant in the Aube served with salt, pepper, finely-minced garlic and a generous sprinkling of fresh herbs – absolutely delicious!

The Route des Vins *Michelin maps 61 and 65*

If you are travelling from the north, you could visit the vineyards concentrated around the ancient town of Sézanne. These can be explored by taking a small road, the D 453, along a gentle ridge of hills through the vineyards to the tiny wine villages of Vindey and Saudoy. The vineyards continue spasmodically as far as the market town of Villenauxe-la-Grande on the N 51.

The regional park of La Forêt d'Orient, immediately to the north of the Route des Vins, is also worth a small detour. It is an extensive, dense forest, around a large lake. There are water-sport facilities at the lakeside village of Mesnil-Saint-Père, or you can enjoy bird watching – and there are plenty of good spots for fishing and picnicking.

The Route des Vins in the Aube is quite well signposted and easy to follow. It is a complete circuit and so can be joined at any convenient place. But a good starting point is the charming town of Bar-sur-Seine, whose narrow streets are lined with medieval houses with timbered façades. The church of Saint Etienne dates from the sixteenth century. The Château des Comtes de Bar above the town has an unusual clock-tower, and there are views of the countryside and the town below from here and from the footpath that leads to it.

Leave the town on the main road, the N 71, going towards Châtillon-sur-Seine (where the archaeological museum displays important Grecian artefacts found locally). After a kilometre or so you'll come to a

A medieval, timbered house, perfectly preserved, in the market town of Bar-sur-Seine

A hostelry in Les Riceys where Champagne and the distinctive local wine, Rosé des Riceys may be bought

small road on the left that leads to the wine village of Merrey-sur-Arce, which has some old houses typical of the region. Continuing on the D 167, you come to the village of Celles-sur-Ource, where there are some important wine establishments whose wines you can sample and buy. The countryside here is quite open with gentle hills, meadows and fields of maize, wheat and barley; the vineyards are confined mainly to the tops and slopes of the slight hills.

After crossing the N 71, take a quiet country road, the D 452, to the village of Polisy at the confluence of the Seine and Laignes rivers. It is a sombre place made up of some rather austere old stone houses, a gloomy sixteenth-century château and a church containing an interesting Virgin and Child and some fine murals. The wine route continues to the hamlet of Balnot-sur-Laignes, which is known for its red and rosé Coteaux Champenois wines, set at the head of a valley. Here the Route des Vins climbs along the side of the valley into the wood of Riceys. A left turn on to the D 142 takes you to the top of a steep hill; from here you can see Les Riceys, a village where the vines are quite extensively cultivated.

Les Riceys is in fact three villages in one. The first you encounter is Ricey-Bas, which has an elegant Renaissance church beside the river Laignes. Nearby is a château, the oldest parts of which date back to the eleventh century. A little further along the road, virtually merged, are Ricey-Haut and Ricey-Haut-Rive, both with distinctive churches. There are several places where you can taste and buy the local Rosé des Riceys and Champagne.

Return to Ricey-Bas, and continue on the wine route along the D 70, crossing the N 71, to the village of Gyé-sur-Seine, which has a twelfth-century church

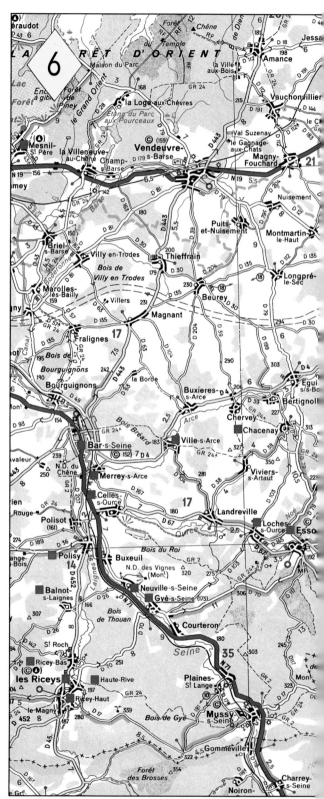

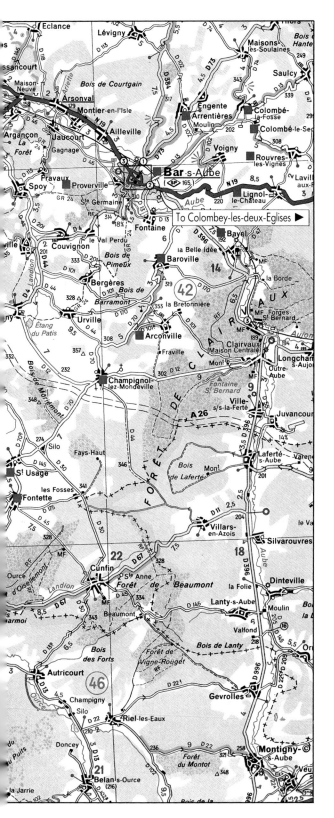

and the remains of a fourteenth-century château. From here, you can make a small detour to Neuville-sur-Seine, which has a Cave Co-opérative and is dominated by a statue of Nôtre Dame des Vignes set on the top of the hill above the village. Now this is the perfect place to lie in the long grass with a *baguette*, a piece of Chaource and a bottle of Rosé des Riceys, and allow the cares of the world to pass you by.

Follow the Route des Vins through a peaceful little valley along the D 103 to Loches-sur-Ource, then cross its Roman bridge and turn on to the D 67 to Essoyes, through which the river Ource meanders. The great Impressionist painter, Pierre-Auguste Renoir, his wife and two famous sons – actor Pierre and film-maker Jean – are buried in the churchyard. The house they lived in between 1897 and 1916 is on the edge of the town, marked with a plaque, and there are plans to open a Maison du Vin here.

There are fine views over the vineyards as the Route des Vins continues along the D 70 to the village of Fontette; there is a Cave Co-opérative here. Just before the next village, St Usage, there is a detour to the high point of the downs giving some breathtaking panoramas over the plateau of Blu. Then on to Champignol-lez-Mondeville, a small village set in a wide valley and surrounded by cornfields, meadows, vineyards and fields of sunflowers. The wine road now continues along the D 101A to Arconville and then to Baroville, where there is a Cave Co-opérative. Continuing along the D 396 you come to Bayel, where you can visit the famous crystal glass works, la Cristallerie de Champagne; they have a shop selling the crystal.

The Route des Vins follows the D 47 to Lignol-le-Château, at the crossroads with the N 19. There are two twelfth-century buildings here – a church and a

château. You can make a detour to the village of Colombey-les-Deux-Eglises, where Charles de Gaulle lived; he is buried in the local cemetery. The next village is Rouvres-les-Vignes, then Colombé-le-Sec, where there is an important Cave Co-opérative. Nearby are the ancient cellars of the Abbaye de Clairvaux; these date back to the twelfth century and can be visited.

Go through the small village of Colombé-la-Fosse to Arrentières, where there are remains of a fourteenth-century castle; it was demolished on the orders of Louis XIII. From here the Route des Vins continues to the bustling market town of Bar-sur-Aube. This ancient town has a number of medieval buildings with timbered façades, an Hôtel de Ville of the seventeenth century, and the twelfth-century Eglise de Saint Pierre whose striking interior includes a wooden gallery. There is a wine-tasting chalet on the outskirts of the town beside the N 19 in the direction of Chaumont.

Vast fields of grain are more common in the Aube than vineyards; the field of burnt stubble (left) lies near the village of Baroville (above)

The route back towards Bar-sur-Seine starts off along the D 4 towards Proverville. Shortly after leaving the town you take a small road to the left to the chapel of Sainte Germaine, set high on the hill above the town and offering splendid views of the valley of the Aube. A delightfully scenic road completes the circuit back to Bar-sur-Seine, passing through a succession of small wine villages such as Meurville, with its twelfth-century church, Chacenay, which has a fifteenth-century château, and Ville-sur-Arce, where there is the Cave Co-opérative of the Coteaux de l'Arce.

Wine Tour N°7

ALSACE

The vineyards of Riquewihr rise high beyond the village rooftops

Borders are made to be disputed, as every student of Alsatian history knows. France's easternmost province has been passed from one régime and ruler to another and back again for thousands of years, from the Celts to the Romans to the Franks and their Merovingian kings. Then there were 700 years of German rule from the tenth century – and a legacy of fine Renaissance architecture remains. The peace and prosperity were followed by several centuries of war, during which time the region was thrown back and forward between France and Germany. Its present status as French dates from the Treaty of Versailles after the 1914–1918 War.

Alsace's landscape is as dramatic as its history: the rugged Vosges mountains with their wooded slopes extend for almost 160 kilometres north to south, running parallel to the River Rhine. Within this domain are crystal-clear lakes, woodland walks, fairy-tale villages and, of course, the vineyards. These are concentrated on the foothills of the Vosges and stretch from the village of Nordheim, near Strasbourg, in the north to Thann, west of Mulhouse, in the south. Understandably, there is a strong German feel to the wines of Alsace, as in its art, architecture, cuisine and landscape.

The wines

The wine of Alsace is predominantly white and, unlike the wines of other regions, is identified primarily by grape type. The main varieties are *Sylvaner, Muscat Riesling, Pinot Gris, Gewürztraminer, Pinot Blanc* and *Pinot Noir* from which red and rosé wines are made. In addition, there is a wine called *Edelzwicker*, which is a blend of various grape types, including the Chasselas; Edelzwicker is the basic, everyday wine of the region, often served in restaurants in the traditional blue-and-white earthenware jug.

The cuisine

The freshly grown produce of Alsace is magnificent: there is a rich variety of grain, vegetable and fruit grown in the fertile Rhine Valley, the lakes and mountains of the Vosges ensure a good supply of fish, while game, beef and dairy products from the mountain meadows and valleys are also abundant.

One of the most famous dishes – and a truly hearty feast – is of course *choucroute à l'Alsacienne*; it is made of sauerkraut and potato and served with a variety of meats including salt pork, smoked ham and sausages. (Incidentally, you can follow the Route de la Choucroute through the countryside where the cabbages are grown.) Another equally rich and substantial speciality is *baekoffe*, a delicious stew made with three types of meat, usually mutton, pork and beef. The pork is very good here: it is smoked, made into sausages, stewed, and eaten roasted with pickled turnips. Geese are raised to make the *terrines* and *pâtés de foie gras truffés* which rival those from Périgord. *Kugelhopf* is another regional speciality; it is a light, sweet, distinctively shaped *brioche*, flavoured with raisins and almonds and dusted with sugar.

Alsace also boasts one of the best – and strongest – cheeses in France: *Munster*. Made from the milk of the cows you see grazing just west of the town the cheese is named after, it is often served with a generous sprinkling of cumin seed and a glass of spicy Gewürztraminer wine.

One of the most renowned French restaurants, the Auberge de l'Ill at Illhauesern, is close to the wine route. And you can enjoy the simple and informal

Kugelhopf, a deliciously light and sweetly spiced brioche which is a speciality of Alsace

winstubs, a cross between German beer kellers and wine bars, which offer good food and wine in cosy surroundings. The friendly Winstub Arnold in Itterswiller, overlooking the vineyards, is particularly worth visiting.

The Route des Vins *Michelin maps 62 and 66*
Marlenheim on the busy N4, a few miles west of Strasbourg, is where the Alsace Route des Vins starts. There are vineyards further north, around Wissembourg, but the main area to explore, and the well-signposted wine route proper, lies to the south of Marlenheim. This town is noted for its rosé wine, called Vorlauf, made from the Pinot Noir grape, and for the important wine festival it holds every September; and there are a number of attractive half-timbered houses near the Hôtel de Ville.

Leaving Marlenheim, the D422 towards Wangen takes you on to the first leg of the official Route des Vins. Here on the rolling hills, you see vineyards side by side with fields of food crops and grazing cattle and sheep. The best time to visit this rich agricultural region is in late autumn when the harvest is taking place and the turning leaves create vivid bursts of colour, as the first dustings of snow cover the more exposed upper slopes of the Vosges. Although tiny tractors have taken the place of horses, the other traditional harvesting methods survive. The grapes are still collected in wooden barrel-like tubs and are loaded on to ancient wooden carts. The vineyards hum with excitement and it seems that the entire population is recruited to help. The narrow, cobbled village streets are constantly jammed with tractors towing cart-loads of grapes; drying tubs are stacked every-

This amazing view looks east towards the Rhine and the thickly-wooded slopes of the Black Forest

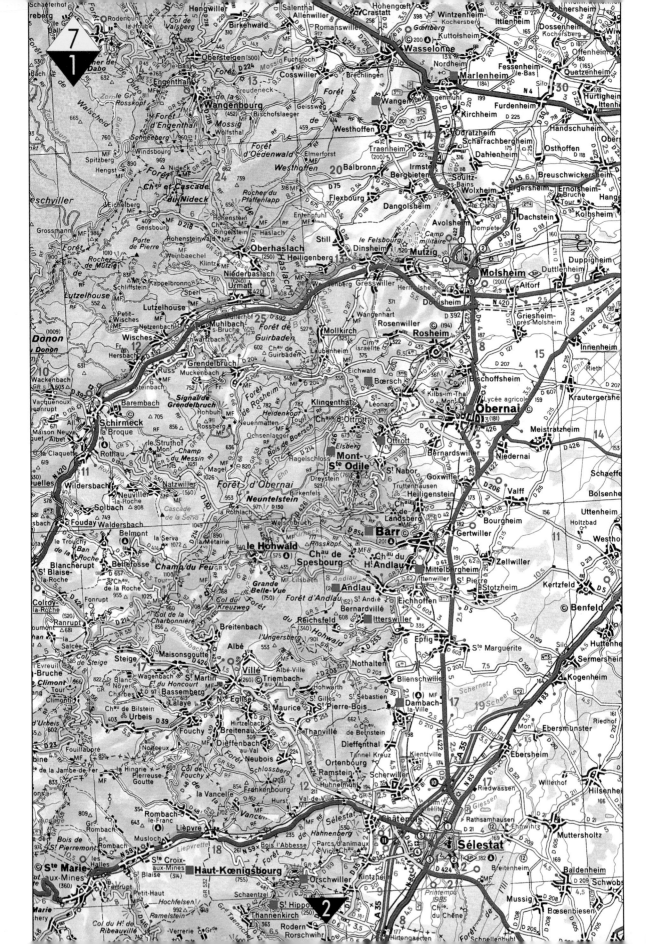

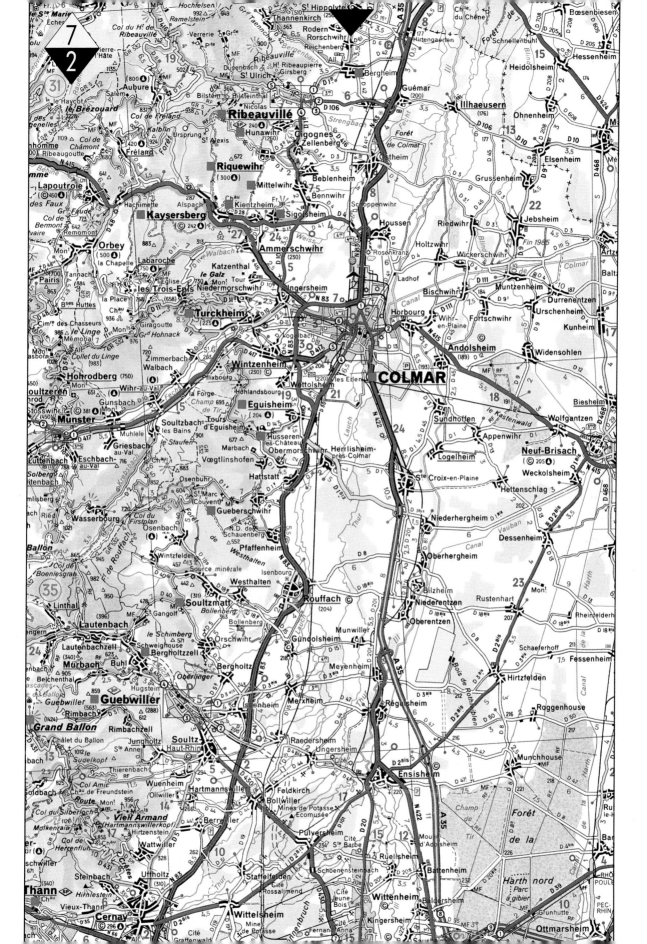

An autumnal vineyard near Itterswiller, the Vosges looming behind

where and the air is heady with the smell of fermenting juice.

The Route des Vins meanders along a quiet country road that twists and turns its way through several small villages to the west of the main road. This region is known as the Bas-Rhin. The university town of Molsheim is situated below the vine-clad Molsheimer Berg on the River Bruche. There is an unusual sixteenth-century Renaissance building, the 'Metzig', which was erected by the butchers' guild and now houses the museum. Obernai, an important market town, has a sixteenth-century corn market and an Hôtel de Ville, and you can look to the forests of Vosges from its medieval ramparts.

A little to the west is the small town of Ottrott, known for its rosé and red wines; nearby Boersch is a slumbering old village with a fortified gateway, many timbered houses and narrow cobbled streets. Barr, an important wine centre, is the next large town on the route and nestles below a steep hill lined with vines. It would make a good base from which to explore the northern part of Alsace, especially in March when

there is a wine fair centred around its seventeenth-century château. Nearby is Mont Ste Odile, a hilltop convent established by Alsace's patron saint, who is buried in the small twelfth-century chapel; it is a spectacular viewpoint and a place of pilgrimage. Two other villages not to be missed, within a short distance are Mittelbergheim and Andlau; the latter is tucked into a niche in a steep-sided green valley. As you follow the wine route a little further south you come to Itterswiller, a welcoming little village perched on the edge of the vineyards, its single, narrow street lined with houses that always seem to be decked with flowers.

The next main town is Dambach-la-Ville, the home of a number of important growers; there are medieval ramparts, three fortified gates and a sixteenth-century town hall to see here as well. Continuing south the road leads you through the small villages of Orsch-willer, St Hippolyte and Bergheim towards Ribeau-villé. Here the Vosges become more rugged and dramatic and the vineyards creep up the lower slopes. You can take a minor detour from Orschwiller up to the castle of Haut-Koenigsbourg; a small road winds up through beautiful woods to the summit of the mountain, from where you can see over the vineyards to the distant Rhine – on a clear day you can even see the Black Forest.

Ribeauvillé is known for its wines – Traminer and Riesling – and its music: on its annual feast day, the first Sunday in September, the fountain in the main square flows with wine, and there is a street festival of strolling musicians. Set in a narrow valley in the foothills of the Vosges, it is ringed with vineyards. The cobbled streets are lined with beautiful old timbered houses and you'll find many places to taste and buy the wines of local growers, as well as *charcuteries, pâtisseries* and *épiceries* to buy the regional culinary specialities. Nearby is the charming small village of Hunawihr, also well worth a visit.

Riquewihr, next on the route, is the pride and joy of Alsace – and undoubtedly one of the loveliest wine villages in France, if at times a little crowded, especially at the height of summer when busloads of tourists descend on it. It has everything a perfectly preserved, historical village should have: ramparts, fortified gates, fifteenth-century houses with sculptured doorways, ornate balconies, wrought-iron signs, cobbled courtyards and winding narrow streets, all a blaze of floral colour. But it's not all show; there are many important growers based here, including Hugel and Dopff. Climb up beyond the village ramparts through the vineyards and look out over to the distant Vosges.

From Riquewihr the wine route continues through the small villages of Mittelwihr, Sigolsheim and Kientzheim to Kaysersberg, at the entrance to the Weiss Valley. This is where Albert Schweitzer was

A farmer cutting his maize for winter cattle and poultry feed near the village of Wettolsheim

born in 1875. The town is dominated by a ruined castle, the streets are lined with medieval and sixteenth-century houses and there is a fifteenth-century fortified bridge incorporating a chapel. The next village is Turckheim, where, as in many other Alsatian villages, a platform has been built high up, usually around a church steeple or tower, in the hope that a pair of storks will build their nest on it; the stork is the local symbol for good luck.

Colmar is the centre of the Alsace wine trade and hosts an important wine fair in mid-August. It is a lovely town set on the River Lauch, with many important old buildings, including the Maison Pfister (a fine example of a carved wooden façade), l'Ancienne Douane (the old customs house) and a medieval guard house. The museum of Unterlinden, in a thirteenth-century Dominican monastery, houses an extensive collection of medieval religious art; the showpiece, though, is Mathias Grünewald's Issenheim altar piece, a superb example of German Renaissance art, and there are works by Picasso and Braque in the modern galleries downstairs. The museum also contains a section on the local wine history: it is a colourful past centred around the *poêles*, private drinking clubs whose exclusive membership demanded exclusive – and excellent – wines. There is a lively weekly market in the old central square, where the local farmers sell their produce, and there are many wine-growers' establishments where the regional wines can be found. Colmar has a number of excellent restaurants, *winstubs*, and hotels too; it is a good base from which to explore the surrounding vineyards and villages.

Continuing south, the Route des Vins leads you to Eguisheim, a Alsatian village which has changed little

Taking a much-needed break during a busy market day in Colmar, the capital of Alsace's wine trade

In Eguisheim (above) the delightful, ancient cobbled streets follow round the encircling ramparts. The vineyards nearby (left), mellow on a late October afternoon, rise onto the lower slopes of the Vosges. Overleaf, the perfectly preserved medieval village of Riquewihr

since the sixteenth century. Its cobbled circular street, which runs around the inside of the rampart walls, is lined with lovely old houses and courtyards. There is a very good Cave Co-opérative here which sells unusual sparkling Blanc de Blancs as well as the more familiar wines of the region; you can eat Alsatian specialities at its restaurant as you sample the local wines.

Further south along the wine road is the village of Husseren-les-Châteaux; the ruins of three châteaux can be seen in the hills to the west overlooking the town. The next villages are Gueberschwihr, Soultz-matt, Bergholtzzell and Guebwiller, the latter at the entrance to the lovely Florival Valley. Near Soultzmatt are the highest vineyards in Alsace, known as the Zinkoepfle. The landscape here is dominated by the Grand Ballon, the highest peak of the Vosges at 1,400 metres.

The town of Thann marks the southern limit of the Alsace vineyards. From here, it's worth travelling a little further west into the Vosges, following the Route des Crêtes, to explore the lakes and forests. There are places here – Gérardmer, le Lac Vert, le Lac Blanc and le Lac Noir, for instance – that seem a world away from the nearby vineyards. They add yet another perspective to this unusual and much disputed corner of France.

CHAMPAGNE

This is a region with a fascinating history and outstanding wine, although the scenery is less interesting. The wine is mostly sold not by geographical district but as one appellation – Champagne. It is marketed as a blended wine by the brand name of the Champagne house that produces it. Small growers and even big Champagne houses do produce unblended single wines but only as an oddity. Blending is the true art of Champagne making. Far from being a technique of mixing indifferent and better quality wine to elevate the general mixture (*coupage*), here blending is an art – *assemblage*. This is the building of a complete picture from individual constituent wines. The best analogy is to regard a single unblended wine as a monochromatic picture and compare it with an *assemblage* of wines as a full-colour picture.

The opportunities to buy the wine are manifold, making advice surprisingly difficult to give. The big companies, mostly centred around Reims, Epernay and Ay, all have efficient publicity departments. They have well-known names and are called the Grandes Marques. They are the significant firms in the Champagne export market. Each Grande Marque will take you on a tour of their cavernous cellars, show you large-scale production of

Champagne, and give you an opportunity to taste and buy. From an architectural point of view, the Roman-dug *crayères* that form part of the cellars of Veuve-Clicquot and Ruinart in Reims are fascinating.

These are the Grandes Marques, town by town. In Ay: Ayala, Bollinger, Deutz and Gelderman. In Epernay: Moët et Chandon, Perrier-Jouet and Pol Roger. In Reims: Besserat de Belleton (owned by the Pernod/Ricard group), Canard Duchêne (owned by Veuve Clicquot), George Goulet, Heidsieck Monopole, Charles Heidsieck (in the Henriot group), Henriot, Krug, Lanson Père et Fils (under the same ownership as Pommery et Greno), Mercier (owned by the Moët-Hennessy group), G H Mumm (owned by Seagrams), Piper-Heidsieck, Pommery et Greno, Louis Roederer, Ruinart Père et Fils (also owned by the Moët-Hennessy group), Taittinger and Veuve Clicquot-Ponsardin. Finally, in Tours-sur-Marne: Laurent-Perrier.

Companies called *Marque Acheteur* or BOB (buyer's own brand) also market Champagne. They are often as big as Grande Marque companies, and are occasionally subsidiaries of them. They make Champagne to be sold under a company's own label and all supermarket, department store, and other such brand-name Champagnes are made by these firms. They tend not to sell champagne under their own names.

In complete contrast there are the smaller *Récoltant-manipulants*. These are small growers who make unblended wine from their own vineyards and sell direct to the local domestic markets. There are also Négociant-manipulants. These are usually fairly small firms which own few, if any, vineyards. They blend the products of different vineyards over a limited locality, often swapping with the more prestigious houses their quality first pressing (*première cuvée*) juice for double the

quantity of lesser *taille* juice.

Of 5,000 champagne producers, only 127 produce more than 50,000 bottles a year (1981 figures).

The Cru classification system

Champagne has a rather peculiar classification system based on vineyard geography, grape variety and price. Of the three main sub-districts of Champagne, the Montagne de Reims tends to grow the Pinot Noir; the Côte de Blancs grows the Chardonnay and the Vallée de la Marne grows the more robust yet less noble Pinot Meunier. The twelve village communes rated as Grand Cru are more concentrated in the Montagne de Reims and the Côte de Blancs because the Pinot Noir and the Chardonnay are the nobler, finer varieties. The price of each of these grapes is fixed annually, at harvest time, at a meeting between growers' representative and a brokers' representative, under the supervision of the *préfet* of the Marne *département*. The price is set by market pressure, stocks available in the cellars and the size of the harvest, and can fluctuate wildly from year to year.

The Grand Cru vineyard grapes fetch 100 per cent of this fixed price per kilo. The Premiers Crus fetch from 99 per cent down to 90 per cent, and the lesser vineyards accordingly down to a minimum of 80 per cent (formerly 77 per cent). So vineyards can be classified in terms of a percentage relating to their grape prices.

What you are buying

The Champagne produced by Grande Marque firms is substantially more expensive than that of the smaller *négociants* and growers because they tend to own or buy in grapes from the better classified vineyards. All Grandes Marques buy in grapes from contract growers because even the biggest, Moët et Chandon, only owns enough vineyards to satisfy a quarter to half of its requirements. In a Grande Marque blend the average classification of the grapes is usually about 97 per cent. Also, when pressing the grapes, the Grandes Marques usually sell off the lesser quality *taille* pressings and only use the *cuvée* juice from the first pressing. Finally, they take a great deal of extra care during production and tend to age the constituent wines of a blend for longer than the legally required minimum for each category of Champagne.

This, however, does not preclude the possibility of finding an exceptionally good growers' wine.

Styles

De-luxe or Cuvées de Prestige Most Grandes Marques produce, in good years, limited quantities of a de-luxe Champagne *cuvée* from their best grapes. The exotic packaging and the quality of the wines in the blend add to the price. The styles can vary from fragrant and delicate to rich and full according to the house style. By and large these wines tend to be of a single vintage.

Vintage Only five or six years in a decade are generally sufficiently good for making a vintage wine. A vintage Champagne is a wine of a single year, although under AC law the admixture of up to 10 per cent of another year is permitted. The wine produced typifies the style of the particular year and so, again, can range from light and delicate to full in taste. Vintage Champagne will, of course, be a blend of wines from different village communes, but all of the same year. Wines of richer years can take on ten years of bottle age to arrive at a more complex character. Vintage Champagne is legally required to have a minimum of three years' ageing.

Non-vintage These are wines made from a blend of grapes of more than one year. Because the Champagne vineyards are so northerly, in some years the grapes do not fully ripen and can only produce thin, tart wines. By blending several years' grapes together, from good to less good, some more mature, some less mature, makers can produce a more balanced wine. The art of blending also allows for consistency in style and quality, year in and year out; a consistency that customers can rely on and that enables a firm's reputation as a brand to be built.

Non-vintage Champagne is legally required to have a minimum of two years' ageing.

Crémant is a sparkling wine with two thirds of the fizziness of normal *méthode champenoise* wines. The term can be applied to vintage or non-vintage sparkling wine, with all the sweet/dry designations. A good one is Mumm's Crémant de Cramant, a *blanc de blancs* from the single Grand Cru village of Cramant.

Sweetness/dryness designations

All champagne is made dry. The sweetness is added at the final stage by putting in a percentage (by

Statue of the celebrated Dom Perignon in Epernay

volume) of a sugar solution in wine. It is up to each firm to decide what percentage of sugar solution is given to each designation but the following is a guide:

Brut Zero or Brut Sauvage 0%
(Popular with dieters and diabetics, but fairly astringent.)
Brut 1–2%
Extra Sec or Extra Dry 2–2½%
Sec 2½–4%
Demi-sec 4–6%
Doux or Rich over 6%

Coteaux Champenois AC

As well as the more famous sparkling white and rosé, you must not forget the still wines that can be red, white or rosé in colour. Although now produced in relatively small quantities, it was these wines that made Champagne a widely known quality appellation prior to the advent of sparkling wines at around the turn of the 17th century.

Some is sold as Coteaux Champenois, but the best red comes from individual communes such as Bouzy. The whites are more common and Moët's Saran Nature and Ruinart's Chardonnay Blanc de Blancs are among the best but, although interesting, these wines will never be as great as the best white Burgundies.

Addresses

Maison Moët et Chandon
20 Avenue de Champagne
51200 Epernay

Pommery et Greno
5 Place Général Gouraud
51100 Reims

Taittinger
9 Place St-Nicaise
51100 Reims

Legras
10 rue des Partelaines
Chouilly
Champagne

Champagne Deutz
BP 9
51160 Ay

THE AUBE

The Aube is the fourth district within the appellation Champagne. While most Champagne purists tend to ignore this sub-district, you should bear in mind that it accounts for 5,500 of the 27,000 hectares of the Champagne vineyards. The wines produced here will never match the quality of those of the Montagne de Reims and the Côte de Blancs, but they are much in demand as less expensive Champagnes.

LES RICEYS

To find and taste the Rosé des Riceys would broaden any amateur's appreciation of wine as it is extremely rare. The red also exists but it is the rosé (both come from the Pinot Noir) that, despite its delicacy, can age gracefully.

ALSACE

This wine region is divided into two halves in the *départements* of Haut-Rhin and Bas-Rhin. The Haut-Rhin, to the south but higher up the Rhine valley, surprisingly produces the better wine. There is only one appellation – Alsace – which has 11,500 hectares of vineyards scattered on the slopes of the foothills of the Vosges. The wines are of an exceptional quality and it is sad that they are not more widely known and appreciated.

The wines are sold, not by geographical area, but under the appellation Alsace, followed by the grape variety. The only blend of varieties is Edelzwicker, made from the less noble Chasselas grape with a mixture of the more noble varieties. This is Alsace's 'jug' wine.

Since 1975 one superior appellation, Alsace Grand Cru, has existed. This is confined to 25 vineyard sites that have been known for generations to produce good wines. The name of the Grand Cru site may appear on the label and is geographically delimited. These Grand Cru wines have to be produced from the lower legal yield of 70 hectolitres per hectare, as opposed to the normal 100 hectos/hectare for Alsace. However, to complicate the picture, it is quite legal to put an individual vineyard name on a label if a wine is genuinely from a single vineyard, even if this vineyard is not a Grand Cru.

As the wines are sold without geographical delimitation within the appellation (Grands Crus aside), the trick is to buy either from specialists in particular grape varieties or from a firm recognized as thoroughly reliable.

Old wooden wine cask and harvesting 'buckets'

Grapes waiting to be loaded into the press

Types of merchant in Alsace

Most of the better houses have been established for many years, some even since the 17th century. These houses may own some vineyard holdings, but they invariably buy in grapes from smaller growers. Here are some of the firms with the name of their village: Léon Beyer (Eguisheim), E. Boekel (Mittelbergheim), Dopff et Irion (Riquewihr), Dopff au Moulin (Riquewihr), Theo Faller (Kayserberg), Heim (Westhalten), Hugel (Riquewihr), Kuentz-Bas (Husseren-les-Châteaux), Gustave Lorentz (Bergheim), Mure (Rouffach), J. Preiss-Zimmer (Riquewihr), F. E. Trimbach (Ribeauvillé).

Fewer than a third of the 9,200 producers own even one hectare of vineyard, so there are a great many very small growers. These growers form themselves into local co-operatives and pool their resources. This means that small operators do not have to provide all the capital for wine-making equipment themselves, but it does tend to produce less individual wines.

Village co-operatives include: Bennwihr, Dambach-la-Ville, Eguisheim and Ingersheim et Environs.

Additional information on label

Most of the better merchants market their better wines with added qualifications such as *Réserve Particulière, Réserve Personelle, Cuvée Spéciale*, or *Cuvée Exceptionelle*; all variations on the same theme. However, these designations are copied by lesser merchants and so are rather meaningless.

Another distinction is *Vendage Tardive*. This covers wines made from grapes picked two or three weeks after normal harvesting. These wines are expensive because of the risk of heavy loss through frost or bad weather. In exceptional years, however, the extra autumn ripening produces wines of great richness and depth that are slightly sweeter than usual in style and can take years to develop fully in bottle.

Eaux-de-vie

Alsace is a great fruit-growing region and makes some of the finest *eaux-de-vie*. Common ones include Poire William from pear and Fraise from strawberry, and there are more exotic ones too, from holly-berry, sorb-apple and cherry, that are well worth finding.

Tasting

It is important to taste Alsace wines, from the plainest and driest to the more aromatic styles. The following order of tasting is recommended: Sylvaner, Pinot Blanc, Tokay (now called Pinot Gris), Riesling, Muscat and finally Gewürztraminer. Taste any Vendage Tardive wine last.

Addresses

These are but a small personal selection of addresses.

Domaine Zind-Humbrecht
34 rue du Maréchal Joffre
Winzenheim
68000 Colmar

Specialist Gewürztraminer and Grand Crus

Hugel
68340 Riquewihr

T. Faller
Domaine Weinbach
68240 Kayserberg

Boeckel
67140 Mittelbergheim

CENTRAL AND EASTERN FRANCE

This region includes the wines of Burgundy, Beaujolais, the Jura and Savoie. There are six wine tours to enjoy in all, through some of the finest wine-producing country France has to offer. Discover the powerful classic wines – both red and white – of Burgundy, the light-bodied red wines of Beaujolais, the distinctive whites of the Jura, with their slightly aromatic after-taste, and the crisp dry wines of the Savoie. The landscape is beautiful and varied, from the gently undulating valleys and hills of the Mâconnais to the forested and mountainous areas of the Jura and Savoie (left near St Badolph). In Central and Eastern France there is wine and scenery to suit all tastes.

Wine Tour N.º 8
CHABLIS AND THE YONNE

Vineyards near the important wine village of Fontenay-près-Chablis,
and (right) a private château in the village of Béru

Driving south from Paris, the first of the great Burgundian vineyards you reach are those of Chablis; it will be another 100 kilometres before you are within sight of those of the Côte d'Or. The small country town of Chablis is 12 kilometres to the east of the A 6 – *Autoroute du Soleil* – near Auxerre. Here and in a few surrounding villages one of the greatest white wines of all is produced. There is nowhere else in the world where the Chardonnay grape – from which Chablis is made – thrives the way it does here on these sunny limestone hills.

While the wine's reputation and importance are immense, the vineyard area where it is produced covers only about 1,500 hectares – and the Grand Crus vineyards are limited to about 100 hectares. However, there are more vineyards in the valley of the Yonne, where other types of Burgundy are produced.

The wines

Chablis is one of the world's best-known wines and has virtually become a generic term for white wine. The true Chablis is made exclusively from the Chardonnay grape – which is used for all the great white wines of Burgundy. Chablis is crisp and dry, making it the ideal accompaniment to seafood and shellfish; it also has a clear, crystalline quality with a greenish tinge and looks as refreshing and pleasing as it tastes.

There are four classifications of Chablis: Grand Cru, Premier Cru, Chablis and Petit Chablis. Seven Grands Crus – Blanchot, Bougros, Les Clos, Grenouilles, Les Preuses, Valmur and Vaudésir – come from the three communes of Chablis, Poinchy and Fyé; the vineyards are on the slopes of the prominent hill immediately to the north east of the town between the D 150 and the D 216. The wines must attain a volume of alcohol of at least 11 per cent and should be kept for at least two or three years; they continue to improve for up to about ten years.

The Premiers Crus – there are twenty-seven of these – come from the next most favourably sited vineyards; they have a similar capacity for ageing and must contain at least 10.5 per cent alcohol. Chablis is produced from nineteen different communes, the best of the remaining vineyards, while Petit Chablis is from the least favourable terrain and is best drunk quite young.

The production of Chablis is fraught with difficulties, since it is an area prone to spring frosts. Considerable effort is made to combat them. Whenever frost is forecast oil-fired stoves are placed

amongst the vines to keep the temperature above freezing point. Another measure involves spraying water from a system of pipes ranged along the vines. The water comes from an artificial lake created specially for this purpose; the principle is that the fine spray of water freezes as it coats the vines and forms a protective barrier of ice.

In addition to Chablis the region is entitled to the *appellation* Bourgogne and red, white and rosé wines are also made from the Gamay, Pinot Noir and Aligoté grapes. A white wine from the Sauvignon grape is made in the village of St Bris-le-Vineux called *Sauvignon de Saint Bris*, and a delightful pale rosé is found in the village of *Irancy*, which also makes a light red wine. An interesting red wine is produced in the village of *Epineuil*, just to the north of Tonnerre.

The cuisine
Gourmets will find all the best influences of Burgundian cuisine in Chablis. The *escargots* are particularly good here; they are often cooked in Chablis. There is a special local *andouillettes à la Chablisienne*, a sausage

made from tripe, and the black puddings and pork pies are excellent. Chablis is used in the local, lighter version of *coq au vin* instead of the usual red wine. Ham from the nearby Morvan is a regular feature of menus, as is the magnificent beef of the Charolais. Chablis is also renowned for its meringues, and for its cherries. Among the excellent cheeses found in the region are *Epoisses*, soft and creamy with a dusty reddish coating, and *Saint-Florentin*, similar in appearance but with a stronger flavour; both are made from cows' milk.

The Route des Vins *Michelin map 65*
The Route des Vins in Chablis and the Yonne valley is not signposted. The route I have suggested takes you to all the most interesting and important villages, mostly along quiet, scenic roads. The town of Chablis is an ideal starting-point for the tour. There are many places where you can sample and buy the wine and, during the summer, the Syndicat d'Initiative mounts a small exhibition of tools, implements, pictures and displays which explain the history and progress of

The tiny village church of Préhy, south of Chablis

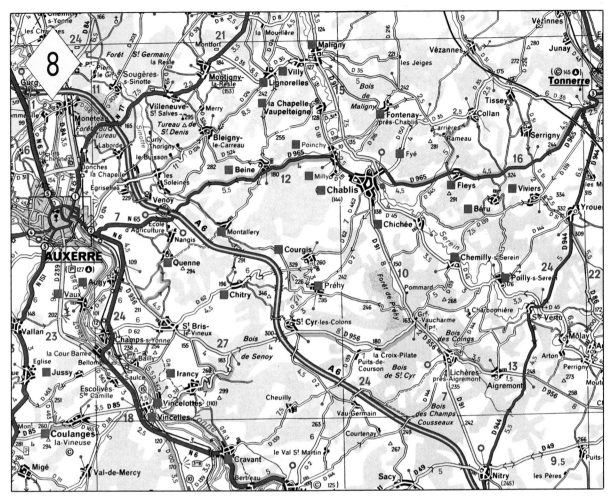

wine-making in the region. A lively market takes place on Sunday mornings, and there is a wine fair on the last Sunday in November. The town itself is small and unassuming with a number of medieval buildings, including the church of Saint-Pierre and the collegiate church of Saint Martin, both dating from the twelfth century.

Leave the town on the D965 heading towards Auxerre. The first wine village is Milly, high up on the hilly slopes to the west; a small road leads up into the village and its surrounding vineyards. A little further along the main road is the Grand Cru commune of Poinchy, designated as a *Village Fleuri* (Flower Village): in the spring and summer every available container – old wine casks, stone troughs, baskets – is crammed with a vivid display of flowers. Here the route leaves the main road and continues along the D131 to the village of la Chapelle Vaupelteigne and

Villy along the banks of the river Serein. The water-meadows are dotted with the large white Charolais cattle grazing under the trees. Then, on to Maligny, where there is an ancient château in the process of restoration.

From here the route climbs up out of the valley towards Fontenay-près-Chablis and then to Fyé, a Grand Cru village in a small valley with the vineyards strung up on the steep slopes about it at a dizzy angle; here you are in the midst of the finest of the Chablis vineyards. Returning briefly to the D965 and heading towards Tonnerre you come to the wine village of Fleys. Just after this, take the small road to the right which leads to Béru, a charming cluster of ancient grey stone houses. The next village is Viviers, a crumbling hamlet in a small valley. The wine road climbs now to the top of the hill towards Poilly-sur-Serein and, as you drive along, there are wonderful views of the vast, open landscape through which the river Serein weaves its gentle course, the rolling hills patterned with vineyards and grain fields.

The road follows the Serein back towards Chablis through the hamlet of Chemilly-sur-Serein and the attractive small village of Chichée. On the outskirts of Chablis take the D 2 through a small wooded valley to Préhy and then Courgis; these two villages with their vineyards spread around the hill slopes mark the western limit of the Chablis vineyards. From here continue along the D 62 towards Chitry, a small town dominated by a fortified church which has a huge round tower. This is the area where the ordinary Burgundy wines are produced. St Bris-le-Vineux, though, makes an unusual dry white wine from the Sauvignon Blanc grape, which is used for the great white wines of Sancerre and Pouilly-sur-Loire, a little further south-west. The wine route here has beautiful and extensive views over the rolling landscape. Next you come to Irancy, situated in an idyllic spot, nestling at the foothills of some steeply sloping hillsides and surrounded by vineyards and orchards; here, a delicate rosé and a light red wine are produced.

From Irancy the wine route continues to the twin towns of Vincelottes and Vincelles, separated by both the river Yonne and the Canal du Nivernais, running side by side. There is a towpath you can walk along and watch the boats and barges making their un-hurried progress along the waterways. If you want to stroll further, the road continues alongside the canal to the old town of Cravant.

Now you must back-track a little to Coulanges-la-Vineuse, an appealing village with a mellow old church set in the middle of vine-clad hills. Here the road turns north through the small wine village of Jussy to Vaux, an old stone village set beside the river Yonne. After you cross the river, take the narrow road back towards Chablis, traversing quiet, almost remote countryside, through the hamlets of Augy, Quenne and Montallery. You rejoin the main road, the D 965, at the busy little wine village of Beine, close to the artificial lake that feeds the vineyard sprinkling system; there are many places to sample the wines of the region here. A little road leads up out of the village over the vine-covered hill to Lignorelles. You complete the circuit by returning through Villy and Poinchy to the town of Chablis.

A summer landscape to the south of the village of Courgis

Wine Tour Nº 9

THE COTE D'OR

The village of Pommard, home of one of the best-known Burgundian wines

One of the most exciting things about exploring the wine roads of France is that every other signpost you encounter seems to carry a familiar and often revered name. This is especially true of the Côte d'Or. You'll see Gevrey-Chambertin, Volnay, Nuits-St-Georges, Montrachet, Vougeot, Meursault, Pommard and Beaune – names that are more familiar in delicate script on the label of a fine bottle of wine – here crudely lettered and scattered casually on roadsigns, walls and plaques.

These famous villages all lie within quite a small area. The Côte d'Or is a ridge of hills that runs almost parallel to the *Autoroute du Soleil*, and the vineyards that pattern its slopes start just south of Dijon and continue in an almost unbroken band to the village of Santenay, some 48 kilometres to the south.

They are divided into two distinctive wine areas: the Côte de Nuits in the northern half, and the Côte de Beaune. The soil here is of a reddish clay with fragments of chalk, with a subsoil rich in minerals. In addition, the disposition of the hills creates an ideal microclimate for the Pinot Noir and Chardonnay grapes, from which the greatest of the Côte d'Or wines are made. This does not mean, however, that wine-making here is a trouble-free occupation. When the first buds appear in April they often have to be protected from hard frosts, while heavy rain in the summer months can easily create the conditions for rot. But the diverse climate and soil in the Côte d'Or mean that there is an extraordinarily rich variety of wine, in terms of character and quality. Often a distance of only a few hundred metres will be the difference between a good wine and a really great one: for this reason, vineyards in the region are called *climats*, since each has its own unique combination of soil, sun, wind and rain. As a general rule the best wines are made from the grapes grown on the middle of the slope.

The wines

Red, white and some rosé wines are made here. The great red Burgundies of the region are made from the Pinot Noir grape and the whites from the Chardonnay. A lesser red wine called *Passe-tout-grains* is made from a mixture of Pinot Noir and Gamay (the red-wine grape of Beaujolais). In addition, the Aligoté grape is used for ordinary white wines.

As well as the fine – and expensive – wines from the famous vineyards and villages of the Côte d'Or there are wines under the *appellations Côte de Nuits* and *Côte de Beaune*, from communes in these general areas; *Côte de Beaune-Villages* and *Côte de Nuits-Villages* from specific communes; and the *Hautes-Côtes de Beaune* and the *Hautes-Côtes de Nuits* from vineyards higher up in the hills beyond the more famous slopes.

The cuisine

Burgundian cuisine is at its richest and heartiest here and red wine features strongly in many dishes. This is where *boeuf à la bourguignonne* and *coq au vin* originate. You'll have plenty of opportunities to eat a real *coq au vin* made with a bird that has spent some time strutting around the farmyard – a far cry from those made with battery-reared chicken. Red wine is also used in *oeufs pochés en meurette*, eggs poached in a wine sauce. *Gougères* are worth looking out for: they are light golden mounds of choux pastry cooked with cheese – when eaten hot the crisp pastry gives way to an oozy, creamy centre. The cheeses include *Cîteaux*, *Saint Florentin* and *Soumaintrain*, all made from cows' milk.

The Route des Vins *Michelin maps 65 and 69*

The Côte d'Or is divided, geographically and by wine types, into two quite separate areas – the Côte de Nuits and the Côte de Beaune – although the vines are virtually continuous. The northern half runs south from Chenôve, a suburb of Dijon. The distance from Chenôve to Corgoloin, where the Côte de Beaune route starts, is little more than 24 kilometres. The countryside on the short northern tour is one you should explore on foot if you have the time, along the tiny lanes that meander up into the vineyards from the villages. You will get a fascinating glimpse of the continuing effort that goes into tending and rearing the vines and, whatever the time of year, something of interest will be happening in the wine calendar.

The Côte de Nuits route starts just outside Dijon, at Chenôve, on the N 74. It is well signposted, rather proudly, as the Route des Grands Crus. From Chenôve the wine road follows the D 122, a small road that winds its way up on to the gentle slopes of the Côte de Nuits towards the village of Marsannay-la-Côte, noted for its rosé; it has its own *appellation*, Bourgogne Rosé de Marsannay. The next village is Fixin, the first of eight major communes of the Côte de Nuits; in the park just above the village is a bronze statue of Napoleon, sculpted in 1846 by François Rude, whose most famous work is the decorative panels of the Arc de Triomphe in Paris.

A few kilometres south is the first of the truly great

Château Clos de Vougeot surrounded by its illustrious, walled vineyard

wine villages of the region, and of the world: Gevrey-Chambertin. Its 3,000 or so inhabitants live in and for the vines, literally; there is a cellar or *cave* underneath most of the houses. Like many other villages on the Côte d'Or, Gevrey has added the name of its most celebrated vineyard, le Chambertin, to its own. There is a second Grand Cru vineyard, Clos-de-Bèze, here too. Just to the west of the village is a medieval château restored in the thirteenth century by the monks of Cluny; it has tasting rooms and cellars, a magnificent hall and a grand staircase. On the other side of Gevrey is the Combe de Lavaux, a dramatic wooded gorge where there are excellent picnic spots. The road that leads to it is one of the routes that winds up into the Hautes-Côtes de Nuits.

The next commune is Morey-St-Denis, a quiet village with its famous walled *climat*, the Clos de Tart, which was planted by the Cistercian monks originally, like the vineyards of the neighbouring village Vougeot. There are four other Grand Cru vineyards in Morey: Clos de la Roche, Clos St-Denis, Clos des Lambrays and, on the southern border of the commune, Les Bonnes Mares. The wine road now leads to the village of Chambolle-Musigny, which nestles at the foot of the Côte de Nuits' highest hill. Although, for the most part, they are not particularly beautiful these Burgundian villages have a sense of their own importance; and this small cluster of mellow stone houses surrounded by carefully manicured vines is no exception.

The next village on the wine route is Vougeot, famous for its château and the walled vineyard of Clos de Vougeot, the largest *climat* in the whole of Burgundy. The fine Renaissance château was built by a

The magnificently sited, Château of La Rochepot, beautifully restored after damage in the French Revolution

sixteenth-century abbot in the middle of what was already an enormous vineyard; it is said that at one time the French army had to present arms as they passed it. Now the château is the headquarters of the Confrérie des Chevaliers du Tastevin, an organization which promotes the wines of Burgundy throughout the world. There is a wine museum in its huge Romanesque cellars with some interesting medieval wine presses.

The village of Vosne-Romanée and the busy town of Nuits-St-Georges are the last of the great communes on the Route des Grands Crus. The former boasts no less than seven Grands Crus. They include Romanée-Conti, which has a reputation for red burgundy that is equalled only by the one Le Montrachet has for its white wine: its scant 2 hectares produce about 3,000 bottles per year. The headquarters of many *négociants-éleveurs* (the merchants who control and market the wine of individual growers) are based in Nuits St-Georges. One of the Apollo astronauts – being a wine lover, or perhaps, a classicist (the ruins of a Gallo-Roman villa were discovered locally) – named a crater on the Moon after the town.

The Côte de Beaune route begins at Corgoloin. One of the first villages you encounter is Aloxe-Corton, a tiny place with few inhabitants and no hotel or restaurant. But it does have two tasting cellars, one in the impressive Château Corton-André (notable for its magnificent gilded mosaic roof), and its red and white wines have an international reputation. In the valley that extends westward from the N 74 is the small commune of Pernand-Vergelesses, nestling at the foot of the Corton hill. Savigny-lès-Beaune lies only a few

Château Corton-André in the tiny wine village of Aloxe-Corton in the Côte de Beaune

hundred metres from the *Autoroute du Soleil* and has a twelfth-century church, two châteaux and many imposing old houses.

And so to Beaune. The capital of the Côte d'Or is a wine town through and through. The leading *négociants-éleveurs* have their headquarters here, and will allow you to tour their vast underground laby-rinths of passages and cellars, many dating from the

fifteenth century, where the great wines of Burgundy are housed. Beaune has a leafy central square, the Place Carnot, and many lovely old streets, ramparts, a bustling and colourful country market, an abundance of tempting wine and food shops and the Hospices de Beaune, known as the Hôtel-Dieu. Built in 1451 by Nicolas Rolin to house the sick, the Hôtel-Dieu is famous for its steep, brightly coloured, mosaic roof; it

Left: The justly celebrated Hospices de Beaune, its famous, brightly coloured, gilded mosaic roof and cobbled courtyard lightly veiled under a sprinkling of snow. Above: Burning the vine prunings

is arranged around a magnificent cobbled courtyard and includes an old pharmacy and a museum, where you can see Roger van der Weyden's polyptych of *The Last Judgement*, painted in 1443. Nicolas Rolin also bequeathed his vineyards to the Hospice, and the wine is sold at the auction held every year in the Hôtel-Dieu on the third Sunday in November. Although these wines frequently reach a ridiculously high price, because the proceeds from their sale go to the Hospice and other charities, nevertheless they also usually dictate the sale price of other Burgundian wines. Thus, if a year's prices for the Hospice wines are generally very high, so too will be the prices for the other wines. The auction draws buyers and wine lovers from all over the world and for the three days it lasts, called *Les Trois Glorieuses*, not a spare bed is to be found in Beaune or the surrounding towns.

Leaving Beaune and heading south you come to a succession of small villages, all of them famous for their wines – Pommard, Volnay, Monthelie, Auxey-Duresses, Meursault, Puligny-Montrachet, Chassagne-Montrachet and Santenay – and you should spend a few hours in each, sampling the local products. A small road from Santenay leads to the old church of St Jean which nestles below a rocky outcrop.

A house in Chassagne near Montrachet. Many of the village houses are wreathed with flowers

You must not miss le Montrachet, the old walled vineyard which produces the world's greatest white wine. It is easy to overlook as there is only a faint inscription on one of the crumbling gateways to signify its presence; it lies mid-way between Puligny-Montrachet and Chassagne-Montrachet, high up on the slopes of the rather stark hill called Mont Rachet, (literally, 'bare mountain'). I was photographing here one bitterly cold January day with snow drifting down on to the vines, when a car stopped and a lightly dressed French couple got out. They gazed reverently at the bleak plot of land for a few minutes. The man was shivering as he turned to get back into his warm car. He caught my eye. '*C'est le Montrachet!*', he said simply.

The vineyards of the Côte d'Or are not only restricted to the prestigious hillsides surrounding these famous villages, and the wine route continues up into the higher terrain known as the Hautes-Côtes de

Beaune. Instead of the preened and regimented vines of Pinot Noir and Chardonnay grapes, you see the rather spindly, untidy Aligoté and Gamay, more suited to the less hospitable soil and climate here but not producing such noble wines.

From Santenay you can follow the signs to small villages such as Dezize-lès-Maranges, and then to the top of the Montagne des Trois Croix, where there are stunning views of the Côte d'Or and the Chalonnais. From here the wine road continues through the villages of Sampigny-lès-Maranges and Change, then on towards Nolay on the D 973. Change is an appealing place with many fine old buildings, including an oak-beamed market. Nearby is a spectacular gorge, le Cirque du Bout du Monde, (World's End), where dramatically sheer cliffs surround a peaceful meadow through which a stream wends its way. At the base of the cliff is a waterfall.

The village of la Rochepot is close by; its spired and turreted château was badly damaged during the French Revolution and was restored last century. From here the Route des Hautes-Côtes winds up towards the highest point in the wine-growing area. You go through Orches, stunningly located beside dramatic rock formations; it is also known for its delicate rosé wine. Near the village of Nantoux, follow a narrow road on a detour up the side of a valley, through precariously sited vineyards, over the steep hill and down into the village of Bouze-lès-Beaune.

Further north, over the *Autoroute* towards the small hamlet of Bouilland, the route goes through what is now the Hautes-Côtes de Nuits and continues up steep-sided, wooded valleys towards Marey-lès-Fussey, where the Maison des Hautes-Côtes is situated. This is a centre that promotes the local wines; you can taste and buy them here and eat the regional culinary specialities in the Maison's restaurant. In these wild and often rugged surroundings, soft fruit, particularly blackcurrants, are grown along with the grapes. Much of the fruit for Cassis, the blackcurrant liqueur for which the region is also famous, is grown here; Kir (named after a former mayor of Lyon who was rather partial to it) is traditionally made with a glass of chilled Bourgogne Aligoté and a dash of Cassis. From here, there's many a lane you can take to get back towards Beaune or the villages along the Route des Grands Crus.

The famous walled vineyard which produces the celebrated white wine of Montrachet

Wine Tour N°10

THE CHALONNAIS

The hilltop village of Aluze, surrounded by thriving vineyards

Herds of brown goats and the large white Charolais cattle graze peacefully on the gentle slopes and meadows of the Chalonnais, shaded by leafy trees. The atmosphere is relaxed after the self-important bustle of the Côte d'Or. And instead of regimented rows of vines extending as far as the eye can see, here the vineyards are often tucked away out of sight among the other crops.

The Chalonnais is an extension of the Côte de Beaune, separated from it by a narrow strip of vineless countryside. It is a small area in terms of vineyard acreage – smaller even than Chablis – and the vines are less intensively cultivated. The vineyards of the Chalonnais extend south from just beyond Chagny to St Boil, on the D 981, a distance of less than 32 kilometres, and they are seldom more than a few kilometres wide.

The wines

The wines of the *Côte Chalonnaise* are less well known than those of the rest of Burgundy, particularly outside France. However, the grape varieties and the soil have much in common with the more illustrious neighbouring vineyards and, while they do not have the same reputation for character and quality, Chalonnais wines have become more popular, perhaps because the high cost of the better-known wines from

Burgundy makes these seem good value. The four major communes are *Rully, Mercurey, Givry* and *Montagny*.

The best white wines are made from the Chardonnay grape and the reds from the Pinot Noir; however the Aligoté thrives well on this terrain and the region's *Bourgogne Aligoté* is highly regarded, in particular that from the commune of Bouzeron. Sparkling wines are also made here by the *méthode champenoise*; in addition there is the *Bourgogne Passe-tout-grains*, a red wine made from a mixture of Pinot Noir and Gamay grapes.

The cuisine

The menus of the Chalonnais are very similar to those of the neighbouring Côte d'Or, with some local variations such as *coquelet au Mercurey* instead of *coq au vin*, and *Charolais au marchand de vin*, a succulent Charolais steak cooked in a red wine sauce with mushrooms and shallots. Among the usual selection of *charcuterie* are a Chalonnais speciality called *rosette*, a spicy saucisson made with red peppers, and *saucisson en brioche*, a spicy pork sausage baked inside a light golden brioche crust. A creamy, mild cows'-milk cheese you will find in the region is *Brillat-Savarin*, a smallish disc with a golden crust named after the

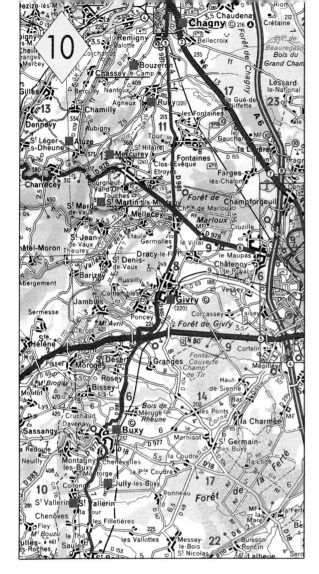

The façade of an old café in the slumbering village of Bouzeron (top). Its Bourgogne Aligoté wine is highly regarded. This creeper-covered farmhouse (above) is hidden away in the tiny village of St Vallerin

nineteenth-century gastronome. There is also *Cîteaux*, a larger cheese with a firmer texture, made from cows' milk. Neighbouring Dijon is famed, among other things, for its mustard, and mustard sauce (*sauce moutarde*) is served often with fish, meat and chicken and of course, with rabbit; the sauce is a creamy combination of Dijon mustard, butter, cream, wine vinegar, egg yolks and stock. You'll also find a special dish of ham and parsley in Dijon, as well as *nonnettes* (iced gingerbread) and *pain d'épice* (gingerbread).

The Route des Vins *Michelin map 69*

The northern gateway to the Chalonnais Route des Vins is the town of Chagny; one of the best restaurants in the region, in the Hôtel Lameloise, is here. You take the D 81 to the first of the four main wine communes, Rully. As you approach the village you will see little evidence of vines, since most of the vineyards are on the hillside behind the village to the west; access is via

a narrow road that leads past an imposing château. Although this was a red wine area originally, today the *vignerons* rely mainly on the Chardonnay grape from which they make a fine white wine that is steadily increasing in both quantity and reputation. A white *méthode champenoise* wine, Crémant de Bourgogne, is also made here from the Aligoté grape.

A short detour from Rully will take you back towards Chagny along a narrow country road through unspoiled, almost deserted countryside to Bouzeron, a sleepy little village of ancient stone houses and crumbling farm buildings. It is known for its white wine made from the Aligoté grape: Bourgogne Aligoté. Driving back along the same road on the D 109 you go through a green valley and the small wine village of Aluze, perched precariously on a hill surrounded by vineyards.

From here the Route des Vins continues towards the second of the major wine centres, Mercurey, a one-

street town ranged along the D 978. But don't be deceived – Mercurey is, in fact, the largest producer of all the Chalonnais communes. Red wines made from the same Pinot Noir grape as the red Burgundies of the Côte d'Or predominate, while a small quantity of white wine from the Chardonnay grape is also produced. There is a tasting cellar where you can sample a variety of these local wines. Before returning to the D 981, it is worth making a small detour to St Martin s/s Montaigu, another village of stone houses surrounded by vine-patterned hills.

As you approach Givry, another important wine town, you'll see signs proclaiming that its wines were Henri IV's favourite tipple. Givry is an old town with a fortified gateway, an ancient covered market, many old houses and a bustling atmosphere; it makes a good base for exploring the region. As in Mercurey, most of the wine here is red, with only a small amount of white being made.

Montagny is the most southerly commune of the Chalonnais appellations. A peculiarity of the Montagny wines is that the term Premier Cru here simply denotes a higher degree of alcohol rather than a superior or specific vineyard, as would normally be the case. This is a white wine area and the vineyards are scattered over the surrounding hillsides, some of which are above 400 metres high. The quiet, narrow lanes that wind in and around the vineyards offer a succession of rural landscapes and will lead you to some quite delightful small villages. Jully-lès-Buxy is one of them – a picturesque cluster of weathered, golden-stone farmhouses – and the nearby village of St Vallerin is also worth a visit. Buxy, which is larger and busier, has a *cave*, called the *Caveau de la Tour Rouge*, where you can taste and buy the local wines. Its restaurant serves regional specialities and is attractively situated in an old tower within the remains of the ramparts.

The imposing Château de Rully on the northern borders of the Chalonnais vineyards. The reputation of its white wine is growing rapidly

Wine Tour N.° 11

THE MACONNAIS

The village church of Vergisson in the heart of the Mâconnais,
and (right) vineyards near the village of Fuissé

Vines have been grown in Mâcon since Roman times, but it wasn't until a brilliant publicity stunt by a local grower in the seventeenth century that they gained wider recognition: Claude Brosse loaded two casks of his wine on to a cart and travelled for thirty-three days until he got to the court at Versailles. Louis XIV was very impressed by him – and by his wine, declaring it to be of a better quality than the Loire wines he had been drinking. In recent years the wines of the Mâconnais have become more and more popular and production has increased accordingly.

Although Mâcon itself is the centre of the region's wine trade, the vineyards are situated further to the west, along a line of low hills rising from the valley of the Saône. Coming from the north, it is around Mâcon that your thoughts start turning towards the Mediterranean. The climate is more southerly, the land lush but rugged and the houses have flatter, red-tiled roofs and open-galleried façades. Indeed, the grapes ripen a week or so earlier here than in the more northerly Burgundian vineyards and the harvest takes place correspondingly sooner.

The wines
Although red, white and rosé wines are all made here,

the dominant type is white, made mostly from the Chardonnay grape, with a small quantity from Aligoté. The red and rosé wines are made mainly from the Gamay, and a little from the Pinot Noir.

The basic classifications of the wines are *Mâcon, Mâcon Supérieur* and *Mâcon-Villages.* The difference between the first two is simply that Mâcon Supérieur has a higher minimum level of alcohol. Mâcon-Villages is made from forty-three specific communes within the region and the quantity of wine allowed to be produced from each hectare of vines is limited, resulting in a better quality wine. In addition there are the named Crus from the small region in the south of the Mâconnais; these are *Pouilly-Fuissé, Pouilly-Vinzelles, Pouilly-Loché* and the most recent appellation, *Saint-Véran.*

The cuisine
The cuisine of the Mâconnais is typically Burgundian, with all the benefits of the superb ingredients from the surrounding countryside: beef from the Charolais, plump yellow chickens from Bresse and superb *charcuterie,* ham and game, as well as wild mushrooms from the Morvan hills and forests to the north. *Escargots à la bourguignonne* are large, tender Bur-

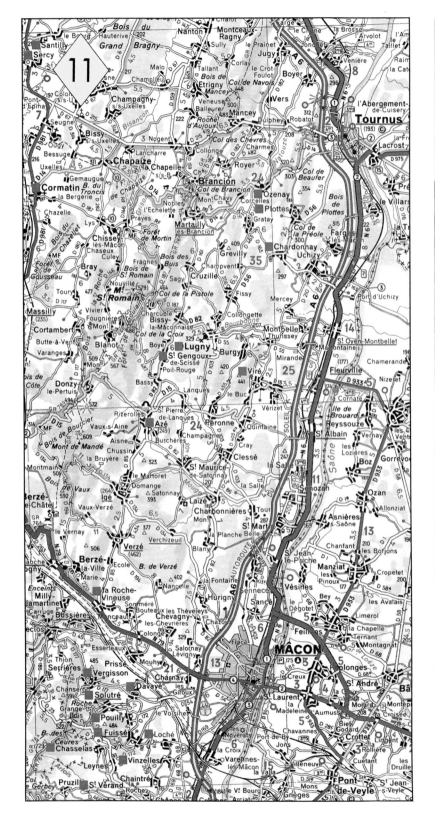

gundian snails which are simmered in a well-seasoned *court-bouillon* laced with dry white wine, then returned to their shells and stuffed with butter, garlic, shallots, ham and parsley. *Potée à la bourguignonne* is a hearty stew made with beef, salt pork, sausage, potatoes, turnips, carrots, cabbage and leeks. Ham is often prepared *à la lie de vin* – in a sauce made from the residues of the wine left in the cask after bottling. The local *andouillettes* and *saucissons* are often served in a sauce made with dry white wine.

The Route des Vins *Michelin maps 69 and 73*

Although the most important wine-growing area is situated immediately to the west of Mâcon, the Route des Vins starts further north, just south of the Chalonnais region beyond Buxy. Drive south on the D981, a quiet road leading to the heart of the Mâconnais through pleasant, undulating countryside. The first towns you reach are St Boil and Sercy; from the road at Sercy a spectacular château is visible. It is well worth making a short detour to St Gengoux, an attractive medieval town with a twelfth-century château, cobbled streets and many old houses. It also has a good Cave Co-opérative where many wines from the Mâconnais and the Chalonnais regions can be tasted. After this, the vineyards become less frequent, but the road is a continuing pleasure with vistas of rolling, wooded landscape. Stop at Cormatin to see the fifteenth-century solid gold Vierge de Pitié in the church. You can also visit the magnificent Renaissance château set in its great park. From here, take the D14 west towards Ozenay where another turreted château can be seen from the roadside. The vineyards begin in earnest again around the village of Plottes, near Ozenay, on the D56.

The road continues through a succession of small wine-growing villages, including Chardonnay, Viré, Lugny and Azé. This is gently contoured, open countryside, criss-crossed by quiet lanes. The meadows and fields are planted with grain and vegetables, while the orderly rows of well-tended vines in the vineyards make pleasing patterns.

Many of the villages have wine co-operatives that it is possible to visit. I was in the one at Viré in late September as convoys of tractors towing cartloads of

The imposing rock of Solutré (top) dominating the vineyards which encircle it. Left: A goatherd leading her small flock home for milking, a colourful but not uncommon sight in this region

greenish-yellow Chardonnay grapes queued up to deposit their loads. In an atmosphere of busy excitement, I asked how the harvest was this year, and received the true Gallic response – with downturned mouth and shoulders shrugged to the ears – '*Moyen, M'sieu, moyen*' (so-so).

Although the vineyards here are less well known than those of the villages further south, much of the good, honest wine (red, white and rosé) sold under the appellation Mâcon-Villages and Mâcon Supérieur is produced from around these sleepy slopes. Further south is the curiously named town of la Roche-Vineuse, where you should go for a walk up the steep, winding lane via the church to the hilltop, from where there is a superb view of the surrounding countryside.

The real heart of the Mâconnais is a small area just south of the N 79. The villages of Pouilly, Fuissé, Solutré, Vergisson, Davayé, Vinzelles, Loché St-Vérand and Chasselas are clustered almost on top of each other, linked by a number of narrow winding roads. They are all quite small and quiet but are full of character. Then there is the medieval village of St Vérand, which is illuminated during the summer months and looks breathtaking after dusk. In addition to the many individual *vignerons* inviting you to visit their *caves*, there are a number of *Caves Co-opératives* that have a deserved reputation for producing fine wines.

The Route des Vins is well marked but this is hardly necessary, since even an aimless drive in this region will take you to most of the important wine villages. The scenic splendour here is matched by the excellence of the wines: Pouilly-Fuissé is considered by many to be one of the greatest white wines of France, certainly of the Mâconnais. The vines which produce this great wine are planted over a landscape of dramatic character and proportion, dominated by two enormous rocky outcrops, Vergisson and Solutré, cathedral-like as they rise above the vineyards.

The rock of Solutré, a natural fortress, was the gathering place for the Gauls during their final battle for autonomy in 511; a huge bonfire of discarded vines is lit on the summit every Midsummer's Day to mark the event. A vast deposit of prehistoric bones – one layer made up entirely of broken horsebones – was found at the base of the rock in 1866: this site is so important that one period of the Palaeolithic era is now known as Solutrian (18,000 – 15,000 BC). Many of the archaeological finds discovered here are on display at

The massive rock of Vergisson, dramatically outlined against a stormy sky, the village of Vergisson nestling at its foot

the Musée des Ursulines in Mâcon.

Although it is not on the official Route des Vins, it would certainly be a pity to bypass Mâcon. Although a busy river port, there is a fine old centre where the Maison du Mâconnais, a restaurant serving the hearty food of the region, and a wine centre are situated.

Wine Tour Nº 12

BEAUJOLAIS

Vineyards near Beaujeu, from which Beaujolais takes its name

Beaujolais is such a perfect name for a wine – suggesting ruddy cheeked joviality and a hearty lust for life – that it might have been thought up by a poetic advertizing executive. In fact, the name is derived from the town of Beaujeu, which lies in the heart of the countryside to the west of the *Autoroute du Soleil*, near Villefranche. The landscape is almost alpine in character with miniature, rounded mountains jostling together, while the country roads wind and climb through them, offering a perpetual display of breathtaking vistas, which is totally captivating.

Protected by the foothills of the Massif Central to the west, the Beaujolais has a mild climate which is ideal for the cultivation of vines, although the mountainous nature of the landscape tends to encourage sudden storms and hail. It is quite a large area, extending from just south of Mâcon to the outskirts of Lyon, and produces a considerable volume of wine – over 11 million cases annually.

The wines
The most important vineyards are situated to the north of Villefranche, where the nine great wine villages of Beaujolais are grouped. In addition to the Crus, much of the Beaujolais-Villages wine is also produced from these vineyards. The less geographi-

cally favoured communes further south are largely responsible for the production of the basic, unnamed Beaujolais. Beaujolais is a red wine produced from the Gamay grape, and is best drunk young; it is often served slightly chilled. There are five basic types of Beaujolais. The most common is known simply as *Beaujolais*; *Beaujolais Supérieur* merely denotes a higher alcohol content, 10 per cent instead of 9. *Beaujolais-Villages* is an *appellation* given to about forty villages in the northern sector of the area and is generally of superior quality to the simple Beaujolais. *Beaujolais Primeur*, or *Nouveau*, is a relatively new phenomenon: fermentation is specially controlled so the wine can be bottled and sold – amidst great publicity – by the middle of November. The most prestigious Beaujolais wines are those bearing the name of one of the nine communes: *Saint-Amour, Juliénas, Chénas, Moulin-à-Vent, Fleurie, Chiroubles, Morgon, Brouilly* and *Côte de Brouilly*.

The cuisine
The cuisine in Beaujolais is notable for its simplicity. As elsewhere in Burgundy, the raw materials are of the highest quality, in particular the game from the wooded mountains, the funghi including *morels* and *ceps*, which are found in abundance in the fields and

100

The region's charm owes as much to its buildings (above, Chessy and right, Col des Truges) as its landscape

woods, and the pike, carp and trout caught in the Rhône. There are fields of corn and other grains growing in the valleys of Beaujolais and black truffles are found in the oak forests. The local *charcuterie*, such as *jambon persillé* and *andouillettes*, is the perfect accompaniment to the wines of Chiroubles or Fleurie. The crayfish are justly celebrated and are usually served *à la crème*.

The Route des Vins *Michelin map 73*
The Route du Beaujolais is signposted in a somewhat random fashion, and as you travel the maze of tiny roads you can easily be led into circles of confusion. But it is an agreeable way of becoming confused admittedly, and the small distances between the villages are such for it not to matter if you become temporarily lost. If you pinpoint exactly where you want to go with the aid of the Michelin map, you can then follow the local signposts to each place. But remember, this is very much a region through which you should meander slowly – even a little aimlessly – in order to appreciate it fully.

It is best to start the Route des Vins at the village of Crêches, near where the Autoroute crosses the N 6, virtually on the border of the Mâconnais and Beaujolais. The division between the two regions is a little blurred here, and you'll see Beaujolais-Villages advertisements for white wines side by side with those for the Pouilly-Fuissé. But look at the vines and you'll know that you are in true Beaujolais country: the tall, gangly vines of the Pinot Chardonnay, from which the white Mâcon wines are made, have given way to the knee-high Gamay vines. Although in other regions the

Top: Harvesting the grapes in the hillside vineyard of Vaux-en-Beaujolais. Above left: An old farmhouse just outside Montmelas. Above right: an elderly *vigneron* breaks from his labours

Gamay often produces inferior wines, it is ideally suited to the soil and climate conditions found here.

St Amour-Bellevue is the first village on the wine route. It has a *cave*, called the Caveau du Cru St-Amour, where you can taste and buy the local wines. From here the wine route leads through a succession of the Crus wine villages. By and large, they are unremarkable, neither particularly quaint nor picturesque; however, they do have a certain quiet, rural charm and are situated in quite beautiful settings. They also provide countless opportunities to sample the wines.

In Juliénas, one of the local *caves* is in a deconsecrated fifteenth-century church and the other, just outside the village, is in the Château du Bois de la Salle, headquarters of the local wine co-operative. At the wine-tasting centre in Chénas, the Cellier de Chénas, there is a sculpture by Renoir depicting workers cutting down a forest of oak trees in readiness for planting the vines. There is scarcely an oak tree to be seen here now. Moulin-à-Vent, where one of the greatest Beaujolais wines is produced, has its tasting cellar close to the vaneless windmill after which the town is named and which is a famous symbol of Beaujolais. There is a fine restaurant, L'Auberge du Cep serving local food, in Fleurie, as well as an excellent Cave Co-opérative.

Of the nine Crus villages, Chiroubles occupies the highest ground, and its vineyards reach to a height of over 400 metres. If you climb – or drive – up this hill, past the vineyards, to its summit, you can sample the wines at the tasting centre and eat the regional specialities in the restaurant while enjoying a breathtaking panorama over the Haut-Beaujolais. The cellars of Villié-Morgon, to the south, are also well

The tranquil village square at Arbuissonas – quite deserted during the grape harvest

Juliénas, one of the Grand Cru villages, which has a *cave* in a local church

worth visiting. Here the tasting is done in the huge vaulted rooms of a château which dates from the fifteenth century.

Brouilly, south of the D 37, boasts two wine châteaux – Château de la Chaize and Château de Pierreux – and two Crus: Brouilly is made in six different villages, while Côte de Brouilly comes from the vines that grow on the sunny southern slopes of Mont Brouilly. On the first Sunday in September a procession winds its way up the mountain to the small chapel of Notre Dame du Raisin on the summit, and there they pray for a successful harvest.

Between Chiroubles and Brouilly make a detour via the Col du Truges and the Col du Fût to Beaujeu. The route is one of the most spectacular in the Beaujolais, with narrow tracks winding along the hillsides by steep plunging valleys at times reminiscent of the roads of Austria and Switzerland. Further south, beyond Brouilly, is Vaux-en-Beaujolais, the village where Gabriel Chevalier set his novel *Clochemerle*. Predictably, an auberge and a tasting cellar honour the connection.

The charms of Beaujolais are not limited to the northerly vineyards and the famous nine villages. The region to the south of Villefranche mainly produces ordinary Beaujolais; and it has much else to offer the traveller. There is a signposted route, called the Route des Pierres Dorées, which leads through beautiful unspoilt countryside to a succession of enchanting golden-stone villages. It begins at Limas, a small suburb of Villefranche. From here the D 70 climbs up along the ridge of a hill towards the village of Charnay; there are wide, sweeping views to the east over the Saône and further to the north towards Beaujeu. A

little further along is Belmont, which in spring and summer is always bedecked with flowers. These villages look very different from those of the more affluent communes not many kilometres north. There are plenty of places along the route where you can stop to taste and buy the simple wines produced here by an apparently limitless number of individual growers.

Châtillon, Chessy and Bagnols, three more small villages within a very small area, are well worth a brief detour; they are quiet, unspoilt and apparently completely unaware of their charm – always an endearing quality. The road north from le Bois-d'Oingt towards Oingt is another route with beautiful views over the diverse landscape. Oingt is walled and has narrow cobbled streets and many honey-coloured houses; there are a number of craft workshops in the streets, a wine-tasting cellar, an old tower and a terrace beside the church with fine views of the surrounding countryside. More obviously 'picturesque' than many of the other villages, it is also more self-conscious.

This part of the Beaujolais is a virtual maze of tiny roads leading to innumerable small villages; a fascinating area to explore. However remote it seems, at no time are you far from the main road, the D 485, which takes you to Lyon, back on to the *Autoroute du Soleil*, or further west towards Roanne and Clermont Ferrand and the vineyards of the Auvergne.

Left: A simple, sturdy castle typical of Beaujolais country, Château Rapatous nestles in the valley below Theize. Above: Gamay grapes from which Beaujolais is produced

Wine Tour N.º 13

THE JURA

Left: A typical crumbling façade in the main street of Arbois.
Above: The Cirque de Baume towers above the Abbey of Baume-les-Messieurs

Driving south on the N 83 from Besançon, you will get your first glimpse of the Jura vineyards a few kilometres north of the town of Arbois, where the rolling hills that signal the approach of the Jura plateau also define the eastern border of the plain of Bresse.

The wines of the Jura have long been regarded with respect. Pliny mentioned them, and they were greatly appreciated by the Romans. They have also graced the tables of many discerning people from the dukes of Burgundy to Rabelais and Brillat-Savarin, the French writer and gastronome. The soil on which the vines are grown is a mixture of limestone often combined with clay, the subsoil being a compacted marl. In the Arbois area the land has a crust of aalian limestone on a foundation of lias, sand and marl which is particularly favourable to the Savagnin and Poulsard grapes. Vine cultivation is hard work in the Jura: many of the vines are planted on terraces cut into the steep hillsides and when the soil is washed down, as often happens during heavy rainfalls, it must be carried back to the vineyards.

The wines

Among the grape varieties grown here are the Ploussard (or Poulsard) from which rosé wines are made, the Trousseau for red, the Savagnin, from which the renowned *Vin Jaune* is made, and the Chardonnay for fine white wines that can be kept for many years. Both the Poulsard and Trousseau and the Chardonnay and Savagnin are often blended during harvesting to produce wines with a considerable variety of colour, from very pale gold through yellow, amber and light pink to rich ruby.

For such a relatively small area, the Jura produces an amazing variety of wine. The regional speciality, *Vin Jaune*, is made by an unusual method, shared by the Spanish Jerez wines. The Savagnin grapes are harvested late, often not until November, and are pressed in the same way as for a conventional white wine, but the juice is then put in barrels and kept for up to ten years (six is the legal minimum). During this period a veil of yeasts develops on its surface, the wine begins to oxidize, creating the characteristic deep yellow colour, and at the same time a subtle and unusual bouquet and flavour develop, often compared to hazelnuts. The exact nature of this transition is not fully understood, nor can it be totally controlled. The natural loss of wine from evaporation in the cask (ullage) is not made up as with normal wines during ageing, and this makes good Vin Jaune a rather

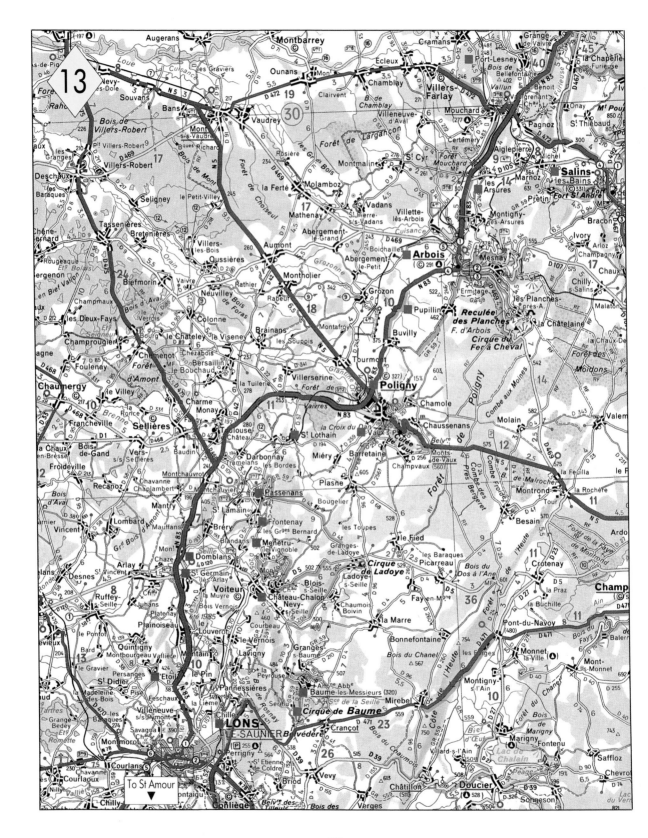

The winter store of maize decorating a farmhouse near Pupillin. Many houses are also decorated with flowers

A *vigneron* pruning the summer vine near the village of Toulouse-le-Château

expensive and relatively rare commodity. It is usually drunk chilled as an apéritif or at room temperature with the local Comte cheese.

Another unusual wine for which the Jura is famous is *Vin de Paille*, or straw wine, so called because the grapes are dried on a bed of straw for three months before pressing. This makes them sweeter and produces a highly alcoholic dessert wine which compares favourably with a Sauternes; it can be kept for fifty years or more. Sparkling wines are also produced in the Jura and Henri Maire extols the virtues of his *Vin Fou*, or mad wine, on hoardings throughout France.

Of the other wines the rosés are of particular interest and are as highly rated as the well-known Rhône wine Tavel. Most rosé wines are left only briefly in contact with the skins of the black grapes to give them colour. But the Poulsard grapes of the Jura have less pigmentation than other varieties, and this means that the juice and skins can be left to ferment together for many days, as they would for a red wine, without losing the delicacy of colour expected of rosé. This gives the Jura rosés well-defined body and flavour and the ability to be kept.

The cuisine

The trout, perch, pike (*brochet*) and carp from the Jura's rivers are excellent, and there is plenty of game found in its forests and hills, including hare, pigeon, woodcock (*bécasse*) and pheasant, which are used to produce some intriguing pâtés and *terrines*. You can find the local smoked hams and *andouillettes* in every *charcuterie*. The dish you will experience most frequently is *coq au vin jaune*, a delicious concoction of chicken in a rich but light sauce made with cream and

Vin Jaune and thickened with egg yolks; in spring it is served with *morels*, dark brown wild funghi which have a quite soft and subtle texture and flavour.

The brown and white cows that graze on the hillsides and meadows provide milk for the region's cheeses. These include the famous *Comte*, much of which is produced in co-opératives – many of the individual herds are quite small and Comte is a very large cheese! At one small co-opérative in a hill-town above Salins-les-Bains, the proprietor showed me the vast copper vats holding over 1,000 litres of milk which, she explained, is made into two cheeses weighing about 45 kilos each.

The Route des Vins *Michelin map 70*

There is no signposted Route des Vins leading through the Jura but the route I suggest will take you through the most satisfying countryside and the most important vineyards and villages. Although most of the vineyards are contained within a narrow strip of land, rarely more than about 5 kilometres wide, between Arbois in the north and St Amour in the south alongside the N 83, it is possible to tour the vineyards all day and hardly be aware that the main road is so near. While the Jura mountains are neither as lofty nor as imposing as the Alps to the south, they nevertheless offer some dramatic and spectacular scenery, particularly on the fissured rim of the plateau, where the rock is broken by precipitous gorges and plunging ravines.

Just north of Arbois and to the east of the N 83, in the valley of the River Furieuse, lies the thermal spa of Salins-les-Bains. This is a good starting point for a tour through the wine-growing area of the Jura. To

reach the town, leave the N 83 a little way north of Arbois; if time allows, make several stops before you get there. Port-Lesney, to the west of the main road on the banks of the river Loue, offers a peaceful retreat for anglers and campers and there are walks along the river and through the surrounding woods. The village of les Arsures, just north of Arbois, is also worth a visit, not only to try its fine wine but also for the seclusion of its quiet lanes and vine-clad hills. I passed a memorable hour here in a meadow just a few hundred metres from the main road, watching a pair of kestrels riding the thermals above my head, with a simple picnic of bread, Morbier cheese and a good bottle of Arbois red wine; I was undisturbed by traffic.

The N 83 takes you right into the centre of Arbois; there are many wine growers around the Place de la Liberté selling their products, and the town's Fruit-

ière Vinicole (the name for the wine co-operatives of the region) is here too. Just along the main street is the imposing Les Deux Tonneaux, owned by Henri Maire, a grower whose wines are known throughout France. Nearby, in a small street behind the Hôtel de Ville, is the recently established wine museum. Try to plan your visit to Arbois to coincide with one of the most spectacular harvest festivals in France, the *Fête de Biou*, which is held in the streets here on the first Sunday in September; the high point of the festival is when about 100 kilogrammes of grapes are carried in procession through the town to the church. Arbois was the boyhood home of Louis Pasteur; the house he lived in on the bank of the River Cuisance is still there. He did much of his experimental work into fermentation and wine-making at a small vineyard in les Rosières, just north of Arbois.

The countryside varies greatly in this region. The land in the Revermont (above) is quiet and flat, contrasting hugely with the mighty and dramatic Cirque de Baume (overleaf)

Continue south from Arbois on the D 246, climbing into the foothills of the Jura towards the little village of Pupillin, which is said to make the best red wine of the region. Here you really know that you are in mountain country, although it is only a few hundred metres above Arbois. Even at the height of summer, there are massive piles of wood stacked against every house in readiness for the cold, dark evenings ahead. And, as if in defiance of the rigours of mountain life, every house will be ablaze with bright geraniums and petunias adorning all available corners and ledges, soaking up every ounce of the summer's warmth and colour as an antidote to the oncoming winter. It was up here in the mountains that an old *vigneron* explained to me that

the Jura vines are among the purest strains in France; only grapes of noble lineage are grown and, he added, if necessary, vineyards are compulsorily uprooted in order to maintain this tradition.

From Pupillin the D 246 rejoins the N 83. Follow this a short distance until you get to the fortified village of Poligny, which is an important wine centre; many growers have establishments in its narrow streets and the Fruitière Vinicole (called the Caveau des Jacobins) is situated in an old church. There are many buildings of architectural interest here, including the seventeenth-century Ursuline convent and the Hotel Dieu with its vaulted halls and kitchens and old pharmacy; there is a superb collection of Burgundian documents in the Church of St-Hippolyte. A few kilometres from Poligny, towards Champagnole, is the beautiful and dramatic wooded gorge at Vaux, from which you have fine views over the surrounding countryside.

A little way further south from Poligny along the N 83 turn left on to the quiet D 57 towards St Lothain, and you will come to a succession of charming villages, including Passenans, Frontenay, Menétru-le-Vignoble and Domblans. You will be able to taste the local wines as you go. This area is known as the Revermont, literally 'the back of the mountain', and some of the more dramatic scenery – wide rolling landscapes with distant views of mountains, sudden surging hills and abrupt escarpments – can be seen at Château-Chalon, a village famed for its Vin Jaune, which is perched on a 460-metre peak overlooking countryside patterned with vineyards. Further south the imposing escarpment of the Cirque de Baume towers above the twelfth-century Romanesque abbey of Baume-les-Messieurs.

To the west of the N 83 lies the village of l'Etoile, where a particularly notable white wine with a remarkable bouquet is made; its appellation also covers Vin Jaune and Vin de Paille. St Germain-lès-Arlay and nearby Château d'Arlay also produce fine white wines. Lons-le-Saunier, the chief town of the region, has been a spa since Roman times; it has a beautiful park which contains the thermal baths and a casino. It is an excellent alternative to Poligny or Arbois as a base from which to explore the Jura vineyards. From here the N 83 takes you further south to the limit of the Jura vineyards at St Amour, a small resort beside the river Besançon which has a lively holiday atmosphere during the summer months.

Wine Tour N⁰ 14

SAVOIE

The bridge spanning the Rhône which divides the town of Seyssel

It is a pity that so little attention is paid to the wines of Savoie, because the vineyards are extensive, the wines distinctive and the countryside most alluring. The wine-growing area of Savoie is concentrated mainly in four regions: on the southern shores of Lake Geneva, along the banks of the Upper Rhône, in the hills around the Lac du Bourget and in the valleys to the south of Chambéry.

The wines
The wines of Savoie are mainly white (often *pétillant*), with some red and little rosé, and are produced from a variety of grape types. The main appellations are *Seyssel*, *Crépy* and *Roussette*.

Roussette de Savoie is a white wine made from a mixture of the Altesse and Mondeuse grape types, which are grown around the towns of Frangy and Seyssel. A little further to the south, a red wine is made from the Mondeuse, Gamay and Pinot Noir grapes in a region called the Chautagne: the villages where the main production is centred are Ruffieux, Chindrieux, Motz and Serrières-en-Chautagne. A red wine made exclusively from the Mondeuse grape is found in the villages of Arbin, Cruet and St Jean-de-la-Porte to the south of Chambéry.

Vin de Savoie, a white wine from the Chasselas grape, is made in the vineyards beside Lake Geneva. The appellation *Crépy* is also from this area, as are the *Marignan*, *Ripaille* and *Ayze* appellations.

The cuisine
Dairy products are a strong feature of Savoie cooking. Cows' milk is used for *Tomme de Savoie* and *Comte* cheeses – large, flat cylinders of firm creamy-coloured cheese with a deliciously nutty flavour and a satisfying texture. *Bleu de Gex* is a blue-veined cheese known as *fromage persillé* because it has a similar marbled appearance to the *jambon persillé* of Burgundy. *Reblochon* is a creamy but firm yellow cheese, while *Saint-Marcellin* is milder, softer and ivory coloured. Cream and cheese are also used in cooking. *Pommes de terre dauphinoise* is a wickedly rich dish of thinly sliced potatoes baked slowly in a shallow dish with butter and cream. In *pommes de terre à la savoyarde* meat stock is used instead of cream and grated Comte cheese is added.

The Route des Vins *Michelin maps 74 and 77*
The Savoie wine route is not a true circuit, although if you use either Aix-les-Bains or Chambéry as a base you can make two separate circuits taking in the entire route. Most of the route I suggest is signposted; it goes

from north to south with the town of Frangy (which is very close to exit 11 on the Autoroute A 40) as the starting point. Frangy is a lively small town astride the N 508 in the valley of the river Usses, and is known for its appellation Roussette de Savoie. Take a small road, the D 310, out of the town towards the hamlet of Desingy (this part of the route is not signposted). The quiet country lane leads through a peaceful, hilly landscape of vineyards and cornfields, woods and meadows. From here continue along the D 31 to Clermont, a village set on the hillside with views towards the Alps, where you can visit the large thirteenth-century château. The route now continues along the D 57 through Droisy and then descends into the valley of the Rhône. The next stop is the little town of Seyssel, which is bisected by the river and famed for its Roussette de Savoie; it received its appellation in 1930 – late recognition for a town mentioned in eleventh-century records for its wine growing. *Méthode champenoise* white wine is also made here from Altesse (or Roussette) and Molette grapes.

Leaving Seyssel, the wine road continues beside the Rhône along the D 981 for a few kilometres until it meets the D 56, a small road that climbs up away from the river through vineyards towards the wine village of Motz. Continue through the hamlet of Chevignay to Ruffieux, where there is a Cave Co-opérative run by the Chautagne producers; there is another one in the neighbouring village, Serrières-en-Chautagne, beside the main road. A worthwhile short detour from Ruffieux takes you up a narrow winding road to the summit of Mont Clergeon, where you can look out over the Rhône valley from the peaceful alpine meadows; just beyond the summit there are wonderful views of the snow-capped Alps to the east.

The next village, Chindrieux, is another commune within the Chautagne appellation; it is immediately to the north of the Lac du Bourget, in marsh-like terrain with brooks, slender trees and reed beds. The Route des Vins now follows the course of the Canal de Savières to Portout, a little village on the canal's bank. Leave the wine route here and follow the D 914, which winds round the side of the mountain above the lake: you will be rewarded with frequent dramatic glimpses

The Château of Miolans overlooking the valley of the Isère

of the blue-green lake far below, through dense woods. From the terrace of the café high in the hills you can see the lake and the Abbaye de Hautecombe far below on its shore: you can reach the abbey via a small road. It was built in the twelfth century by Cluniac monks but was heavily restored in the eighteenth and nineteenth centuries, in a somewhat extravagant style. The lakeside road now joins the main road. Turn off for the Col du Chat and begin to retrace your path along the wine route to the north of the lake. When you reach the top of the Col du Chat, the Route des Vins follows a small road, the D 210, leading off to the right to the wine villages of Monthoux and Billième. The small villages here are quiet and undistinguished but have a rugged charm, the crumbling stone walls of the ancient houses and farms in strange contrast to the gleaming stacks of shrink-wrapped, virgin wine bottles awaiting use. The vineyards cling to the steep hillsides and the there are frequent signs along the road, particularly in Billième, inviting you to stop and sample the local wines. The road descends now to the valley floor towards Lucey and the meadows of maize (which is used as cattle feed).

The Route des Vins continues along by the river on the D 921 to the village of Chanaz. Like its neighbour, Portout, it is situated beside the Canal de Savières and has a number of waterside restaurants and cafés. Take the main road, the D 991, along the eastern shore of the Lac du Bourget to the small but important wine-growing community around Brison-St Innocent. The village is, in fact, a residential suburb of Aix-les-Bains and the vineyards are cultivated between the gardens of the smart villas: the local climate is ideal.

There are no vineyards of significance now until you reach those south of Chambéry; to get there it is easiest to take the N 201 into the centre of the town. It would be a pity, however, not to linger a while in the elegant resort of Aix-les-Bains. It has a long tree-lined lakeside promenade with cafés and restaurants. All the usual seaside facilities are available here, from sunbathing on the beach to windsurfing, swimming and boating, and the modern thermal establishment is renowned for the treatment of rheumatism and sciatica.

Jean-Jacques Rousseau lived at Chambéry for a while, and you can visit Les Charmettes, the house he

Mountainside vineyards near the village of St Pierre – d'Albigny

The village of Myans which nestles beneath the splendour of Mont Granier

stayed in and described in his *Confessions*; it is set in a quiet wooded hillside on the edge of the town. The wine route is signposted again from the suburb of Barberaz along the D 201, a quiet road which leads through the wine villages that nestle below the peak of Mont Granier. The two appellations in this region are the white wines of Apremont and Abîmes; the five communes of St Badolph, les Marches, Myans, Apremont and Chapareillan are the centres of production. There are many places where you can taste and buy the local wines and visitors are welcomed at the *caves*.

The appeal of these wine villages, small, rather haphazard collections of old stone houses and farms criss-crossed by narrow streets, lies mainly in the wines they make and their beautiful mountain settings: it is worth taking one of the many small roads that climb up into the vineyards above the villages, from where there are stunning views of the distant valley of the Isère and the mountains beyond. To enjoy the mountain scenery to the full you should also make a detour to the top of the very dramatic Col du Granier. You get to it via a narrow road that literally hugs its way around the side of the mountain providing a constant display of staggering views over the sheer side to the valley below and distant Chambéry.

From les Marches the Route des Vins crosses the Autoroute A 41 and the main road, the N 90, to the town of Montmélian. There is a large Cave Coopérative here where you can taste and buy a variety of Savoie wines, including Mondeuse. The next stops are the wine villages of Arbin and Cruet, known for their red Mondeuse. The road follows the Isère Valley, climbing higher as it nears the villages of St Jean-de-la-Porte, St Pierre-d'Albigny, Miolans and Fréterive,

the latter marking the limit of the wine route. The silvery Isère shimmers below you and the dramatic snow-capped peaks of the Massif de la Vanoise are clearly visible in the distance. An essential small detour here is to the Château de Miolans, perched high up on the hill; a small road climbs up to it.

If you retrace your steps to Cruet another narrow road, the D 11, winds up through the vineyards to the secluded lake of Thuile, an oval of limpid blue-green water surrounded by gently sloping meadows and ringed with reeds. From here there is a gentle drive through a series of small valleys back to the wine villages of Chignin and finally St Jeoire-Prieuré on the main road (the N 6), which will take you back into Chambéry or south to Grenoble and beyond.

The vineyards beside Lake Geneva are quite small in area and are concentrated around the towns of Evian, Thonon and Douvaine. *Vin de Savoie* is to be found at Ripaille and Marignan and the appellation *Crépy* in the communes of Douvaine, Loisin and Ballaison. I have not included these vineyards in the wine tour because they are not very extensive and are rather cut off from the rest of the wine-growing region. However it is worth making a small detour to taste these distinctive wines, and you will be made very welcome at the *caves*. One of particular interest is the Tour de Marignan, where there are fascinating ancient cellars in a fortified house dating back to the eleventh century. Not far from Lake Geneva are the appellations *Marignan* and *Ayez* in the valley of the Arve near the town of Bonneville.

Below: Maize drying from the eaves of a farmhouse in the village of Ruffieux is a common sight in the Savoie. Right: The remote and peaceful Lac de Thuile, a popular spot with anglers. Overleaf: The Abbaye de Hautcombe and the Lac du Bourget, shrouded in mist

CENTRAL AND EASTERN FRANCE
Wine-buying Guide

Making Comte cheese near Salins-les-Bains

CHABLIS AND THE YONNE

This region's name is so well known that it is copied in other vineyards outside the protective legislation of the EEC. This worldwide fame has led to steep increases in prices over the past few years as demand has outstripped harvest yields. This means that Chablis wines, although quite delicious, no longer represent very good value for money.

Appellations Contrôlées

Chablis Grand Cru The seven Grand Cru vineyards are arranged on slopes between the town of Chablis itself and the village of Fyé. The same slopes also grow the grapes for Chablis Moutonne, a brand name owned by Joseph Drouhin which, although not a Grand Cru itself, is acknowledged as being of similar standard.
 The Grands Crus, particularly in good years, must be given three or four years' bottle ageing to show their true colours.

Chablis Premier Cru Of the 27 Premier Cru vineyards, perhaps the most famous are Fourchaume, Vaulorent, Montée de Tonnerre, Monts de Milieu, Vosgros, Vaugiraud, Monts Mains, Les Fôrets, Vaillons and Côte de Léchet.
 These wines are less intense than the Grands Crus but still need two or three years in bottle to develop. Here, perhaps, the biggest influence on quality is the method of vinification, namely whether oak casks or stainless steel vats are used.

Chablis The general appellation of the district covering the remaining vineyard area. This wine is of slightly weaker alcohol content than the Premiers and Grands Crus.

Petit Chablis The most humble wine of the appellation.

Other Appellations Contrôlées

Bourgogne Aligoté A dry white wine made from the less noble Aligoté grape throughout the entire Burgundy region but only allowed this appellation. In the Chablis area it produces a particularly crisp wine

that is delightful to drink locally but is less interesting if taken home.

Bourgogne Irancy Red and rosé wines made from the Pinot Noir grape and local varieties César and Tressot. The rosé is better than the red because in poor years ripening is a problem and the wine is thin and stalky.

VDQS

Sauvignon-St-Bris A white wine only, making an excellent apéritif. Drink as young as possible.

Generic ACs covering all Burgundy including Yonne

Bourgogne Rosé Made from Pinot Noir, César and Tressot grape varieties, but not common now.

Crémant-de-Bourgogne A white or rosé sparkling wine made by the *méthode champenoise* throughout the Burgundy region. Like *crémant* in Champagne, this has two-thirds the normal CO_2 pressure.

Vin de Pays

Vin de Pays de l' Yonne Light, dry white wines only.

Addresses

For all Chablis:
Lamblin et Fils
Maligny
89800 Chablis

For Grand Cru:
William Fèvre
Rue Jules Ratier
89800 Chablis

For Aligoté, Chardonnay:
Domaine Bersan
20 rue de l'Eglise
St Bris-le-Vineux
89530 Chablis

In the town of Chablis there is a wine shop belonging to Domaine Laroche where you can see a full range.

THE CÔTE D'OR

The two districts of the Côte d'Or are markedly different. The Côte de

Nuits produces very little white wine, and its reds are masculine with more colour, tannin and backbone than those of the Côte de Beaune.

The wines of the Côte de Beaune are both red and white. Here, stretched between Fixin and Santenay, are all the great names of Burgundy. Some village communes are more noble and so better known than others.

The problem in purchasing is quantity. The well-known names have to satisfy a worldwide demand for their production and this means that some wines are sold at prices well beyond their actual worth. Even in the area it is impossible to buy the great wines cheaply. The generic appellation wines such as *Bourgogne Rouge* or *Blanc* often offer the best value. If purchased from a *négociant* skilled at blending or from an individual grower, these wines can be excellent even if you forgo the possibility of pinpointing the vineyard of production on a map.

Cru classification system

The vineyards of Burgundy are divided first into village communes and then into individual patches called *climats*. Each *climat* has its own soil and microclimate conditions and so produces its own unique wine. Because of the historical inheritance laws in Burgundy, whereby each child had an equal share in his father's estate, the vineyard holdings have become broken up. Nowadays, through intermarriage and the purchase of vineyard plots, people owning a *domaine* may well have several separate plots within many *climats* spread over several village communes.

Of these *climats*, those producing the most superior wines are designated Grand Cru. These *climats* are so well known that they do not need to use the village name on the wine label. Indeed, a village often annexes the name of such a *climat* to its own to develop more self-importance. Thus the village of Gevrey became Gevrey-Chambertin.

Other very good *climats* are designated Premier Cru. The Premiers and Grands Crus form a belt occupying the best parts (the

middle) of the Côte d'Or slope. Lesser *climats* are given over to producing lesser wines within the village commune appellation.

Here is an example from the commune Gevrey-Chambertin.

CHAMBERTIN
A Grand Cru wine from the Le Chambertin *climat*.

GEVREY-CHAMBERTIN
Clos St Jacques.
A Premier Cru wine from the Clos St Jacques *climat*.

GEVREY-CHAMBERTIN
Premier Cru.
A blend of wines but only from Premier Cru *climats*.

GEVREY-CHAMBERTIN
The village wine blended from anywhere within the commune.

NB Wines from the commune of Gevrey-Chambertin may not be declassified to Côte-de-Nuits-Villages.

It is fairly common for a Grand Cru *climat* to be shared between two communes.

THE CÔTE DE NUITS

Appellations Contrôlées

Rather than list the wines in order of classification it is perhaps best to discuss them in geographical order from north to south.

Marsannay-la-Côte A small amount of red wine is produced as Bourgogne Rouge, but it is the rosé, Rosé de Marsannay, that this commune is famous for.

Fixin A small village commune with no Grands Crus and only six Premier Cru *climats*: Les Meix-Bas, Le Clos-du-Chapitre, Aux Cheusots, La Perrière, Les Arvalets and Les Hervelets. Although white wines are allowed only red is made. It can be quite long-lived.

Brochon This commune only produces lesser wines not sold under the commune name but contributing to Bourgogne Rouge and Côte-de-Nuits-Villages blends.

Gevrey-Chambertin A big commune with two major Grands Crus: Chambertin and Chambertin-Clos-de-Bèze, which are surrounded by the other Grands Crus of Charmes-Chambertin (also called Mazoyères-Chambertin), Chappelle-Chambertin, Griotte-Chambertin, Latricières-Chambertin, Mazis-Chambertin and Ruchottes-Chambertin. All are rich reds needing several years' ageing.

The Premier Crus, which may put their name after the words Gevrey-Chambertin, number 25 of which the best known are Clos St Jacques, Aux-Combottes and Combe-aux-Moines.

Even the commune wine, Gevrey-Chambertin, can be outstanding.

Morey-St-Denis The Grands Crus are Bonnes-Mares (part of which is also in neighbouring Chambolle-Musigny), Clos-St-Denis, Clos-de-la-Roche and Clos-de-Tart. There are 26 Premier Cru *climats* of which the best known are Clos Bussière and Les Fremières. Again, Morey-St-Denis also makes an excellent village wine.

Chambolle-Musigny The Grands Crus are Le Musigny (divided into Les Petits Musigny and Les Musigny) and the remaining part of Bonnes Mares. A little white Musigny exists and is well worth finding, but it will be expensive.

There are 20 Premier Cru *climats* of which the best known are Les Charmes and Les Combottes (not to be confused with Aux-Combottes in Gevrey-Chambertin).

Again, the village wine, Chambolle-Musigny, can also be quite outstanding.

Vougeot The only Grand Cru is Clos-de-Vougeot, the largest single *climat* in Burgundy with 52 hectares. In one corner is the Château de Vougeot, the headquarters and meeting place for the *Confrérie des Chevaliers du Tastevin*, founded in 1933. This *climat* accounts for the majority of the vineyard of the commune, but there are four Premiers Crus which are not often seen. Some white wine also exists in the Premier Cru *climats*. Even the village wine is rare because the remaining vineyard area of the commune is much smaller than the Grand Cru.

Flagey-Echezeaux This commune used to be considered as part of Vosne-Romanée, but in fact it is a commune in its own right. Displaced about 1 kilometre to the west of the village are the Grands Crus; Grands Echezeaux and Les Echezeaux. The only Premier Cru *climat*, Les Beaux-Monts, is shared between this commune and the neighbouring Vosne-Romanée. The wine is red only.

Vosne-Romanée The Grands Crus are La Romanée-Conti, Le Richeborg, La Romanée, La Tâche and Romanée-St-Vivant. Perhaps the most important *domaine* here is the Domaine Romanée-Conti, which has holdings in all these Grands Crus, and is owned jointly by Mme Bize-Leroy and A. P. de Villaine.

There are two Premiers Crus of which the best known are Les Suchots and Aux-Malconsorts. There is also the excellent village wine of Vosne-Romanée.

Nuits-St-Georges A large, well-known commune with no Grands Crus but 29 Premiers Crus. The best known of these are Les-Saint-Georges, Aux-Damodes, Aux-Champ-Perdrix and La Perrière (not to be confused with the *climat* of the same name in Fixin). Some of the Premiers Crus are actually in the adjacent commune of Prémeaux (see below).

A white wine does exist in this commune but it is extremely rare.

Prémeaux This is in fact a separate commune but all its Premiers Crus are classified as Nuits-St-Georges.

The best known are Clos-de-la-Maréchale, Clos Arlots (where the rare white is grown), Aux Perdrix and Clos-des-Fôrets.

There is no village wine of Prémeaux.

Generic appellations

Côte de Nuits-Villages This is a general appellation that can be blended from several communes of the Côte de Nuits; Fixin, Brochon, Prissey, Comblachien and Corgoloin. Wines from the other communes mentioned above may never be sold as Côte de Nuits-Villages. This appellation exists for both red and white wines but in fact is predominantly red.

Hautes Côtes de Nuits An appellation covering blends from the less good upper slopes of the Côte and Arrière Côte to the West.

THE CÔTE DE BEAUNE

Appellations Contrôlée

Ladoix-Serrigny This appellation makes red and white wines under the names Ladoix Rouge and Ladoix Blanc. The white is by far the superior. There are two rare Grands Crus; Les Vergennes (part is only rated Premier Cru) and Le Rognet-Corton (often deemed to be a Grand Cru of neighbouring Aloxe-Corton). The six Premiers Crus are also rare, and these too are deemed to belong to Aloxe-Corton.

Aloxe-Corton This commune has the famous Grand Cru red wine Corton (shared with neighbouring Pernand-Vergelesses), subdivided into Le Corton, Corton-Clos-du-Roi, Corton Renardes, Corton-les-Bressandes and Corton-les-Perrières, among others. There are also two Grands Crus producing only white wines; Charlemagne and Corton-Charlemagne (part of which is also in neighbouring Pernand-Vergelesses).

There are eight Premiers Crus making mostly red wine with a tiny amount of white. The village wine is both red and white.

Pernand-Vergelesses This commune

shares the white Grand Cru Corton-Charlemagne and the red Corton with Aloxe-Corton. It also has five Premiers Crus of which the best known is Ile-des-Vergelesses. The wines are both red and white and tend to be a bit harder and firmer than their neighbours.

Savigny-lès-Beaune This commune has no Grands Crus but has 24 Premiers Crus of which the best known are Les Peuillets and Les Lavières.

The wines in this commune are red and quite light and soft. There is no white.

Chorey-lès-Beaune This small commune only produces a village wine. It is mostly a soft, light red; there is no white.

Beaune Despite its worldwide fame, this large commune has no Grands Crus. Of the 34 Premiers Crus the best known are Le Clos-des-Mouches, Clos-du-Roi, Les Cents Vignes, Les Grèves, Les Marconnets, Les Teurons and Les Vignes-Franches. The Premiers Crus make mainly red wines but the white exists in reasonable quantities. Beaune Premier Cru, a blend of more than one Premier Cru *climat*, is quite common. There is also a straight village wine and a small area with a separate appellation, Côte de Beaune, making red and white wines. Do not confuse this with the name for the whole district or the appellation, Côte de Beaune-Villages.

Pommard Again, a famous commune with no Grands Crus. Of the 26 Premiers Crus the best known are Les Épenots and Les Rugiens. This commune makes only red wine.

Volnay No Grands Crus but 27 Premiers Crus of which the best known are Les Caillerets, Taille-Pieds and En Chevret.

This commune also produces red wine in the lighter, more rounded style.

(Note that Volnay-Santenots is in fact in Meursault: see Meursault.)

Monthélie A small commune to the south-west of Volnay with 11 Premier

Cru *climats*, all bordering Volnay or Auxey-Duresses to the south. It produces mostly red wine. This appellation deserves to be better known, but at the moment its obscurity means that its wines are excellent value.

Meursault A large commune with no Grands Crus but 21 Premiers Crus, of which the best known are Le Poruzot, La Goutte d'Or, Les Genevrières and Les Charmes. The commune produces mostly white wines but also some red.

Where a Premier Cru *climat* produces a red wine it has to borrow the neighbouring village's name because there is no appellation for red Premier Cru Meursault. Thus Volnay-Santenots and Blagny La-Pièce-sous-le-Bois are in fact red wines produced by Premier Cru *climats* in Meursault.

The white wines are rich and full.

Blagny This tiny commune does produce a village wine under its own name, but the Premier Cru *climats* come under Meursault when they produce white wines (see Meursault). The wines can be sold as Meursault-Blagny, Puligny-Blagny or as one of the Meursault Premiers Crus if from the *climats* La Jennelotte, La Pièce-sous-le-Bois or Sur-le-Dos-d'Ane.

Auxey-Duresses This commune makes both red and white wines of good quality but of less intensity than those of neighbouring Meursault. There are no Grands Crus but eight Premiers Crus including Les Duresses (shared with Monthélie) and Les Grands Champs. Prior to the advent of AC law these wines were sold as Volnay and Pommard without diminishing the reputations of those two wines.

St-Romain A tiny commune up the slopes from Auxey-Duresses and Meursault making only a village wine. The wine is mostly white, and only rarely red. The white wine can be extremely good value when compared to the price of its neighbours.

Puligny-Montrachet This commune shares the white wine Grands Crus of

Loading grapes into the press at Mercurey in the Chalonnais

Le Montrachet and Bâtard-Montrachet with Chassagne-Montrachet, but also has the white Grands Crus of Chevalier-Montrachet and Bienvenues-Bâtard-Montrachet.

Le Montrachet is the pinnacle of white Burgundy and is regarded by many as France's finest white wine.

There are 11 Premier Cru *climats* making mostly white wine of which the best known are Les Folatières and Les Combettes.

The straight village white wine is also very fine and the red is interesting but quite rare.

Chassagne-Montrachet This commune shares the Grands Crus of Le Montrachet and Bâtard-Montrachet with Puligny-Montrachet, but also has the tiny Criots-Bâtard-Montrachet.

There are 12 Premiers Crus making both red and white wines, of which the best known are Clos-St-Jean and Abbaye-de-Morgeot.

The village wine is also good in both red and white and is a little fuller than neighbouring Puligny-Montrachet.

St Aubin This small commune, to the west of Chassagne-Montrachet, produces red and white wines. There are eight Premier Cru climats.

Santenay This commune has seven

Premiers Crus *climats* producing both red and white wines of which the best known are Les Gravières and La Comme.

The red wines of Santenay are lighter and softer than most in the Côte de Beaune. The whites are fuller and can be quite delicious.

Cheilly, Dezize and Sampigny-lès-Maranges These are lesser communes around the end of the Côte de Beaune. Between these three appellations there are four Premier Cru *climats* of which one, Les Maranges, is shared by all three communes.

Generic appellations

Côte de Beaune-Villages This appellation is only for red wine blended from all the above communes except Aloxe-Corton, Pommard and Volnay. It is usually light and fruity and can be drunk relatively young.

Hautes-Côtes de Beaune A lesser AC, blended from the top of the Côte and the Arrière Côte.

Addresses

Négociants:

Joseph Drouhin (cellar visits can be arranged by appointment)
7 rue d'Enfer
21201 Beaune-Cedex

Louis Latour
18 rue des Tonneliers
21204 Beaune

Louis Jadot
Rue Samuel Legay
21200 Beaune

Some growers known for quality who will greet the passer-by and sell him wines direct are:

Domaine René Lamy-Pillot
Route de Santenay
Chassagne Montrachet
21190 Meursault

Bernard Delagrange
Domaine Gagnard-Delagrange
Chassagne Montrachet
21190 Meursault

Philippe Leclerc
13 rue des Halles
21220 Gevrey Chambertin

Domaine Francois German
Château de Chorey-lès-Beaune
21200 Beaune

Domaine René Monnier
6 rue Docteur Rolland
21190 Meursault

Domaine Chartron
Chartron et Trebuchet
13 Grande Rue
21190 Puligny Montrachet

Domaine J. J. Confuron
Prémeaux
21700 Nuits-St-Georges

Domaine Arlaud
Morey-St-Denis
21200 Gevrey Chambertin

THE CHALONNAIS

This region, also called La Région de Mercurey, consists of scattered vineyards spread among areas of other agricultural activity. Until the 1970s these wines were not exported to the UK and they are still not as well known as they deserve to be. Although lacking the class of the Côte d'Or wines, the Chalonnais wines have a lightness and fruitiness that makes them attractive in their own right. Those from good years, after two or three years in bottle, can be confused with more famous appellations, which makes them good value. The village of Bouzeron, around which the best of the

Bourgogne Aligoté is grown, is in this region. The Cave Co-opérative at Buxy also makes very good generic wines as well as wines from the four main appellations.

Appellations Contrôlées

Rully Predominantly white wines are produced here although the red does exist in tiny quantities. There are 19 Premier Cru *climats* but these in no way match the Premiers Crus of the Côte d'Or. Much of the production here is used to make Crémant de Bourgogne.

Mercurey This commune makes almost entirely red wine. The white is very rare. There are five Premier Cru *climats* producing what is generally judged to be the finest red of the whole region.

Givry Another commune producing predominantly red wine. The wines are pleasantly fresh and fruity, and are surprisingly good value. They can be drunk quite young.

Montagny Produces mostly a white wine that is regarded as the best of the region. The Beaune shipper, Louis Latour, led the way with this appellation and now most merchants list it. In good vintages, such as 1983, this wine will develop a lovely *goût de miel* (honey-taste).

Generic appellations

Bourgogne Passe-Tout-Grains Red or rosé wines made from a mixture of two-thirds Gamay grapes and one-third Pinot Noir. This AC is found throughout Burgundy but is mostly produced in the Chalonnais and Mâconnais regions.

Addresses

Caves des Vignerons de Buxy
Les Vignes de la Croix
St Gengous-le-Nuit
71390 Buxy
Apart from all the local appellations they produce excellent Mâcon Rouge and Aligoté.

M. Bernard Michel
Saint Vallerin
71390 Buxy

M. Millet
Montagny-lès-Buxy
71390 Buxy

M. Arnoux
71390 Buxy

Rully:
Domaine de la Folie
71150 Chagny

Givry:
Domaine du Baron Thénard
Givry
Chalons-sur-Saône

They own a part of the great Le Montrachet, but will not sell to visitors. However, their Givry red and white are exceptional.

THE MACONNAIS

Although the countryside here is more dramatic, the wines are not as good as those of the Chalonnais or the Côte d'Or districts. All the reds and some of the whites within the appellation are sold without geographical origin.

Appellations for red wine

Mâcon Rouge and Mâcon Supérieur Essentially these are fairly pedestrian wines, a cut above *vin ordinaire*, but they are widely known and popular as everyday wines. Coming mostly from the Gamay grape, but with some Pinot Noir, these wines tend to be more earthy and rustic than the wines of Beaujolais. *Supérieur* just indicates an extra degree of alcohol.

Appellations for white wine

Pouilly-Fuissé, Pouilly-Loché and Pouilly-Vinzelles Pouilly Fuissé is the most famous white wine of the region, produced to the west of the villages of Pouilly and Pouilly-Solutré. This wine has recently become fashionable with Americans and their avid purchasing has caused almost incredible price rises. The wine now fetches nearly as much as the whites in the Côte de Beaune and

no longer represents value for money. However, the very similar neighbouring wines Pouilly-Loché and Pouilly-Vinzelles, made from the same Chardonnay grape, are still worth finding. A visit to the Caves des Grands Crus Blancs at Vinzelles would be very rewarding.

St-Véran This is a new appellation changing its name from Beaujolais Blanc in 1971. The boundaries between Mâcon and Beaujolais are sufficiently indistinct to have allowed this to happen. This white wine is produced from seven communes around Fuissé towards St Vérand. It is still relatively unknown and so is very good value.

Individual Mâcon village wines The appellation Mâcon-Villages is only for white wine blended from any of the 43 communes entitled to use the appellation. Some of these villages make a classier, more individual wine and are therefore entitled to use their name after the word Mâcon.

Mâcon-Lugny, Mâcon-Clessé, Mâcon-Prissé and Mâcon-Viré are among the best known. Not so well known but still worth finding are Mâcon-Ige, Mâcon-Uchizy and the rare Mâcon-Fuissé.

An excellent white Mâcon is made at the Château de Chaintré.

Mâcon Blanc The more ordinary wines go under this generic appellation, but generally Mâcon Blanc is better than Mâcon Rouge.

The largest viticultural district of Burgundy is Beaujolais, accounting for two-thirds of the region's production. However, the Beaujolais district is very different from the rest of Burgundy viticulturally, climatically and oenologically. The scenery is rural and quite beautiful and its character is matched by the liveliness and fruitiness of the wines.

When tasting from the distinctive glasses (shaped like brandy glasses) that are used in the district, look for assertive wines with good fruit, acidity and tannin, and if you want a keeping wine, ask for a *vin de garde*.

Appellations Contrôlées

In the northern half of the district are nine village communes, each allowed to use its own name, which produce the better wines known as Cru Beaujolais: *St-Amour, Juliénas, Chenas, Moulin-à-Vent, Fleurie, Chiroubles, Morgon, Brouilly and Côte-de-Brouilly*. Most benefit from keeping for two to three years, especially in good vintages. Moulin-à-Vent, Chenas and Morgon are thought to keep the longest. When these wines age, they lose their purple colour, freshness and fruitiness and start to resemble Pinot Noir wines from more noble appellations.

Beaujolais-Villages This wine is red only. It is blended from 39 communes in the north of Beaujolais, including the nine Crus and some communes in the hazy Beaujolais/Mâconnais border. The wines must have the same alcoholic strength as Beaujolais Supérieur (10°). The quality is usually above average and, if skilfully blended, can be better than a poorly made Cru.

Beaujolais Supérieur and Beaujolais These appellations cover the rest of the district. Only about 1 per cent of the production is white, with an equally tiny proportion of rosé. Beaujolais Supérieur must have one degree of alcohol more than straight Beaujolais but in both appellations the quality can and often does vary enormously.

VDQS

Coteaux du Lyonnais VDQS Red, dry white and rosé wines produced around Lyon, to the south of Beaujolais. The whites are the rarest.

Addresses

Caves des Producteurs Juliénas
Château du Bois de la Salle
69840 Juliénas-en-Beaujolais

Cave du Château de Chenas
69840 Juliénas

Cave Co-Opérative des Grands Vins de Fleurie
69820 Fleurie

Cave Beaujolaise de Saint Véran
69620 Le Bois d'Oingt

THE JURA

This wine region is under the commercial domination of a company founded centuries ago, Henri Maire. There are also many small individual growers. However, despite the efforts of Henri Maire, the Jura wines are not well known in the UK, perhaps because they lack the body for its fickle climate.

Appellations Contrôlées

Arbois This appellation produces red, dry white and a *gris* rosé. The reds are made from Pinot Noir and the local grape varieties Trousseau and Poulsard, either alone or blended.

The Trousseau variety lends rich colour and tannin, suitable for a *vin de garde*, while the Poulsard is lightly coloured and makes a rosé even when vinified like a red wine. These rosés derive enough tannin for short-term keeping. The white wines are made from the Savagnin grape (not to be confused with the Sauvignon), the Chardonnay and the Pinot Blanc. The Savagnin can make deeply coloured, sherry-like wines.

The local specialities are Vin de Paille and Vin Jaune, and these are both a must. Neither are appellations. Vin de Paille is an expensive rarity produced from sugar-rich, sun-dried grapes, dried on *lits de pailles* (straw mats). This is sold only in small bottles called *pots*. Vin Jaune is a cask-aged wine exposed, rather like sherry, to air and a *flor* yeast. Having survived this, the Vin Jaune is expensive, complex in flavour and virtually indestructible. It is sold in a small squat bottle called a *clavelin*. The best Vin Jaune comes from *Château Châlon*.

Under the Arbois AC, *mousseux* wines are also produced.

Jura Again, red, dry white and *gris* rosé wines produced from the same grapes as in Arbois. There is also *mousseux*.

Arbois Pupillin These are red, dry white and rosé wines from the commune of Pupillin. They have an added intensity of flavour.

L'Etoile White wine with a little more finesse than straight Arbois. An excellent *mousseux* also exists.

Addresses

Apart from Henri Marie, there are three other establishments well worth a visit.

Henri Maire
Les Tonneaux
Rue de l'Hôtel de Ville
39600 Arbois

Domaine Rolet
Montigny
39600 Arbois

Château d'Arlay
Arlay
39140 Bletterans

Caveau des Jacobins
Poliguy
39600 Arbois

SAVOIE

Although this is an area of great gastronomy and spectacular scenery, few of the wines are good enough to sell well outside the region. The delightful vermouth apéritif Chambéry comes from here. Its flowery delicacy and flavour make it distinctly superior to its Italian counterparts.

Appellations Contrôlées

Crépy This appellation produces dry white wines that are faintly sparkling (*perlant* or *pétillant*). These low-alcohol wines from Chasselas grapes are refreshing but not of great interest.

Rousette de Savoie This appellation produces only white wine from the Altesse and Chardonnay grapes (Chardonnay is known locally as the Petite-Sainte-Marie) with Mondeuse

own names, for example, *Chautagne* and Ripaille.

White and rosé *mousseux* is also produced as well as a non-appellation sparkling wine made from wines bought in from outside the district.

Vin de Savoie Ayze Mousseux A similar appellation.

VDQS

Vin de Bugey A tiny but growing production of red, dry white and rosé. *Mousseux* and *pétillant* are also made.

Vin de Pays

Balmes Dauphinoises Red, dry white and rosé of which the white wines are best.

Coteaux du Grésivaudan Similar to Balmes Dauphinoises.

Franche-Comté

Vin de Pays de l' Ain A tiny production of what would otherwise be Vin de Bugey.

Addresses

Varichon et Clerc
Château des Sechallets
014120 Seyssel
Ain

Left: *Cave Co-Opérative* in Poligny. Below: A *vigneron*

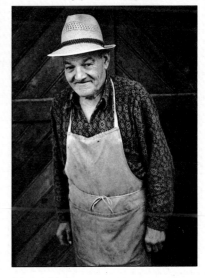

varieties. The wine is very dry and has some finesse. It is an excellent accompaniment to the local freshwater fish.

This AC also has individual Crus which are communes that may add their own name, but little is seen of them outside their district.

Seyssel Dry white wines and a particularly good *mousseux*. The wine is light and perfumed with a floral bouquet.

Vin de Savoie This produces red, dry white and rosé wines that should be drunk young. The white wines are the best. Like Rousette de Savoie, there are several communes that have been allowed since 1973 to add their

SOUTHERN FRANCE

For many years, Southern France has been a favourite holiday destination for both European and American tourists (Collioure in Roussillon, left, is still idyllic despite them). In their appreciation of the almost constant sun and the scenic smörgåsbord, the great variety of excellent wines the five areas of this region produce, go almost unnoticed. But anyone who tastes the classic reds of the Rhône, the cheap and eminently drinkable *vins de table* of Languedoc, the full-bodied rosés of Roussillon which complement the Catalan-style cuisine so well, the full red wines of Cahors and the superb rosés of Provence, will return to Southern France again and again.

Wine Tour Nº 15
THE RHONE

The walled, hilltop village of Caromb

Running south from Lyon – between the Savoie Alps to the East and the Massif Central to the West – towards the sprawling estuary beyond Avignon where it spills into the Mediterranean, the powerful Rhône River traverses a wide variety of landscape, from ruggedly dramatic, steep-sided valleys to flatter pastoral farm and meadowland. For over 200 kilometres, the banks of the Rhône are lined with vineyards, some teetering on precarious terraces high above the river, and others spread flat and wide as far as the eye can see. This is a region of great wines – of deep reds such as Châteauneuf-du-Pape and the very rare Côte Rôtie, of Travel and Lirac, the two best rosés in the world, and the lovely spicy white wines of Condrieu and Château Grillet. The range is as enormous as the landscape is dramatic.

The wines
The 138 communes which make up the Rhône region produce a rich variety of wine, in terms of both quality and character. Some wines are made in such small quantities that a bottle almost becomes a collector's item. Others are produced on such a vast scale that huge machines are needed to harvest the grapes and the wine co-operatives look like oil refineries. The colour of the wines range from the deepest blood red through delicate pink to the palest gold. So, Côtes du Rhône' covers a huge variety of wines.

The Appellation Contrôlée wines within the department of the Rhône are: *Côtes du Rhône* (red, white and rosé); *Côtes du Rhône-Rhône* (red and white); *Condrieu* (white); *Côte Rôtie* (red); *Côtes du Rhône-Loire* (red and white); *Château-Grillet* (white); *Côtes du Rhône-Ardèche* (red and white); *Cornas* (red); Saint-Peray (white; *mousseux* as well as still); *Côtes du Rhône-Drôme* (red and white); *Crozes-Hermitage* (red and white); *Saint-Joseph* (red and white); *Hermitage* (red and white); *Vin de Paille* (white); *Die* (white sparkling): *Tavel* (rosé); *Châteauneuf-du-Pape* (red and white); *Côtes du Rhône-Gigondas* (red, white and rosé); *Côtes du Rhône-Cairanne* (red, white and rosé); *Côtes du Rhône-Laudun* (red, white and rosé); *Côtes du Rhône-Chusclan* (rosé); *Côtes du Rhône-Vacqueyras* (red, white and rosé) *Côtes du Rhône-Vinsobres* (red, white and rosé); *Rasteau* (red, white and rosé dessert wines and *rancio*); *Beaumes de Venise* (red wines and white dessert wines) and *Lirac* (red, white and rosé). In addition there are *marcs* and brandies and a number of VDQS wines.

The cuisine
The restaurants in Lyon are magnificent – they are

The lush green Rhône valley

owned and run by the most famous chefs in France. This city in the north of the Rhône region is renowned for all kinds of sausages, for its *quenelles* (fish balls) made of pike, for its tripe and chicken dishes and for sweets such as acacia-blossom fritters. Further south, the food takes on a distinctive southern character: the flavours are stronger, more garlic and olive oil are used. Perhaps the speciality of the southern Rhône area is the *bouillabaisse*, the great fish stew of Marseilles. There are many versions but they all should include a mixture of firm, white-fleshed fish, olive oil, garlic and onions, with saffron added for flavour and colour. Then there are the *daubes*, hearty stews of lamb or beef cooked slowly with wine, garlic and tomatoes and seasoned with aromatic herbs. *Pieds et paquets* are sausage-like parcels of lambs' trotters and tripe stuffed with bacon, garlic and herbs and cooked in white wine. For those with a sweet tooth, the world-famous Montélimar nougat is not to be missed.

The Route des Vins *Michelin maps 73, 74, 77, 80 and 81.*
Just 30 kilometres south of Lyon is Vienne, the starting point for the wine tour down the Rhône. The main wine road is the N 86, which follows the course of the river for about 70 kilometres. The first village on the Route des Vins is Ampuis, which produces the rare Côte Rôtie, a full-bodied, deep red wine that benefits considerably from ageing. The hillsides here rise sharply from the river, almost like cliffs, and the vines are grown on narrow terraces, many of which date from Roman times. Ampuis itself was founded in 600 BC by the Phoenicians. The Syrah grapes grown on these steep slopes, which face south west, are bathed in sunshine all day long, hence the name Côte Rôtie (literally, 'roasted slope'). A tiny road, the D 615, twists its way up the hillside behind the village and from it you get an excellent view over the terraced slopes to the Rhône far below.

The wines produced in the next two villages, Condrieu and Château-Grillet, in contrast, are heavily scented whites made from the Viognier grape. Both these wines are produced in very small quantities – Château-Grillet is one of the smallest appellation areas in France, with only about 3 hectares of vineyards – and consequently appeal as much for their rarity and snob value as for their character and quality. One place you can try them is at the two-star Beau Rivage restaurant which overlooks the Rhône at Condrieu.

There are no vineyards of interest now until Tournon. Across the river from here you can see a huge granite rock towering above the town of Tain-

The ancient, ochre-coloured, hilltop town of Roussillon,
which has breathtaking views of the surrounding country

On a good day he could produce up to 500 litres, he said. I tasted a sample of his work – and it was fiery indeed. He showed me, with some pride, a picture of a beautiful copper and brass still on cart-wheels. He used it until fairly recently, but is keeping it safe now. It's his pension, he explained wrily.

Once back at Tain, you cross to the west bank of the Rhône, where the N 86 continues through a succession of small wine-growing villages: St-Joseph, Cornas and St Peray, where red and white wines are made; St Peray also produces a sparkling white wine. There is a scenic detour at Cornas, up a small road that climbs towards St Romain de Lerps, where there is a ruined tower. You can return to the N 86 either by doubling back a little via the village of Plats and taking the D 219 into Mauves, or by turning left on to the D 287 and driving down into St Peray.

These villages mark the limit of the northern Rhône vineyards and now it is some 90 kilometres before you reach the next wine areas. However, there are a number of detours off the N 86 which will make this an interesting journey. La Voulte is a fascinating old village perched on a rock topped by a sixteenth-century chapel. Further south, in one of the most beautiful spots in the Rhône Valley, is the village of Rochemaure. There is a fortified gate at each end of the centre of the village. If you stop to explore the ruins of the feudal castle here you will see that there is a split in the rock upon which it is built.

The N 86 continues south through the towns of Viviers and Bourg-St-Andeol to what is virtually the gateway of the sourthern Côtes du Rhône, Pont-St Esprit. This old market town is dramatically situated beside the torrential Rhône, its waters swollen by the confluence with the powerful Ardèche just to the north. The town is named after its thirteenth-century bridge, built by the Frères Pontifs, which spans the river. From here you can explore the southern Rhône vineyards and the wild and majestic gorges of the Ardèche, which lie a little to the west.

The Route des Vins now goes in three different directions. Crossing to the east bank you can follow the route from just outside Bollène towards the village of Ste-Cécile-les-Vignes. Here the terrain is flat and the vines stretch towards the horizon like a patterned green carpet. Although there is a maze of small roads criss-crossing the vineyards and leading to innumerable small villages, the Route des Vins is extremely well signposted – so much so that you can virtually

l'Hermitage, named after a knight crusader who 'retired' here and made wine. Its vineyards of Hermitage and Crozes-Hermitage produce a strong and full-bodied red wine from Syrah grapes which seem to thrive in the rough, rocky soil.

At Tain you could make a detour and follow a signposted route that takes you around the wine-growing communities of la Roche de Glun, Pont-de-l'Isère, Beaumont-Monteux, Chanos-Curson, Mercurol, Crozes-Hermitage, Larnage, Serves, Erôme, Gervans and then back to Tain. It is not all vineyards. There are rich, flat meadows beside the river where a wide variety of fruit and vegetables is grown. In a layby outside Mercurol I met a man with a huge, black, greasy machine called an *alambic* (a still); it looked like an ancient traction engine and had a Heath Robinson air about it. He told me that he spent three months of the year towing it around the local *communes* and converting apples, plums and pears into *eau de vie*.

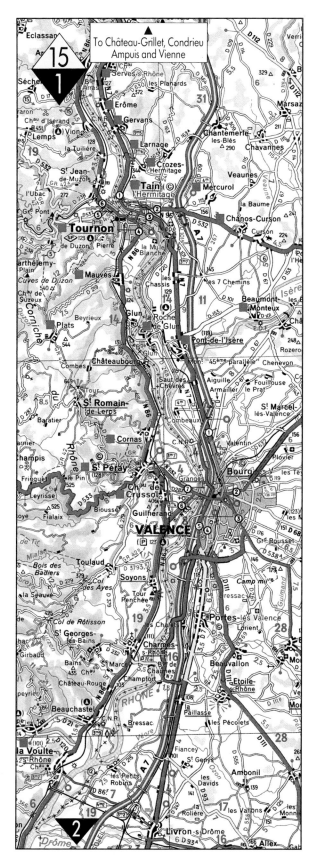

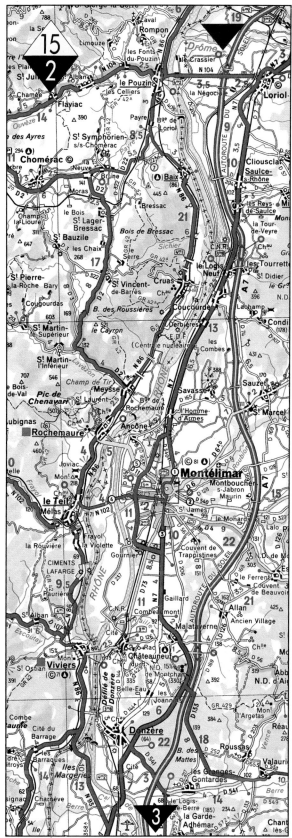

To Village des Bories

ignore the map and simply follow the signs to a succession of fascinating places. At Suze-la-Rousse, for example, there is a university of wine based in a vast château which towers above the small town, and many of the villages, including Bouchet, Cairanne and Roaix, have old fortifications, abbeys, châteaux and often wonderful views from their hill-top settings.

As you travel further to the east a range of jagged mountains begins to loom in the distance. These are the Dentelles de Montmirail; at their foot is Gigondas. It is a handsome mountain village and produces a wonderful full-bodied, deep red wine from the Grenache, Mourvèdre and Syrah grapes that grow here. There is a small road that climbs up and through the mountain giving spectacular views towards the western Cévennes ranges and Mont Ventoux to the east. A little north of Gigondas is Séguret, one of the many little hill-top villages in the area but perhaps more self-conscious than most, having been taken up – and renovated – chiefly by wealthy Parisians.

A little further along the southern edge of the Dentelles de Montmirail are the wine villages of Vacqueyras and Beaumes-de-Venise. They both make good red wines, while Beaumes-de-Venise is famed for its heady Muscat, a rich, naturally sweet white wine which chilled can be served as an apéritif or more regularly with a dessert. A complete circuit of the Dentelles de Montmirail can be made by continuing round towards Malaucène and Vaison-la-Romaine.

Alternatively you can follow the signs for the Côtes du Ventoux from Malaucène. This route leads south through wonderfully scenic countryside, where the vineyards are mingled with lavender fields and the mountains are always in sight. Just outside the small walled village of Caromb is a Cave Co-opérative which also houses a small wine museum. You could stay overnight here in a little hôtel called Le Beffroi, which also has a restaurant. Bédouin and Flassan are two villages worth visiting; the latter is a very evocative example of a Provençal village with its orangey-pink stone and red-tiled houses perched high above the surrounding countryside.

Continue through the village of Villes-sur-Auzon and then westward again via Mormoiron and Mazan to Carpentras, a bustling market town, the medieval capital of the region until Pope Clement V decided that Avignon was more convenient. From here you can follow a circuit of the more southerly wine-growing villages. Of particular interest on this route are the hilltop towns of Venasque and Roussillon, one of the most superbly sited villages in Provence, its ochre and red houses set on the brink of a sheer, rust-coloured cliff. From the village there are breathtaking panoramas over the Côtes du Ventoux. Nearby, close to Gordes, is the ancient Village des Bories, made up of curious conical houses built from flat stones and perfectly preserved.

Heading towards Avignon, make a detour via the

Left: The vineyard of Clos du Pape and the ruined wall and tower which is all that remains of its papal château. The vines, which produce the celebrated Châteauneuf du Pape, thrive in an unlikely soil comprised largely of round stones. Centre: A typical landscape in the mountainous region of the Dentelles de Montmirail. Right: The walls of the village of Cornillon rise straight up from the cliff on which it is built

wine town of Bédarrides to Châteauneuf-du-Pape. All that is left of its papal château is a ruined wall and tower. Up to thirteen different grape varieties are used in the making of the village's famous rich red wine; they grow in a soil studded with round white stones, like small boulders, which store the heat of the sun and release it at night.

Of course you must stop in Avignon. Its medieval Palais des Papes was the home of seven French popes; it is an imposing fortress-like structure with a strong Mediterranean character. The famous Pont d'Avignon has only four of its twenty-two arches now, but retains its chapel. Avignon holds a music and theatre festival in high summer every year and it attracts some world-famous performers.

The circuit on the western side of the Rhône starts from Villeneuve-lès-Avignon, a suburb of the city. There are two routes. You can travel north, following the river upstream. The first two villages are Lirac and Tavel: they produce some of the best rosé wines of France. A little further along the Route des Vins you come to the old, walled village of St Laurent-des

Arbres. Next is St-Victor-la-Coste; looming high above it is an extraordinary huge part-ruined, part-occupied, fortification called le Castella. From here the road continues back northwards past the small wine villages of Laudun and Chusclan and then for a while along the river bank into Pont-St Esprit.

The alternative route goes west from Villeneuve-lès-Avignon through the villages of Saze, Domazan, Théziers and then northward via Pouzilhac (on the N 86), Gaujac and Thesque to the town of Bagnols-sur-Cèze. This is a beautiful, quiet rural route and like all the Côtes du Rhône circuits, it is very well signposted. Instead of returning directly to Pont-St Espirit along the N 86, a really delightful detour can be made by following the route through St Gervais, St Michel-d'Euzet and St Laurent de Carnois to la Roque-sur-Cèze, a little village perched on high. Nearby, at the Cascade du Sautadet, the river spills into a series of rocky crevices; flat rocks beside the cascade invite you to sit and dream. A little further along the D 980 is Cornillon, its walls rising up from the sheer cliff on which it is built. Doubling back a little towards Bagnols-sur-Cèze you will find a small road on the left, the D 23, which winds up through the village of St Laurent-de-Carnois and into a wooded valley to the Chartreuse de Valbonne. You can visit the château and buy the wines of the region at a small *caveau* here. Finally, follow the D 23 back into Pont-St Esprit to rejoin the N 86 and the other wine routes.

Wine Tour Nº 16

LANGUEDOC

Vineyards in early spring, near St Nazaire-de-Ladarex

Languedoc enjoys the warm, sunny climate of the Mediterranean in which the grape vine thrives. This is one of the main wine-producing regions in France, the origin of millions of bottles of Vin de Table and a major contributor to the wine lake. Its wine is known more for its quantity than for its quality. However, although no truly great wines are produced in Languedoc, there are many good and satisfying ones to be tried and the traveller will find the countryside and villages fascinating to explore. The Mediterranean coast is always crowded in the summer months, but even a short distance inland there is a wild and spectacular landscape largely undiscovered by tourists.

Ironically, in view of its lack of great wines, Languedoc is considered to be the birthplace of the French wine industry. The vine is probably indigenous to the area, but its cultivation dates from the Roman occupation in the second century BC. Then, wine was imported from Italy through the Roman port of Narbo Martius, now Narbonne; it is this trade which encouraged the Narbonnais to cultivate the vine and produce their own wine. Wine-making became so important to the region that legend has it that when the Visigoths invaded the city of Béziers in the fifth century they met no resistance because everyone was out in the vineyards harvesting the grapes.

The area's Roman heritage is also evident in a wealth of architectural remains: there are ruined ramparts, aqueducts, amphitheatres, bridges and churches throughout the region. The Roman amphitheatre in Nîmes, for example, is the most perfectly preserved in the world.

The region's name is derived from its mother tongue, literally the *Langue d'Oc, oc* being the regional word for 'yes'; the northern parts of France, where 'yes' was *oil*, now *oui*, was known as the *Langue d'Oil*.

The wines

There is a considerable variety of wine to be found in the region. As well as reds, whites and rosés of varying quality and character, there are also a number of dessert or Vin Doux Naturel wines with the Appellation Contrôlée classification, such as *Muscat de Frontignan, Muscat de Lunel* and *Muscat de Mireval*, as well as sparkling wines and brandies. There are several other Appellation Contrôlée wines such as *Clairette de Bellegarde, Clairette du Languedoc* and *Fitou* but most of the good wines produced here are classified as VDQS, including *Minervois, Corbières, La Clape, Picpoul-de-Pinet, Coteaux de Saint Christol, Saint Saturnin, Montpeyroux, Faugères,* and *Saint Chinian.*

The main volume of the production, however, is Vin de Table and Vin de Pays, and some wine goes into the manufacture of vermouths and apéritif wines such as *Byhrr*. There is a large number of different grape types used, because of the widely varying nature of the soil and location of the vineyards; they include the Carignan, Grenache, Aramon, Cinsaut and Macabeo. The Muscat is used for much of the dessert wine.

The cuisine

Perhaps the best-known dish of the region is *cassoulet*, named after the covered dish in which it is cooked, the *cassolle*. It is a very rich combination of meats such as lamb, duck or goose *confits*, pork or bacon and sausages, baked with onions, garlic and tomatoes and white beans. Then there are the famous Toulouse sausages, *anchoide* (anchovy paste) from Nîmes, game and pâtés, wild mushrooms and wonderful vegetable stews. Fresh and saltwater fish are found in abundance, but the people of Languedoc are still fond of dried salt cod; in *Morue à la minervoise* it is cooked with the red Minervois wine, onions, olive oil, garlic, anchovies and olives. *Pelardon* is a favourite goats'-milk cheese of the region; it is sold in small discs and has a soft texture and delicate nutty flavour.

The Route des Vins *Michelin map 83*

The Route des Vins is very extensive, stretching south from Nîmes nearly to Carcassonne. It is best to divide it into four separate tours; of course, you can combine two or more of them to suit your own interests. The route is quite well signposted – the signs are rather small but are sensibly sited. In places the route is quite

The village of Puéchabon. Its small church overlooking a cluster of houses is very typical of the region

The precariously sited village St Guilhem-le-Désert; it is perched beside the spectacular Gorges de Hérault

circuitous and a certain amount of backtracking is necessary, but the countryside is so splendid that this simply increases the pleasure of the journey.

There are other wine communities outside the official wine route that are also worth visiting – for instance, those producing Vin de Sable (literally, wine of the sand) in the sandy soil around the medieval, fortified town of Aigues-Mortes on the edge of the Camargue, or Costières du Gard, made just south of Nîmes. Clairette de Bellegarde, a dry white Appellation Contrôlée wine, comes from the same area, while Muscat de Lunel, a dessert wine, is produced nearby.

The first circuit begins just to the west of Nîmes, in the small wine village of Langlade. Here, the vineyards are not intensively cultivated and the broad valley through which the road sweeps is chequered with a patchwork of vineyards, meadows and crops such as asparagus and rapeseed; the hills on either side, although quite steep, are not very high. As you travel westwards the land becomes more undulating and the distant mountains more dominant. Pass the small walled town of Sommières on the banks of the river Vidourle and continue south on the D 105 through St Christol, St Geniès and Vérargues; the hillsides here are more densely covered with vines. As the Route des Vins turns northwards towards the wine villages of St Drézéry and Fontanès the landscape begins to change, taking on a wilder and more rugged character with steep, rocky outcrops and the dense, wiry *maquis* dotted with pine trees. Soon the large, distant, conical shape of the Pic St Loup appears to the west. The road continues northward to the small villages of Valflaunès, Lauret and Claret, on the D 17, which now

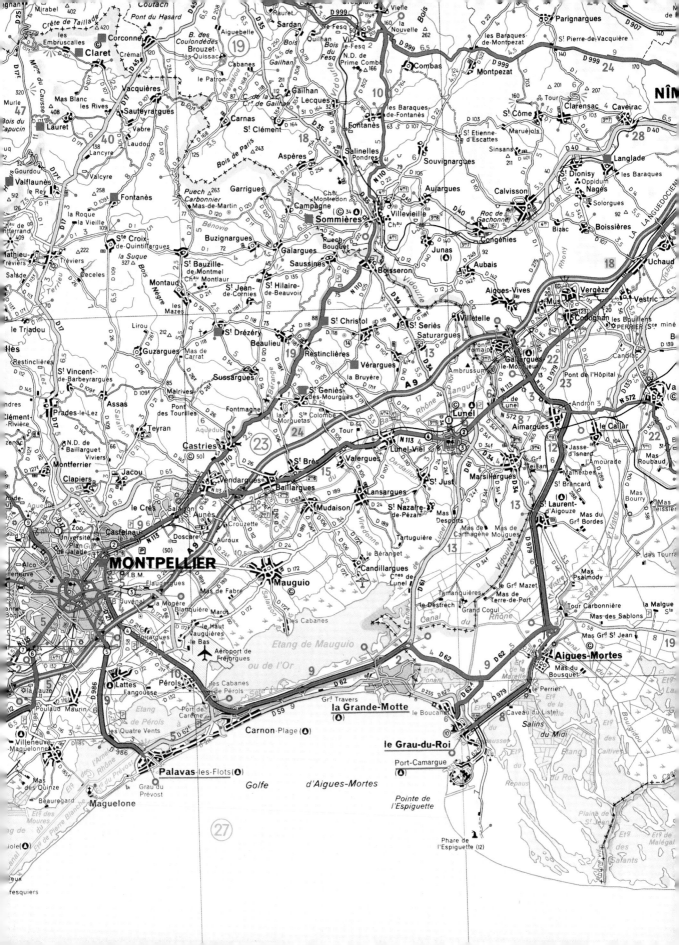

One of the many signs offering wine for sale, tempting the visitor to an often worthwhile detour

winds its way through dense pine forests. This is an ideally tranquil place in which to stretch your legs or have a picnic lunch. Corconne, the most northerly point of this part of the wine route, is a charming small village of old stone houses set at the foot of two cliffs in a ravine.

From here follow the same road back to Valflaunès, where a small road, the D 1e, branches off to wind around the dramatic Pic St Loup. This countryside is full of colour; the steep, rocky hillsides are covered with *maquis*, wild flowers and herbs and shaded by pine trees; it is popular with the local people, who come here to walk, climb and picnic at the weekends. In the nearby village of Nôtre-Dame-de-Londres is a small twelfth-century château.

The Route des Vins now leads to the small villages of St Mathieu-de-Tréviers, Cazevieille and St Jean-de-Cuculles, the latter teetering on a hilltop. The quiet road through this region weaves through steep, rocky hillsides with pine forests and there are frequent beautiful views, with the Pic St Loup constantly dominating the landscape. It's worth visiting the little medieval village of les Matelles; its ramparts, fortified gateways, narrow, steeply winding streets, archways and tunnels are all in miniature.

The next important wine village, some way to the west, is Montpeyroux, which produces well-respected VDQS reds and rosés, as does the nearby village of St Saturnin. An essential minor detour here is to the Gorges de l'Hérault and the village of St Guilhem-le-Désert. Although these gorges are not as deep and extensive as those of say Verdun or the Tarn, nonetheless they are very impressive. You can climb down to

the riverside quite easily in many places and enjoy the solitude surrounded by the majestic rocks. The village of St Guilhem is built along a deep cleft in the side of the gorges, its tiny, narrow, stone houses with their brown-tiled roofs nestling under a massive rock looming high above. The Grotte de Clamouse is close by; you should linger here for a while.

Another worthwhile detour in this region is to the lake of Salagou, where you can windsurf, sail and canoe; there are also camping facilities. Nearby is the Cirque de Mourèze, a place with strange dolomitic pinnacles with a tiny village in the middle. This is the most westerly point of the first circuit and the route now begins to head back towards Montpellier through the wine villages of Aspiran, Lézignan-la-Cèbe, Montbazin, Pignan and Lavérune, the latter virtually a suburb of the city. The lovely Abbaye de Valmagne, one of the most beautiful buildings in Languedoc, is situated between the villages of Montagnac and Ville-veyrac. Montpellier has been an important wine centre for many centuries and was also a leading producer of liqueurs. Today its importance is just as great as it houses the Ecole Nationale Supérieure Agronomique, the Ecole d'Oenologie (College of Wine) and the Ecole de Viticulture, and as such is the main centre in France for the study of the cultivation of the vine.

The second circuit of the Côtes du Languedoc Route des Vins starts just north of the town of Agde in the small wine village of Pinet, which produces a wine called Picpoul-de-Pinet. The Picpoul is a grape used to produce the rather thin wine from which Cognac is distilled, but here the soil and climate combine favourably to produce a well-thought-of dry white wine. The wine road continues northward on the D 161 towards the town of Pézenas, an attractive old town with narrow streets and some distinguished buildings, where Molière spent several winters. In nearby Caux there is a twelfth-century church and the remains of ramparts from the sixth century. From Pézenas the Route des Vins continues along the D 13 through the wine villages of Roujan and Gabian towards Faugères; there are extensive vineyards along this road, and many opportunities to stop and taste the wine. Just north of Roujan; set among the vineyards, is the charming château of Cassan. As in the rest of the

The rather rugged countryside of this part of the region is dotted with tiny hamlets like Nôtre-Dame-de-Londres (above). The Lac du Salagou (below) offers many sporting opportunities and ideal conditions for windsurfing and sailing

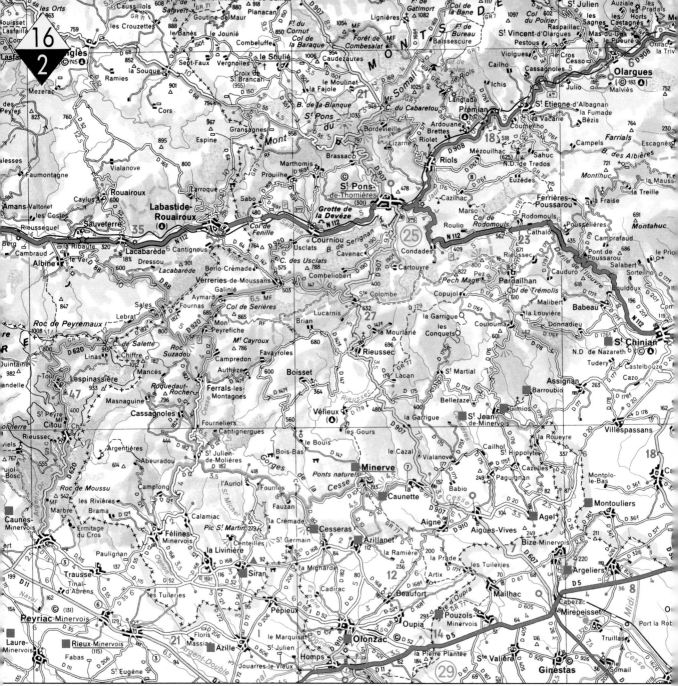

Languedoc, most of the wine here is made by small producers who own only a few hectares. Consequently the Cave Co-opérative plays an important economic role; sometimes these vast establishments almost dwarf the tiny villages that give them their name. A few kilometres off the main wine route, along tiny country lanes, there are many small wine-producing villages, such as Fos and Roquessels, which is perched on a pinnacle of rock. If you take these small detours you will discover some tranquil countryside – a beautiful stretch of road with splendid views is the

D15 from Neffiès to Cabrières, while the *caveau* in Nizas, north of Pézenas, is in an attractive château in the centre of the village.

Faugères, a very small and quiet village, is an important wine centre for the surrounding producers and makes excellent red and rosé wines. The nearby small town of Laurens has steep, narrow streets surmounted by an imposing château. The Château de Grezan, close by, is well worth a visit; the restored building was once a Templars fortress and it stands in the middle of extensive vineyards with a backdrop of

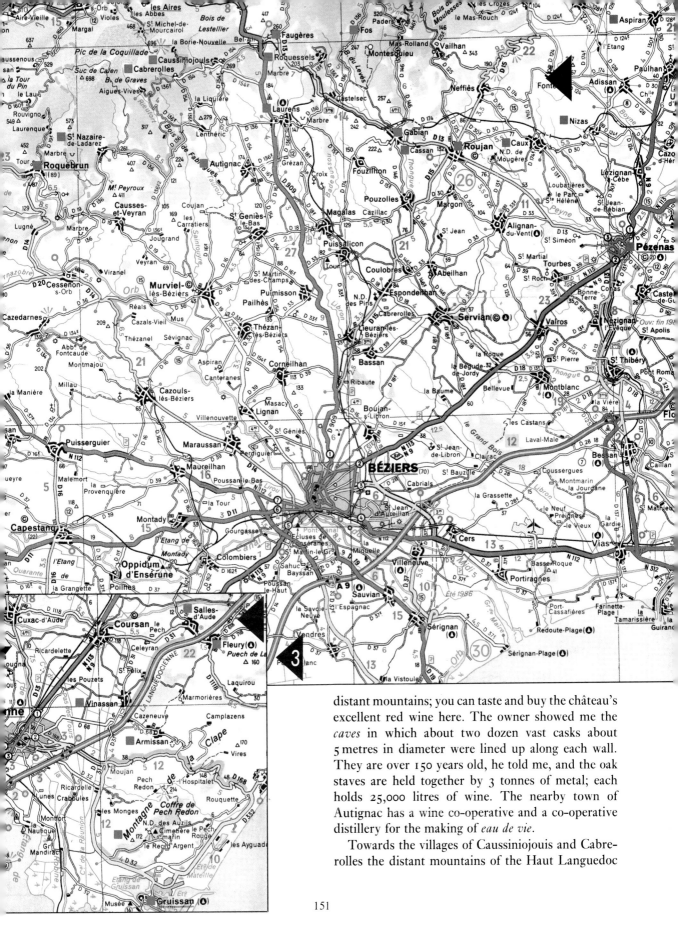

distant mountains; you can taste and buy the château's excellent red wine here. The owner showed me the *caves* in which about two dozen vast casks about 5 metres in diameter were lined up along each wall. They are over 150 years old, he told me, and the oak staves are held together by 3 tonnes of metal; each holds 25,000 litres of wine. The nearby town of Autignac has a wine co-operative and a co-operative distillery for the making of *eau de vie*.

Towards the villages of Caussiniojouis and Cabrerolles the distant mountains of the Haut Languedoc

An ancient, shuttered shop front in the small village of Azille in the Minervois

begin to loom larger and the countryside becomes hillier and more rugged. The region has magnificent scenery and there are unexpected vistas at every twist and turn of the narrow, winding road. It is very quiet – you can drive for an hour or more without meeting another car or even seeing a house – and there is virtually no sign of habitation except for the well-tended vineyards which pattern the hillsides.

From St Nazaire-de-Ladarex to Roquebrun the wine road follows the course of the river Orb. The small village of Roquebrun, at the head of the valley nestling below the mountain, spreads up the hillside to a ruined tower. Follow the wine route to Vieussan, another dramatically sited village – this time above a steep cliff beside the river where the hillsides are so steep that the vineyards are terraced, with dry stone walls to hold the soil. Both these villages have a microclimate in which oranges and mimosa as well as the vines flourish and the landscape becomes almost alpine in character. The road continues now along the D 177 towards the village of Berlou. As you wind up out of the valley to the top of the mountain there are a series of quite spectacular panoramas. After St Chinian, which is an important wine centre, the Route des Vins continues along the main road, the N 112, to Cébazan and south to Quarante, the last village on this leg of the wine route.

The wine-growing region of the Minervois is adjacent to St Chinian and has its own small, signposted circuit. The most convenient place to start the Minervois circuit is in the small village of Montouliers, near Quarante, the last village on the previous tour. Head towards St Jean-de-Minervois through landscape that is quite different from that covered in the previous

tour. Nearby are the curious, tiny wine villages of Gimios and Barroubio with houses built of large, rough, white stones; the vineyards in this region are also covered with white, flinty stones, which at times create the illusion of a snowfall. From here, the wine road continues through the villages of Agel and la Caunette towards Minèrve. The Romanesque church at Minerve contains an altar dated 456, supposed to be the oldest altar in France. There is an archaeological museum here and the remains of medieval fortifications. The route continues through the villages of Azillanet, Cesseras and Siran towards Caunes-Minervois. The vineyards here, in what is now a much flatter landscape, are very extensive and opportunities to stop and taste wine are frequent. The grottoes of Limousis are close by; they can be visited with a guide on Sundays and holidays only in the afternoons. The Minervois Route des Vins completes its circuit via the wine villages of Laure, Rieux-Minervois (where there is an interesting octagonal church), Azille, Olonzac, Pouzols and Argeliers back to Montouliers.

The final part of the Languedoc Route des Vins is concentrated in the Montagne de la Clape, a region very near the sea, between Narbonne and Narbonne-Plage. The circuit winds through the small villages of Salles-d'Aude, Fleury, Gruissan, Armissan and Vinassan. The Massif de la Clape is a strange hump of a hill set on the flat coastal plain from which it rises quite dramatically. It is a quite curious landscape; on top it is rocky, rugged and even a little bleak, covered with *maquis* and dotted with pine trees. It has a rather remote and not-of-this-world atmosphere. There are some impressive views from the small road that leads to the village of Armissan displaying the unusual nature of the landscape of la Clape. The wines here have an excellent reputation, particularly the white VDQS wine with its dry but fruity character well suited to the seafood which is available in abundance in the region. The route is by the sea around Gruissan, an old circular fortified town which in fact stands on a lagoon, and there are lovely pine forests between the water and the mountain. Close by is the Château de Bouis, one of many places where you can taste and buy the local wines. From here it is a short distance to the Autoroute A 9 which will take you back northwards or on to Perpignan to explore the Côtes de Roussillon.

The village of Vieussan perched above the valley of the Orb

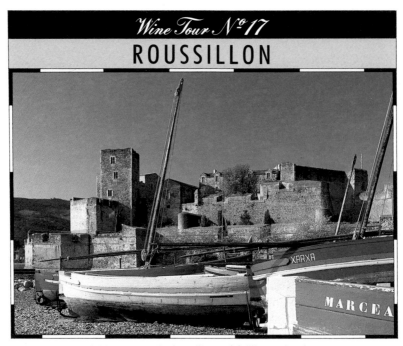

Wine Tour N° 17

ROUSSILLON

The fishing port and wine village of Collioure, its character
undiminished by tourism

Ringed on three sides by mountains – the Pyrenees to the west, the Corbières to the north and the Albères to the south – and on the fourth by the warm, blue waters of the Mediterranean, Roussillon seems a world apart. It is the most southern region of France; just across the Spanish border is the Costa Brava. Through its long history of invaders and foreign rulers, including Greeks, Romans, Visigoths, Moors and, of course, Spaniards, the region has developed a proudly partisan character quite unlike the rest of France. Its language and culture are similar to those of Catalonia: the folklore and the cuisine are alike, the *sardane* is danced here, as it is in north-east Spain (where it is called the *sardana*), and there are bull-fights during the summer months. You will notice that place names are written in both French and Catalan. Scenically, it is a richly endowed region, with dramatic snow-capped mountains, rivers, shimmering lakes, dense forests and a beautiful coastline. The climate, too, is extraordinary – it averages 325 sunny days a year. This is wine-making country.

The grape vine flourishes in the warm climate of Roussillon and there is a long history of cultivation here: grains of vine pollen were found in the grottoes of Tautavel, where the first Europeans lived 500,000 years ago. The vineyards are often established on steep hillsides, where they are extensively terraced.

The wines
A considerable variety of wine is produced in the Roussillon. The white Appellation Contrôlée *Côtes de Roussillon*, a light, dry wine made from the Macabeo grape, goes well with the local seafood and shellfish, and the fruity, full-bodied rosé is an ideal accompaniment to the Catalan *charcuterie*. In addition, there are the Appellation Contrôlée *Côtes de Roussillon-Villages*, red wines made primarily from the Carignan grape to which other varieties, such as the Grenache Noir, Cinsault and Syrah, are added according to the soil and location, and dessert and Vin Doux Naturel wines such as *Maury*, *Banyuls* and *Muscat de Rivesaltes*.

The cuisine
In these rich, fertile plains many varieties of fruit – apricots, cherries, strawberries, lemons and peaches – are ripe much earlier than in other parts of France. There is an abundance of wild game, seafood and freshwater fish and the Roussillon cuisine reflects this in local specialities such as *sanglier de Fenouillèdes*, a wild boar stew, *perdreau à la catalane*, wild partridge

cooked in the Catalan style with onions, tomatoes and peppers, and *bolas de picolat*, meatballs flavoured with garlic, green olives and parsley. The anchovies of Collioure are also a regional delicacy and are often served as a first course, as part of a *salade composée*. A local temptation for the sweet-toothed is *touron*, a confection made from candied fruits, pistachio nuts, hazelnuts and almonds.

The Route des Vins *Michelin map 86*

Ideally, the Route des Vins of Roussillon should be explored from a central base such as Perpignan; it is not really a circuit, but rather a series of excursions into different regions. On the inland parts of the route in the north, hotel accommodation is quite limited; however you are never more than an hour or so away from the coast and its resort areas.

Perpignan is the centre of the Roussillon wine industry and also the region's capital. It is a city of wide tree-lined boulevards, leafy squares, smart shops, stately old buildings and monuments and a lively social calendar. The Palace of the Kings of Majorca is a magnificent thirteenth-century building situated in the old centre of the city, the cathedral of Saint Jean is fourteenth century, while the Rue des Mercaders contains many old houses from medieval times. The Castillet, a crenellated fourteenth-century, red-brick fortress, houses the Casa Pairal, the Catalonian Museum of Popular Arts and Traditions; from its terrace there are views of the city, the sea and the mountains.

The first part of the Route des Vins explores the Aspres region. The small town of Thuir is the centre of this wine-producing area; it has the largest wine cellars in Europe. Beyond the pretty hilltop village of Camélas nearby, there is a tenth-century retreat hidden in the hillside. Also close by is Castelnou, a picturesque medieval village in a wonderful setting – perched on a hilltop, surrounded by vineyards, against a breath-taking backdrop of mountains. There is a château and ramparts here dating from the tenth century, the thirteenth-century of Ste Marie, which has been restored, and a centre for arts and crafts, where exhibitions and concerts are held.

The village of Castelnou, dominated by the Massif du Canigou

The Mediterranean photographed from the scenic route

A number of small wine villages on the plain, including Banyuls-dels-Aspres, Trouillas, St Genis-des-Fontaines (which has a ruined Benedictine abbey) and Bages, all have *caves* where the local wines can be tasted. Continue towards the coast to Argelès, a lively fortified town with many ancient remains; it is also a busy summer resort with an extensive beach.

Along the valley of the river Tech is the busy town of Céret; the fourteenth-century bridge, Pont du Diable, spans the river, and there are old town gates and a fourteenth-century church. Céret's museum of modern art contains works by painters who have lived here, most notably Dufy, Picasso, Chagall, Gris, Braque and Matisse. The town is also known as the cherry capital of France, as its orchards produce the first fruit of the year, and there is a *sardane* festival here every August. At the nearby Château d'Aubiry you can taste and buy the local wine.

The second section of the wine route is centred around Banyuls-sur-Mer. Although quite small, this region has a varied landscape. The lure of the warm climate, sea, wines and food, could tempt you to linger here. Collioure is the first town on this route. You approach it along a road that winds around the steep hillsides lining the coast. The vineyards here are

planted precariously on the terraced slopes, some of which plunge straight down to the sea. Collioure is a lovely town, one of the most attractive seaside villages on the Mediterranean. Henri Matisse and André Derain spent the summer of 1906 painting here, at the high point of their Fauvist collaboration. In spite of the obvious tourist appeal, Collioure has lost little of its charm or character. Be warned, however, that in July and August it can become very crowded. It has a tiny, turreted church overlooking a small shingle beach, which is populated by a small fleet of coloured fishing boats and café tables and chairs spilling over from the small cobbled promenade. High above the other side of the harbour is the majestic Château Royal, a former residence of the kings of Majorca.

The spectacular coast road continues winding its way round the hills to Port-Vendres, the ancient Port of Venus. Now a busy town with a bustling harbour and many sea-front cafés and restaurants, it has a large *cave* called the Cellier des Templiers. Continue along the coast to the small town of Banyuls-sur-Mer. Noisy and colourful, with a busy harbour, it has its own Appellation and a highly regarded red Vin Doux Naturel ranging from sweet to very dry. In the town itself and along the roadside there are many opportunities to taste the wines. From here the Route des Vins continues, with views that constantly surprise and delight, to the town of Cerbère, almost on the Spanish border.

The Banyuls wine route follows the small roads that climb up into the mountains beyond the coastline; although they are signposted, they are quite easy to miss (the Michelin map 86 shows them clearly). The first is just before you reach Collioure; the second a kilometre or so south of Port-Vendres at the top of the hill, and the third starts in Banyuls, at the Grande Cave des Templiers: these roads all link up, so you only need to find one of them. Be prepared for some quite spectacular scenery. As you climb higher into the mountain the views, both towards the sea and inland to the mountains, are breathtaking. There are vineyards covering every useful piece of land, held up by dry-stone terraces, and there is a network of ingenious drainage ditches that create strange patterns on the slopes; these were originally developed by the Knights

Templars. Soon you will be deep into a landscape that seems far removed from the busy Mediterranean towns a few kilometres away. The air is full of honey-bees and butterflies, and birds, and when you drive along the tiny road, scarcely wider than a car, through the wild and remote landscape, you see only the vineyards and an occasional small barn or hut. Stop at the Table d'Orientation on the road between Port-Vendres and Banyuls; from here you have a panoramic view from Narbonne-Plage in the north to Cerbère and Spain in the south.

The road climbs higher still, to the tower of Madeloc, where the view is even more spectacular. Unless you have nerves of steel get out and walk at this point, as the road has become nothing more than a track and it is very steep and narrow with tight hairpin bends and a sheer drop on one side. Another place of interest on the road between Collioure and Port-Vendres is Nôtre-Dame-de-Consolation, a seventeenth-century hermitage and chapel.

The most northerly section of the Route des Vins, around Salses, north of Perpignan, also has some scenic delights in store. It is not a neat circuit and the signposted route is convoluted, but distances are not very great and it is perfect countryside in which to meander. Salses itself is an unremarkable wine village set between the Etang de Salses and the hills. It has, however, a remarkable fifteenth-century fortress, the Fort de Salses, a fine example of military architecture, guarding the route Hannibal took in 218 BC. Its pinkish stone and domed construction seem to belong to the Sahara desert rather than rural France.

Nearby Rivesaltes is the birthplace of Marshall Joffre and an important wine community with many *caves* for tasting. It is known particularly for its Vin Doux Naturel, Muscat de Rivesaltes. In the small town of Baixas are ruined ramparts, fortified gateways and many old buildings, including a Gothic church. I was walking through the village with my camera when I was accosted by a little old lady, apparently the church custodian, who insisted that I see inside the church, and then tottered off for the key. Once inside she showed me, with great pride, the magnificent gilded Baroque *retable* (reredos) which dates from the seventeenth century. At Espira de l'Agly, close by, there is another notable church with beautiful interior features, including twelfth-century furniture and carved wood reliefs.

At the village of Cases-de-Pène, with its Hermitage

Above: Vineyards photographed in early spring from the D17 which winds through the mountains above the village of Cassagnes. Below: The remarkably well-preserved fifteenth-century Fort de Salses

de Nôtre-Dame de Pène, a small road (the D 59) climbs out of the valley of the river Agly towards the small wine village of Tautaval. The road winds around the top of an escarpment and you can look down on the floor of the valley, far below, carpeted with neatly patterned vineyards. This route now becomes even more spectacular as you twist down through the gorge of the river Verdouble. Tautavel has a Cave Co-opérative, Les Maîtres Vignerons de Tautavel, and is known also for its museum of prehistory. Many important anthropological finds have been made

around here; the most famous is the skull of the Caune de l'Arago man, believed to be 500,000 years old. The wine road continues to the head of the valley, to Vingrau, a village surrounded by vineyards and mountains with a thirteenth-century Romanesque church at its centre.

Returning to the main road, the D 117, the next town is Estagel, the birthplace of Dominique François, the nineteenth-century astronomer and physicist, who is honoured with a monument in the square. There is an exhibition of Catalan history here. A very

worthwhile short detour is to the Château de Quéribus, an imposing grey fortress set, quite improbably, on the ridge of the sheer, rugged mountain; it appears to be carved out of the rock. There is a narrow road, winding up to the castle, from which there are superb views.

The Route des Vins continues through the village of Maury, known for its Vin Doux Naturel, to St Paul-de-Fenouillet, the centre of this region and the western route. About 5 kilometres from the town are the Gorges de Galamus – vast, jagged clefts in the rock, surrounded by sheer cliffs and chasms, while the silvery thread of a river is visible way below. In the summer there is a *caveau* at the entrance to the gorges, and you can visit the tiny hermitage of St Antoine de Galamus tucked into the side of the gorge about half-way down. If you have time, about an hour's drive away along a lovely scenic route to the north-west on the D 118 is the wine town of Limoux, known mainly for its excellent sparkling wine, Blanquette de Limoux.

From St Paul-de-Fenouillet, follow the wine road

The whitewashed village of Caramany (above) sitting in tiers in the mountains above the valley of the river Agly. After the winter pruning and and before the vines have begun to shoot, vineyards (as left between Cases-de-Pène and Tautavel) look remarkably unattractive and barren. Overleaf: The beautiful hilltop village of Montalba-le-Château

into the mountains to the south, along a small scenic route through the villages of St Martin-de-Fenouillet, Ansignan and Sournia to the wine village of Caramany. (There is a Roman aqueduct-viaduct near Ansignan which is still in use, carrying water to the vineyards in the valley and the tunnel bridge below it allows people to cross the small river.) Caramany is curiously situated, its small red-tiled houses stacked up like a house of cards. The route continues through remote countryside, where the tranquil atmosphere is disturbed occasionally by quail and partridges fluttering across the road. Montalba-le-Château is a beautiful village perched on top of the mountain, surrounded by vineyards, with views of the distant, often snow-capped Pyrenean peaks in the background; there is a wine museum in the small château here. This part of the route is completed by returning to the coastal plain via the villages of Bélesta, Cassagnes, Latour-de-France, with its Appellation Contrôlée Côtes de Roussillon-Villages, Montner, with the nearby chapel of Forca Réal, and Corneilla-la-Rivière.

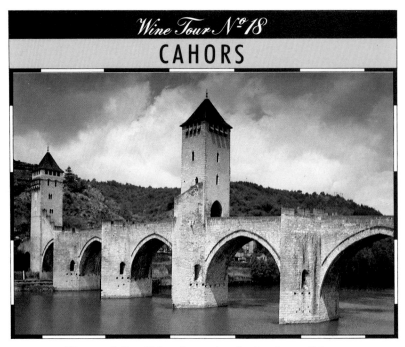

Wine Tour N° 18
CAHORS

The superb Pont Valentré spanning the river Lot at Cahors

The city of Cahors is at the very heart of rural France. It is situated in the lovely valley of the river Lot, which threads its way through the Dordogne in a series of winding loops and curves. Once the thriving capital of the old kingdom of Quercy, Cahors is situated in one of these loops, which almost encircles the city in the shape of a horseshoe; its fortifications and dominant position made it virtually impregnable. So much so that during the Hundred Years' War, when the British took possession of all the other towns in Quercy, only Cahors resisted. Today it is an elegant town with broad tree-lined streets and squares shading the pavement cafés, and here you begin to feel some of the atmosphere of the Mediterranean life and climate.

Much of Cahors' wealth during the Middle Ages came from trade and banking, but wine has always been an important part of its commercial life and the region has long been famous for its vineyards. During the Roman occupation, the Emperor Dolmitian ordered the vines to be uprooted as a penalty for an attempted uprising and for two centuries no wine was produced. Later the deep red wine of Cahors became very popular in England, where it was often preferred to Bordeaux wines, despite that region's attempts to prevent it being shipped. Legend has it that the Popes insisted on its use for the celebration of Mass.

The wines
The best wines of Cahors are made from the vineyards in the lower Lot Valley beside the river between Cahors and Fumel to the west. The rich red soil, often scattered with limestone pebbles, is planted primarily with Malbec, Merlot and Jurançon grapes. The deep red wines which they produce, classified Appellation Contrôlée, are often matured for three years or more in oak casks, improving still further with age in the bottle.

The lesser wines, such as the *Coteaux de Quercy* and *Coteaux de Glanes*, red, white and rosé, are produced from a wider area away from the river and this countryside is well worth exploring.

The cuisine
This is one of the principal areas where black truffles are found. They feature in many dishes, most notably in *pâté de foie gras truffé*, produced from the frequently encountered gaggles of geese, and are also excellent cooked in Champagne or in cream. *Confit d'oie* and *confit de canard* can often be bought directly from the farms. *Foie gas à la quercynoise* is goose-liver served in thin slices with a sauce made by simmering finely chopped vegetables and herbs in stock and white wine and flavoured with cognac and truffles. *Rillettes d'oie*, a

wonderful pâté made from goose, is another local speciality to look out for, as are the small, round creamy goat cheeses called *Cabécou*.

The Route des Vins *Michelin map 79*

The official Route des Vins is clearly signposted, and starts and ends in Cahors although it can, of course, be picked up from any point. There is a fine old quarter in the town with magnificent medieval buildings and ruined ramparts. Of particular note is the Maison de Roaldès, sometimes called the Mansion of Henri IV because the king was reputed to have stayed there during the siege of 1580, and also the twelfth-century Cathedral of St Etienne. The medieval Pont Valentré is Cahors' *pièce de résistance*, however. It is fortified and spans the river Lot, supported by three towers; it is considered to be one of the finest examples of French military architecture and the bridge is the recommended starting point for the wine route.

Cross the bridge to the south bank of the river and follow the signs to the first wine village of Pradines. The next small community is Douelle; in earlier times this was where the Cahors wines were loaded on to flat-bottomed boats to be transported down river to Bordeaux. Nearby is the ruined château of Cessac.

At this point the valley is quite wide and the vineyards lie between the road and the river. There are several important growers in the next village, Parnac, which is almost beside the river, and you can go for a walk on a track that runs along the river bank. Nearby, near the main road, is the large Cave Co-opérative of the Côtes d'Olt, where you can taste the local Appellation Contrôlée wines. You can also buy Vin de Table and Vin de Pays in large plastic containers (*en vrac*). Take a short detour to St Vincent Rive d'Olt (Olt is the old name for the river), then go on to Luzech. Here, the river forms a characteristic loop, but this time so dramatic that it almost seems as if the town is an

A weatherbeaten *vigneron* of the region

island. It is a pleasant place with some impressive old buildings, including a twelfth-century chapel, and there are remarkable views over the river towards the vineyards, which can be reached by a small road that climbs up out of the village to the hilltop called Impernal.

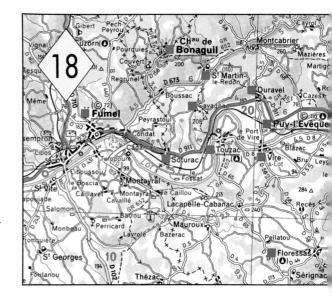

The road curves round to Albas, with its tiny red-tiled houses built on a large rock beside the river dominated by the church. The hills are getting steeper now and the valley narrower, and from the winding road there is an inspiring succession of views. At Grézels, a small wine village, there is another detour up a narrow, steep road that climbs out of the valley through a wooded hillside towards the village of Floressas, where the Château Chambert is situated; you can taste and buy some wine at the château. Go back to Grézels and follow the Route des Vins through small communities such as Pescadoires, often no more than a cluster of small stone houses and a church. The landscape is changing now. You'll see fruit trees and meadows and fields of sunflowers scattered among the vineyards, and gentle hills crowned with copses.

Puy l'Evêque, on the north bank, is the next large town. Tiers of mellow old houses tumble down the steep hillside to the water's edge. The church stands on the summit; it has a fortified belfry and a doorway decorated with statues. There is a spectacular view of the Lot Valley from the esplanade beside the remains of a thirteenth-century castle.

At this point the Route des Vins crosses the river and continues through Duravel, a village of mellow stone houses topped by a small château. From here the wine road winds up and away from the river through a wooded hillside to St Martin-le-Redon, which is little more than a cluster of crumbling, yellow stone houses surrounding a small church, and makes few visible concessions to the twentieth century. The next village, Cavagnac, is situated high up the hillside and is full of rather curious little houses with porches and eaves. The vineyards are not so evident here and the land is quite densely wooded with rolling hills and charming small valleys. It has a tranquil quality, and a much sparser population than the region closer to the river.

Follow the wine route to the Château de Bonaguile, a splendid example of fifteenth-century military architecture; it was strongly fortified with no less than three defence lines. Strangely, it looks terribly romantic set on a hilltop overlooking a small wooded valley and could easily be the setting for a fairy story or a Gothic

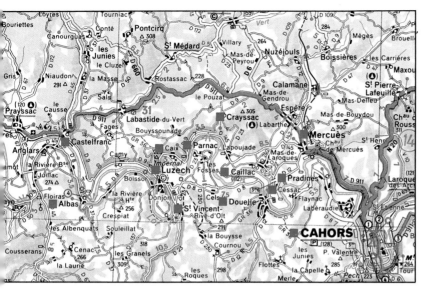

Top: The village of Albas, built on a large rock beside the Lot. The rich countryside plays host to both flowers (left) and cereals (above, near the village of Lalbenque) as well as to vines

novel. Walk along a little road that winds through the wooded hillside to the east of the château to a small clearing where you get a sudden and quite spectacular view of the building. This is just 6 kilometres from the industrial town of Fumel, which marks the western limit of the circuit. The return route is along the main road (the D 911) for a short distance past Soturac, then crosses back over the river to the wine village of Touzac.

At Vire-sur-Lot the wine road turns south on to the D 58 through a quiet valley patterned with vineyards and then back to Puy-l'Evêque and the north bank of the river. On the return journey to Cahors, the road stays near the river, passing through the small villages

A crumbling farmhouse (above) and (right) the Château de Bonaguile, both in the region of the little hillside village of St Martin-le-Redon

of Prayssac and Castelfranc, then on the D 9 to Caix, Crayssac and Caillac. Rejoin the main road, the D 911, at Mercuès, where there is the imposing thirteenth-century Château de Mercuès. Once the property of the counts of Cahors, it was rebuilt in the last century and is now a luxury hotel. From here the main road leads back into the centre of Cahors.

The total circuit is only about 120 kilometres long, but it would be easy to spend several days exploring the countryside and there are several other places not on our official route that are well worth visiting. One of the most important vineyards in the region is that of Georges Vigouroux near Lalbenque (off the N 20, south of Cahors), a village renowned for its truffle market as well as its wine. The countryside due south of the Lot Valley vineyards is where much of the Vin de Table, Vin de Pays and the VDQS Coteaux de Quercy is produced, in the vicinity of such villages as Montcuq and Castelnau-Montratier. A tour through this peaceful region of old, traditional Quercy farms and buildings can be made by following the Circuit de Quercy Blanc, a route which is signposted from the N 20 south of Cahors, or from the village of St Vincent Rive d'Olt on the Route des Vins.

Although it is not in the wine-growing area, it would be almost unthinkable to visit the Cahors area and not see the village of St Cirq-Lapopie, about 30 minutes' drive east along a beautiful scenic road through the upper Lot Valley. St Cirq-Lapopie is the showpiece of France's tourist industry: it has quaint old brown-tiled houses, narrow hilly streets, a fifteenth-century church and a ruined château. What more could you want?

Wine Tour Nº 19
PROVENCE

A vineyard between Carcès and Montfort-sur-Argens

Endless blue skies, olive groves, wild thyme and lavender fields, garlic, pine trees, parched rust-coloured soil, sea, sea, sea ... this is Provence. It is hardly surprising that the south of France has been one of the most popular European tourist destinations for generations. Provence has one of the most beautiful stretches of coastline in the whole of the Mediterranean. It also has majestic mountains, wild gorges and cascading rivers, as well as vast forests and green, fertile valleys. Its cultural heritage is fascinating and there is a wealth of small, unspoilt villages, many in spectacular settings. Added to all this is the perennial attraction of the powerful Mediterranean sun and the warm and benevolent climate it creates.

Provence also possesses extensive vineyards which produce a range of good wines. The other, more obvious, attractions of the region are so appealing, however, that many visitors remain virtually unaware of what the vineyards offer. The principal wine-growing area of Provence is in the region of the Var, bordered by Toulon in the west and Fréjus in the east and extending as far north as Draguignan. Within this area the wine route offers the traveller every aspect of the Provençal countryside, from breathtakingly beautiful coastal scenery to wild and rugged mountainscapes and peaceful, pastoral valleys.

The wines

The predominant wines of Provence, *Côtes de Provence*, have an Appellation Contrôlée classification, although red, white and rosé are all made. The region is best known for its rosés and indeed some are among the best made in France; they are very dry with a high alcohol content, a good body and a fruity aroma. VDQS rosés (and some undistinguished reds and whites) come from the vineyards of *Coteaux d'Aix-en-Provence*, *Coteaux de Pierrevert* and *Coteaux des Baux-en-Provence*. There are a number of other Appellation Contrôlée wines such as *Cassis*, *Bandol*, *Bellet* and *Palette*, and some Vin de Pays including *Les Maures*, *Coteaux Varois*, *Mont Caume* and *Argens*.

Cinsaut, Grenache, Carignane, Tibouren and Peccoui Touar grapes are used to make the rosés and reds; the white wines are made from the Picpoul, Clairette, Semillon and Ugni Blanc grapes.

The cuisine

Grapes are not the only important crop in Provence: the olive tree is almost as plentiful (there is a Route de l'huile d'olive) and olive oil is essential to the region's cuisine. *Aïoli*, a garlic-flavoured mayonnaise made with olive oil, is served with seafood or raw vegetables. There are wonderful vegetable stews such as *ratatou-*

ille of aubergines and peppers cooked in olive oil. *Salade niçoise* is a combination of tomatoes, olives, capers, potatoes, beans, lettuce, anchovies and tuna. *Pan bagna* is a *baguette* filled with anchovies, tomato and capers. The rich, tangy sauce called *tapenade* is made with olives, capers, tuna and anchovies; it is delicious with hard-boiled eggs. *Sauce provençale* is served with fish, meat and vegetable dishes; tomatoes, garlic and shallots are gently simmered in white wine and olive oil, and seasoned with parsley and basil. *Pissaladière* is a flat bread dough covered with olives, anchovies, onions and tomatoes, which is similar to the Italian *pizza*.

With all of these regional specialities you should drink a chilled Côtes de Provence rosé. Another speciality of the region, traditionally served at Easter and Christmas, is Vin Cuit (cooked wine), made by boiling newly pressed, unfermented grape juice until it is reduced to about a third of its volume and adding a measure of *marc* or *eau de vie*.

The Route des Vins *Michelin map 84*

The Route des Vins is quite extensive and it would take several weeks to explore it properly. Although the distances may not appear great on the map, most of the roads are very narrow and winding, with numerous hairpin bends, and it can often take an hour or two to cover only 10 kilometres – especially when there are so many temptations to stop and admire the views or to explore tiny villages. The route is well signposted and is essentially a circular tour, but it incorporates a number of detours. If you are staying on the coast, you could begin the tour at either St Tropez or Hyères; if travelling on the Autoroute A 8 (*La Provençale*) start at

Mellow houses in the peaceful square in the village of Lorgues

The old quarter of the ancient market town of Draguignon

Brignoles or Fréjus.

Officially the Route des Vins begins in Toulon, a busy port and the main French naval base (established by Louis XIV). It leads to Hyères, a resort town that was fashionable as long ago as the eighteenth century; there are a number of important *domaines* with *caves* here where you can sample the wines, and just off the coast are the beautiful islands of Porquerolles, Levant and Port-Cros. The wine road leaves the coast at this point and crosses the wide, fertile valley of the river Réal Martin to Pierrefeu-du-Var. The landscape is quite flat and the vineyards are extensive here, and you can see the mountains in the distance. It is particularly handsome in springtime when the new shoots of the vines and the trees in blossom contrast vividly with the rich, red-brown soil. From Pierrefeu the road leads to Cuers, which has a number of interesting old buildings, including a sixteenth-century church, as well as a Cave Co-opérative and some private *caves*. The wine road continues along the main road, the N 97, through the wine villages of Puget-Ville with its thirteenth-century Saracen tower, Carnoules and Pignans, from which you can make a small detour to the viewpoint of Nôtre Dame des Anges. The next village is Gonfaron, where, legend has it, a donkey once flew, and then you come to le Luc, a colourful town on the busy N 7. It is an important wine centre, and there are nine *caves* that you can visit. Also of interest are the twelfth-century clocktower and a Romanesque chapel.

The wine route now doubles back along the N 7 to the wine village of Flassans-sur-Issole, built around the ruins of an old village and dominated by a privately owned feudal castle. Here the wine road heads north again on the D 13 to Cabasse and Carcès, an old olive oil-milling town. From here a detour can be made to

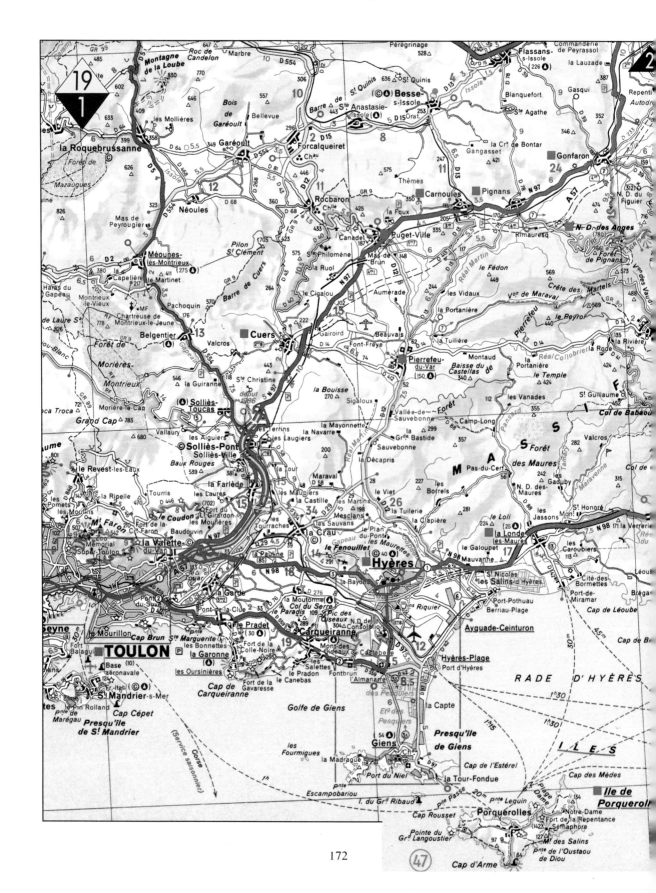

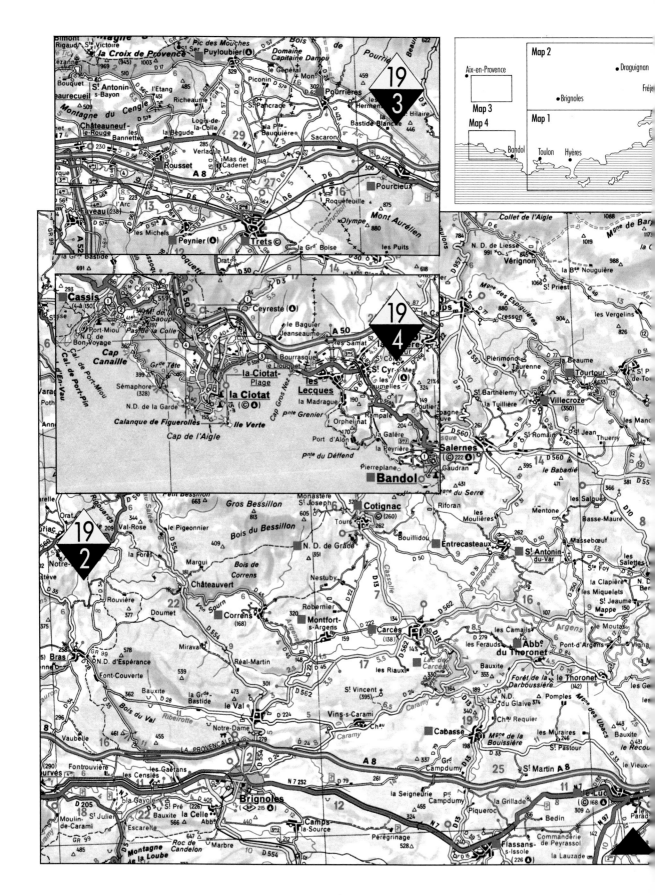

the famous twelfth-century Abbaye de Thoronet, a superb example of Romanesque architecture, built by the Cistercians and restored by order of Prosper Mérimée, the nineteenth-century novelist who was also Inspector-General of Historic Monuments. Just before Carcès the road circumnavigates the Lac de Carcès, an artificial lake that supplies water to many of the coastal resorts. This is excellent countryside for picnicking. Nearby are the jagged red cliffs and quarries of the bauxite mines, which lend a rather surrealist air to the landscape.

The route continues west to Montfort-sur-Argens, almost as noteworthy for being the home of Louis-Joseph Lambart, the man who invented reinforced

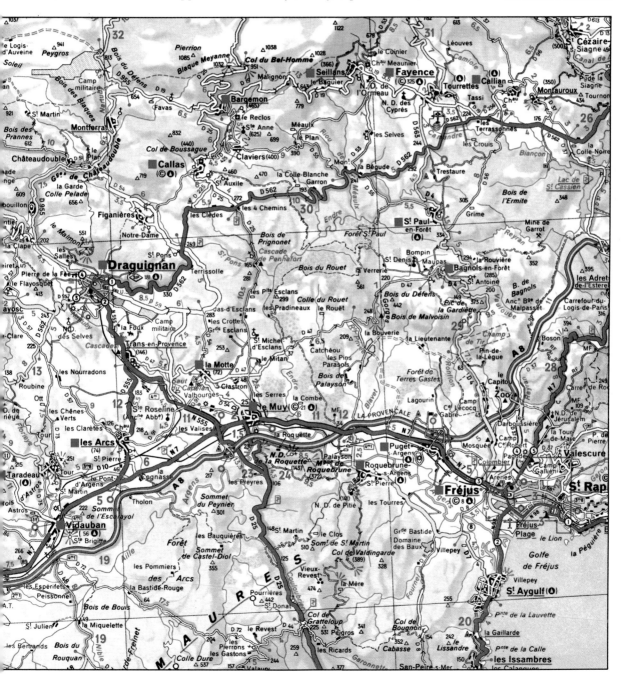

concrete, as for its Templar castle and twelfth-century church. You can take a detour here to the tiny village of Correns, set in a peaceful vine-clad valley beside the little Argens river. The main route continues north to Cotignac, set at the foot of a high, sheer cliff under a ruined watchtower. Sit in an outdoor café shaded by enormous plane trees on Cotignac's broad main street and really absorb the Provençal atmosphere. There are caves cut into the cliffs, an eleventh-century priory church and the remains of an oil mill, and the Chapel of Nôtre-Dame de Grâce, a famous sanctuary since the time of Louis XIII, set on a hill opposite the village; it can be reached by a small road near the bridge.

From Cotignac the Route des Vins follows the D 50. The narrow country roads are lined with dry-stone walls, which are also used to terrace the vineyards and olive groves. When the wild flowers and herbs are in full bloom and the air is heady with their fragrance, everything seems absolutely perfect. You get to the hilltown of Entrecasteaux next. It is dominated by an eleventh-century château, which is privately owned but allows visitors, and two old churches and a chapel that are built above it. As you drive towards St Antonin du Var, look back at the village – it is very dramatic against the steep wooded hillsides.

The route continues towards Draguignan via the village of Lorgues, where there are many interesting old buildings including a Saracen gate, ancient ramparts and towers and an old oil mill now used as an art gallery. You can make several detours from here. Go to Flayosc to see a typical village of the region; its village square is shaded by plane trees and there is an ancient fountain, which is quintessentially Provençal. Visit Villecroze (to the north-west along the D 10), a high mountain village, for its wine and for the spectacular views over the surrounding landscape. And walk up the narrow winding streets of nearby Tourtour, which is at an altitude of 1630 metres, and enjoy the views; it also has a private château and a few old towers.

The shady streets and squares of old Draguignan

contain some fine buildings, including an Ursuline convent that houses the town's museum and library, a Roman gate and a sixteenth-century clock-tower. From here a detour can be made through the enchanting medieval hill villages of Callas, Bargemon, Seillans, Fayence and Callian; each twist and turn of the road which connects them reveals a new and breathtaking vista. Callian and Seillans are very small and delightful; the latter has a Saracen gate and an eleventh-century feudal castle perched high up above its tiny houses. Continue south on the D 4 through the villages of St Paul-en-Forêt and Bagnols-en-Forêt, which, as their names suggest, are set deep in the cork forest that borders the mountains of the Esterel. There are many good picnic spots on the first part of the drive

Below: The Château de Entrecasteaux, a small village north of Carcès. Below left: A dramatic, sun-baked ravine, situated to the west of Bagnols-en-Fôret. Bottom: The hilltop village of Seillans has an eleventh-century feudal castle

through forested hillsides then, as it winds round the sides of the mountains, the road becomes more austere and mountainous with panoramic views of the valleys below. At Bagnols-en-Forêt you rejoin the main wine route to Trans-en-Provence and la Motte along the D 47. This too is a ruggedly beautiful road through forests and mountains. At one point, where the road runs alongside a rugged, red gorge, just a short distance from the road, you can see a dramatic outcrop of rock and impressive views down into the gorge.

From Bagnols-en-Forêt the road winds down towards the coast and the town of Fréjus, the oldest Roman city in Gaul. Julius Caesar founded it, Augustus built up its harbour and Agricola was born here. There are many important Roman remains, including an amphitheatre where bullfights are held in summer, part of an aqueduct and ramparts. Fréjus was destroyed in the tenth century, but got a new lease of life 500 years later when its fine cathedral was built.

The wine road continues west along the N 7 through the wine villages of Puget-sur-Argens and le Muy to les Arcs, an important wine centre. Take a short detour to Roquebrune-sur-Argens where the biggest mulberry tree in the South of France grows. The village is situated beneath a red rock which rises from the flat coastal plain, and you can drive around it through the surrounding vineyards, or walk through its wooded slopes to a small chapel nestling in a cleft half-way up. From les Arcs the route continues through the small wine village of Taradeau to Vidauban, with its seventeenth-century château. The Routes des Vins continues on the D 48 through the Massif des Maures; there are dramatic views at every turn as the road winds steeply through forested hillsides. The ancient hilltop villages of la Garde-Freinet and Grimaud are a delight, particularly Grimaud, a medieval walled town with a Renaissance chapel and a ruined eleventh-century castle. A short detour to the west from la Garde-Freinet takes you to the Roches Blanches, where there are superb views over the village and surrounding countryside. A second detour can be made, this time to the east, over the Col de Vignon to the village of Plan-de-la-Tour.

The sophisticated and crowded St Tropez is the next town on the wine route. Early this century, long before Brigitte Bardot, it was a favourite summer resort of the Neo-Impressionist painters, including Bonnard and Matisse. You should visit the Coopérative du Golfe de St Tropez, and the important *domaine* of Château de Minuty, which is nearby. Every May, St Tropez honours its patron saint in a street procession that is quite unique to this part of France – a wonderful spectacle. From here a small scenic road winds up into the mountains above the town through Gassin, where the views over the gulf are awe-inspiring. The road continues to the hilltown of Ramatuelle, a lovely medieval village where a large, ancient elm tree grows in the square. Follow the route over the Col de Collebasse to la Croix-Valmer, with spectacular views down to the sea.

There are two options now: you can continue along the coast through the resorts of Cavalaire-sur-Mer and Rayol to le Lavandou and Bormes-les-Mimosas, or you can return inland and follow the N 98 to Cogolin and la Môle. On the coastal route, the road follows the beautiful coastline. The walled town of Bormes-les-Mimosas is particularly pretty, built on the side of a steeply sloping hillside a few kilometres from the sea. This stretch of road will be very crowded and congested in the summer months, though, and perhaps should be avoided then.

The alternative route runs along the valley of the river Môle, whose banks are lined with tall reeds.

These are cut and dried and made into clarinet reeds and pipes in Cogolin, which is also known for its carpets and silk yarn. From la Môle you can take a winding scenic road over the Col du Canadel to the sea; at the top there is a sudden, almost startling view of the sea far down below. The Route des Vins

A vineyard near Plan-de-la-Tour (left) photographed in early spring when the first shoots are appearing. The vineyards (above) on the slopes of the dramatic rock formation, the Montagne de Roquebrune, are at a later stage in their cycle

completes its circuit after passing through la Londe-les-Maures, on the N 98.

In addition to the main wine circuit there is a small tour further west towards Aix-en-Provence, through the small wine villages of Puyloubier, Pourrières, Pourcieux, Trets, Peynier and Rousset, in the foothills of the Montagne Sainte Victoire. The small wine-growing communities in the coastal resorts of Bandol and Cassis, between Toulon and Marseille, and in the region of Bellet in the Var valley near Nice, are also worth visiting both for their interesting wines and for their delightful locations.

SOUTHERN FRANCE
Wine-buying Guide

THE RHONE

Viticulturally the Rhône can be split into three regions; the Northern Rhône, the Middle Rhône, and the Southern Rhône. Recently, Rhône wines have been gaining the recognition they undoubtedly deserve, with worldwide interest following the excellent 1983 vintage. This means that the prices for the best wines are now beginning to rise to realistic levels, but for the moment they are still outstanding value.

THE NORTHERN RHONE

Appellation Contrôlées

Côte Rôtie Here steep slopes grow the Syrah grape that makes a rich yet elegant, perfumed red wine. The region is divided by two distinct soil types into the Côte Brune and the Côte Blonde. Normally the two wines are blended and sold as Côte Rotie, but they also exist individually. Look out too for Guigal's La Mouline and La Landonne. Both are stunning – in quality and also in price.

Under this appellation the red Syrah's richness is granted extra elegance and perfume by the admixture of up to 15 per cent of the aromatic Viognier grape.

Maison Delas, now owned by large vineyard holders and shippers Champagne Deutz and Gelderman, have opened a cellar for visitors next to their establishment in Tournon, where all the northern Rhône wines can be purchased.

Hermitage A tiny amount of white wine is produced from the Marsanne and Rousanne grapes, but the red wine from Syrah is king here. The granite mountain gives a richness and sturdiness to the wine that is virtually unequalled in the rest of France. The best comes from the tiny *climat La Chapelle*, perched on top of the mountain and owned by Paul Jaboulet Aîné.

Crozes-Hermitage Both red and white wines are made on more fertile ground around the bottom of the Hermitage mountain. Less rich and complex than Hermitage, but nevertheless good value.

Cornas This appellation is for red wine only, from the Syrah, making the deepest and richest coloured red wine in France. Needs at least five years' ageing to smooth out the tannin and develop its blackcurrant fruit. The production is small but extremely good value.

St Joseph A more general appellation covering much of the west bank of the northern Rhône. The red wines are more common than the white, but the white is more elegant than the rustic red.

Condrieu A most elegant, expensive and extremely good quality white wine from the low-yielding, aromatic Viognier grape. Very little of the permitted area is cultivated with vines because of the steepness of the slopes, so this wine is fairly rare. It has a haunting bouquet of apricots and wild flowers and ought not to be missed.

With Condrieu is the smallest appellation in France, *Château Grillet*. Here the Viognier is cask-aged, giving greater complexity but losing the smell of wild flowers. However, as the production is only 3–4,000 bottles per year, it is extremely expensive and unlikely to be seen outside the district.

St Péray A dry white only, from near Valence. Most is drunk locally, but its full-bodied, lively style makes it worth finding. A *mousseux* is also made here.

THE MIDDLE RHONE

Appellations Contrôlées

Clairette-de-Die Dry to sweet sparkling wine is produced here. The dry wine (brut) is made by the *méthode champenoise*, principally from the Clairette grape. The sweeter style (Tradition) is made by the *méthode dioise* or *méthode rurale* with at least 50 per cent Muscat grapes. The sweeter Tradition preserves the grapiness of the Muscat.

A still white wine is also made from the Clairette alone.

Châtillon-en-Diois Red and rosé wines made from a mixture of Burgundian and Rhône red grapes, as well as white wines from the

Chardonnay and Aligoté grapes of Burgundy. All are fairly ordinary.

Coteaux du Tricastin An up-and-coming appellation, growing in both size and reputation. The classic Rhône varieties of grape are planted, making a full, rich, fruity red wine, a small amount of rosé and a still smaller amount of white.

VDQS

Côtes du Vivarais Red, dry white and rosé wine of which the reds are the best and the whites the rarest.

Haut-Comtat Red and rosé only, not seen much nowadays.

THE SOUTHERN RHONE

Appellations Contrôlées

Châteauneuf-du-Pape This appellation is famous for its red wine, but white accounts for about 2 per cent of its production. There are 13 legal grape varieties (four of which are white) that can be used to make the red wine, but Grenache, Syrah and Mourvèdre are the most important.

There are two different schools of thought on the making of red wine. The traditionalists in specialized *domaines* made a big, rich, meaty, tannic wine that requires laying down for a main minimum of five years and usually more. The modern trend is to use more Grenache in the *encépagement* to make a less coloured, less tannic, lighter wine that is ready to drink in about three to four years.

The wines produced by the Reflets growers' club are worth looking at, and there are both new and old styles. (The Reflets are a group of about 20 *domaines* who apply more stringent rules to the making of their wine and have the papal cross-keys symbol on their bottles.)

Gigondas Red and rosé wines are produced here, and the rich yet fruity reds are the most interesting. The better wines resemble nearby Châteauneuf-du-Pape.

Vacqueyras Good value, rich red wines. Some can take lengthy ageing

along with the better wines of Châteauneuf-du-Pape and Gigondas.

Lirac Red, dry white and rosé wines are all made in this appellation, but the red and the rosé are superior. These wines are well worth finding.

Tavel Dry rosé only. Made principally from the Grenache grape with some Cinsault, the styles vary from oak-aged orangey rosés to the younger, fresher, pink ones.

Individual Rhône village appellations

Beaumes de Venise Good red wines, and a more famous *vin doux naturel* made from the Muscat grape.

Top: The market town of Pont-St Esprit. Below: The University of Wine in the village of Suze-la-Russe

Cairanne Rich, deeply coloured, spicy red wines with a small amount of rosé and white.

Chusclan Used to be famous for its rosé but now produces mainly red wine.

Laudun Excellent white wines as well as rosé and red.

Rasteau Some rosé and white wine but the good full-bodied red is more common. However, this appellation is perhaps better known for the red *vin*

doux naturel made from the Grenache grape.

Roaix Mostly red wines.

Rochegude Plummy, deep-coloured red wines only.

Rousset A tiny production, quite rare.

Sablet Mostly red wines.

Saint-Gervais Elegant red wines, but none are great.

Séguret Robust red wines.

Saint-Maurice-sur-Eygues Mostly red wines.

Saint-Pantaléon-les-Vignes Fruity red wines to drink young.

Valréas Dark, velvety red wines.

Vinsobres Full-bodied red wines.

Visan Full, rich, alcoholic red wines and some white.

General appellations

Côtes du Ventoux Making red, dry white and rosé wines of increasingly good quality.

Côtes du Rhône-Villages Red, dry white and rosé wines from 17 specific communes, making better wine than straight Côtes du Rhône. A good value appellation.

Côtes du Rhône This appellation applies to the whole of the Rhône valley, but not much wine is made in the north where the steepness of the slopes precludes inexpensive, commercial production. The quality can vary immensely within this appellation but most is good quaffing wine.

VDQS

Côtes du Lubéron Red, dry white and rosé wines made east of Avignon in very similar styles to Côtes du Rhône.

Vin de Pays

Vin de Pays de l'Ardèche One of the better Vin de Pays and improving all the time. Red, dry white and rosé wine. (Also Vin de Pays des Coteaux de l'Ardèche.)

Vin de Pays de la Drome, Vin de Pays de Vaucluse, Collines Rhêdaniennes, Comté de Grignan, Coteaux de Baronnies All make red, dry white and rosé wine.

Principauté d'Orange Red and rosé only.

Addresses

Domaine de Mont Redon
84230 Châteauneuf-du-Pape

Château Redortier
84190 Beaumes de Venise

Maison Delas
Saint-Jean-de-Muzois
07300 Tournon-sur-Rhône

Domaine André Mejan
Place du President le Roy
30126 Tavel

LANGUEDOC

This is a region where the wines range from the ordinary to good honest wines. None, however, are great, although research into modern production techniques is elevating the general quality.

Appellations Contrôlées

See also *Vins Doux Naturels*

Minervois Well-known red wines and some rosé produced here. This was deservedly promoted from a VDQS to an AC in 1985. The reds are deep, rich and quite robust. Although the majority of the production is done by Caves Co-opératives, there are some growers who make a better, more complex wine using oak *foudres*. These wines can take four or five years' bottle ageing.

Faugères A tiny production of dry white wine from the Clairette grape, but the robust, rich red from Carignan, Cinsault and Grenache varieties is best known.

Clairette de Languedoc Dry and semi-sweet white wine only, much higher in alcohol than the Clairette-de-Die wines.

St Chinian The largest appellation in Languedoc, producing only fairly inexpensive red wine.

Clairette de Bellegarde A dry white wine from the Clairette grape to drink young.

An ancient mobile wine press in Caromb

VDQS

Costières du Gard Quite a big production, mostly from co-operatives, of red, dry white and rosé wines.

Cabrières Rosé only and the best in Languedoc.

Coteaux de la Méjanelle, Coteaux de St-Christol, Saint-Drézery, St Georges d'Orques Red wines only.

Coteaux de Vérargues, Coteaux du Languedoc, Montpeyroux, Saint-Saturnin Red and rosé wines only.

La Clape, Pic-Saint-Loup, Quatourze Red, dry white and rosé wines.

Picpoul de Pinet A fragrant, fruity, dry white wine from coastal vineyards that grow Picpoul, Clairette and Terret Blanc.

Vin de Pays

Vin de Pays du Gard Red, dry white and rosé wines made from Rhône grape varieties but now also with the Bordeaux varieties of Cabernet Sauvignon and Merlot. These wines are generally well made and good value at the more modest end of the scale.

Coteaux Cévenols, Coteaux de Cèze, Coteaux du Pont-du-Gard, Coteaux du Vidourle, Coteaux Flaviens, Côtes du Salavès, Mont Bouquet, Serre de Coiran, Uzège, Vaunage, Vistrenque All produce red, dry white and rosé in the *département* of Gard.

Vin de Pays des Sables du Golfe du Lyon A large area of vineyard, planted on sandbanks and dunes recovered from the sea in the Golfe du Lion, and stretching across the *départements* of Gard, Hérault and Bouches-du-Rhône. Here a government-backed SICA (similar to a co-operative), known by its brand-name Listel, is leading experimentation into new methods of planting and wine production. Listel make both single-grape-variety wines and blends in red, dry white and *gris* rosé styles, as well as sparkling wine made by the Charmat method.

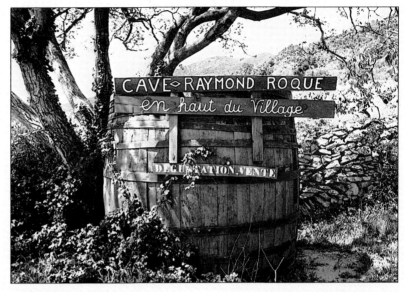

Vin de Pays de l'Hérault A massive production of red, dry white and rosé wines mostly from Caves Co-opératives. Within this Vin de Pays are many smaller zonal Vin de Pays. The following produce only red and rosé wines: *Ardaillon, Bénovie, Cassan, Cessenon, Coteaux de Murviel, Coteaux de Peyriac, Coteaux du Salagou, Côtes de Brian,* and *Haute Vallée de l'Orb.*

These produce red, white and rosé wines: *Bérange, Bessans, Caux, Collines de la Moure, Coteaux d'Enserune, Coteaux de Fontcaude, Coteaux de Laurens, Coteaux de Libron, Coteaux de Céresscu, Côtes de Thau, Côtes de Thongue, Gorges de l'Hérault, Littoral Orb-Hérault, Mont Baudile, Monts de la Grage, Pézanas, Val de Montferrand* and *Vicomté d'Aumelas.*

Vins Doux Naturels

Vin Doux Naturel is not wine but fortified grape juice. The grape juice must have a natural sugar content which, if fermented, would result in an alcohol concentration of $14°$. The fermentation is initiated and allowed to proceed to a level of about $7°$ of alcohol. It is then arrested by the addition of 6–10 per cent by volume of grape alcohol at $90°$. This alcohol addition (called *mutage*) stops fermentation by killing the yeasts. The resulting product is a sweet beverage of about $21°$ of alcohol.

The *Vins Doux Naturels* of Languedoc are richer, more alcoholic and less aromatic than the famous Muscat-de-Beaumes-de-Venise *Vin Doux Naturel* of the Rhône valley.

Muscat de Lunel and Muscat de Mireval White only, from the Muscat grape.

Muscat de Frontignan The best of the Languedoc white *Vin Doux Naturel.*

Muscat de Saint-Jean-de-Minervois

Addresses

Listel:
Compagnie des Salins du Midi
30220 Aigues-Mortes

Muscat:
Cave Co-opérative du Muscat
34110 Frontignan

Cave Co-opérative du Muscat
34400 Vérargues (Lunel)

Cave Co-opérative du Muscat
34840 Mireval

Cave Co-opérative de St Jean-du-Minervois
34360 St Jean-du-Minervois

Coteaux du Languedoc:
SICA les Vignerons des Quatres Vents
34360 St Chinian

Chateaux
Chateau de Blomac
Blomac 11700

Carcassonne, *Coteaux de Termenès,
Côtes de Lastours, Côtes de Pérignan,
Côtes de Prouille, Haute Vallée de
l'Aude, Hautrive en Pays de l'Aude,
Val de Cesse, Val de Dagne* and *Val
d'Orbieu.*

Vin de Pays des Pyrénées-Orientales
Red, dry white and rosé wines made
throughout the *département* mostly by
Caves Co-opératives. There are also
smaller zonal Vins de Pays within
this designation, all of which produce
red, dry white and rosé wines: *Vin de
Pays d'Oc, Catalan, Coteaux des
Fenouilledes, Côtes Catalanes, Val
d'Agly.*

Vins Doux Naturels

Banyuls Red and tawny *Vins Doux
Naturels* made primarily from
Grenache grapes. These may be aged
to achieve the designations *vieux* or
rancio. Banyuls Grand Cru also
exists.

Côtes d'Agly Red, white and rosé.

Maury Mostly red.

Muscat de Rivesaltes White only,
from Muscat grapes.

Rivesaltes Red, white and rosé.

Addresses

Corbières:
Château Vaugelas
Pierre Bouffet
Fabrezau
11200 Lézignan-Corbières

Fitou:
Cave Co-opérative
11350 Tuchan

Blanquette de Limoux:
Cave Co-opérative
11300 Limoux

Côtes du Roussillon:
Jaubert et Noury
St Jean-Lasseille 66300

Vignerons Catalans
Route de Thuir RN2
Perpignan 66011

Colliure and Banyuls:
Groupement Interproducteur du Cru
Banyuls
66660 Port-Vendres

ROUSSILLON

The surrounding districts of Limoux,
Corbières and Fitou are also included
in this section.

Appellations Contrôlées

Blanquette de Limoux This
appellation makes still, dry, white
wine but the *mousseux* made by the
méthode champenoise is both more
common and better known. The
grapes are Mauzac and Clairette but
some Chardonnay is now found.
Most of the production comes from
the Cave Co-opérative.

Corbières and Corbières-Supérieur
This wine was deservedly promoted
from VDQS to AC in 1985. A tiny
proportion of the production is white
and rosé, but the majority is red. The
Corbières-Supérieur designation is
for red and white wines with an extra
degree of alcohol.
    At Château Vaugelas, in Lézignan-
Corbières, a high quality red wine,
matured in oak casks, is made.

Fitou This appellation makes only
red wine and it is some of the best of
the region. The wines are dark,
sturdy and pungent in bouquet.

Colliure Red wine only, from steeply
terraced vineyards surrounding the
fishing port. The wine is deeply
coloured, velvety and quite rich, and
the heavier *cuvées* can take five to ten
years' ageing. Banyuls *Vin Doux
Naturel* is also grown in the same
area.

Côtes du Roussillon Red, dry white
and rosé wines that come mainly
from Caves Co-opératives.

Côtes du Roussillon-Villages Red
wines only, from the better sites in
the valley of the river Agly. Better
quality than straight Roussillon and
so good value.

VDQS

Cabardès Red and rosé wines only,
mostly from Rhône grape varieties.
Some of the Bordeaux varieties are
now also grown here.

Côtes de la Malepère Red and rosé
wines from around Carcassonne.

Vin de Pays

Vin de Pays de l'Aude Massive
production of red, dry white and rosé
wine mostly by co-operatives. Within
this designation are several smaller
zonal Vins de Pays. The following
produce only red and rosé wines:
*Coteaux Cathares, Coteaux de la
Cabrerisse, Coteaux du Lézignanais,
Coteaux de Miramont, Coteaux de
Narbonne, Coteaux du Littoral
Audois, Cucugnan, Hauts Badens* and
Vallée de Paradis.
    These produce red, dry white and
rosé wines: *Coteaux de la Cité de*

CAHORS

This appellation is perhaps the best of the many small appellations scattered throughout south-western France. Many of these regions have been producing wines for hundreds of years but have only recently achieved recognition and AC status. Cahors become an AC in 1971.

Cahors Red wine only, from an *encépagement* that must have a minimum of 70 per cent Malbec grapes (also known as Cot Noir or Auxerrois), a maximum of 20 per cent Merlot and Tannat with 10 per cent of Jurançon Noir. Formerly these were extremely robust, tannic, 'black' wines but now the style is lighter and more subtle to accommodate modern tastes.

Wines designated *vieux* must be aged for more than three years in wood.

Vin de Pays

Coteaux de Quercy Red and rosé wines only, from the Lot valley.

Addresses

Cahors:
Georges Vigouroux
Château de Haute Serre
Cieurac
46003 Cahors

Domaine de Cèdre
Vire-sur-Lot
46700 Puy-l'Evêque

Co-opérative à Parnac
46140 Luzech

PROVENCE

This is a region famous for its rosé wine. It is exquisitely refreshing in the heat of the Mediterranean sun, but is somewhat lost in other climates.

Appellations Contrôlées

Palette A tiny area with one major producer, Château Simone. Red, dry white and rosé wines are made, all of which are expensive and need some ageing.

Bandol Coastal appellation producing red, dry white and rosé wine. The best is the red wine which can be very well made and quite expensive. The best estates, Domaine Tempier and Château Vannières, produce wines that need laying down for at least five years.

Cassis Red, dry white and rosé wines are produced here immediately to the east of Marseille. The white is an excellent accompaniment to the local fish and *bouillabaisse* (fish soup).

Bellet A very small appellation near Nice producing red and white wine. The best estate is Château de Crémat, making a rich, tannic, oak-aged red wine and a white with a scent of wild flowers.

Côtes de Provence A large area producing red, dry white and rosé wines. The rosés are the best known but now the red wines may be made with up to 60 per cent Cabernet Sauvignon, which radically alters the Provence style but produces finer wines. This became AC in 1977 and the quality varies from good ordinary to quite good.

VDQS

Coteaux d'Aix-en-Provence and Coteaux des Baux-en-Provence Both are satellite vineyards of Côtes de Provence, making similar red, dry white and rosé wines. Both are being promoted to AC in 1986 and are excellent value.

Coteaux de Pierrevert A smaller production of red, dry white and rosé wines, again similar to Côtes de Provence.

Vin de Pays

Vin de Pays des Alpes-de-Haute-Provence, Vin de Pays des Alpes-Maritimes, Vin de Pays des Bouches-du-Rhône, Vin de Pays du Var, Argens, Coteaux Varois, Maures Red, white and rosé wine.

Mont Caume Red and rosé only.

Petite Crau Red, dry white and rosé.

Addresses

Palette:
M. Rougier
Château Simone
Meyreuil
Bouches-du-Rhône

Bandol:
Domaine Tempier
Château de Vannières
La Cadière d'Azur
Var

Bellet:
Jean Bagnis
Château de Crémat
06200 Bellet-de-Nice

Coteaux d'Aix en Provence:
Château Vignelaure
Rians

Côtes de Provence:
Les Maitres Vignerons de la Presqu'Ile de St Tropez.

SOUTH–WEST
FRANCE

The seven areas of the South West include the wines of St Emilion, St Julien and Château Margaux; the countryside ranges from the grandeur of the Pyrenees to the simplicity of St Emilion (left), yet the region remains remarkably free of tourists. The discerning visitor can savour the great red wines of the Médoc and North Bordelais; the classic sweet white wines of South Bordelais and Bergerac; the unassuming wines of Madiran/Tursan and finish with the great brandies of Cognac and Armagnac. To explore South-West France is to discover a subtle and imaginative cuisine, unspoilt surroundings and some legendary wines.

Wine Tour Nº 20
THE NORTHERN BORDELAIS

Château de la Rivière, north of the village of Fronsac

Indisputedly, the wine capital of the world is Bordeaux, an ancient city and river port once the headquarters for Roman troops in Gaul. It lies on the banks of the Gironde and for over 2,000 years has been involved in the wine trade.

To the north of the city are the extensive and highly prized vineyards which start along the northern bank of the Gironde facing the Médoc and reach eastwards beyond Libourne until they give way to the vineyards of Bergerac. This area includes the Côtes de Blaye, Côtes de Bourg, Fronsac, Graves de Vayres, Pomerol, St Emilion and Côtes de Castillon and produces some of the greatest wines of France. The town of Libourne, built on the banks of the Dordogne, more or less in the centre of this region, is second only to Bordeaux in importance as a wine centre. It, too, was an ancient river port, from which the area's wines were exported, and the town has retained its reputation as a wine capital.

The wines
All the truly great wines of this region are red. However both white and some rosé wines are made under the general Bordeaux appellation as well as *Côtes de Blaye* (white) and *Graves de Vayres* (red and white), which is just across the River Dordogne opposite Libourne. The main grape types used for the red wines are Cabernet Sauvignon, Cabernet Franc and Merlot, while the Sauvignon Blanc is used predominantly for white wines. Another wine of this region which has its own appellation is *Clairet*, a light red wine which is deeper in colour and more full-bodied than a rosé.

Undoubtedly the finest wines of this region are to be found in the small area immediately around Libourne, St Emilion and the surrounding villages of Puisseguin, Montagne, Lussac, St Georges and Parsac, all of which are hyphenated with the name St-Emilion, as well as Fronsac, Canon Fronsac, Pomerol and Lalande-de-Pomerol.

The cuisine
One of the most typical dishes of this region is *lamproie à la bordelaise*, which is an eel-like, freshwater fish (lamprey) casseroled in a rich, red wine sauce. There is a rich onion soup called *tourin*, which is thickened with egg yolks and cream and served over garlicky bread; often it is enriched with red wine. Among the many types of game found here is *marcassin* (young wild boar); this is delicious when cooked slowly in red wine. The oysters for which the region is famed are often stewed gently in white wine with small sausages called

crépinettes. If you have a sweet tooth you must try the *macarons de St-Emilion*, a delicious confection made from ground almonds, egg whites and sweet white wine, which you can buy by the box and make ideal gifts for friends when you get home.

The Route des Vins *Michelin maps 71 and 75*
The route given here is not a signposted Route des Vins and not a circuit as such, but it takes you through the most important villages and vineyards and can easily be extended to the regions of Bergerac, Graves or Entre-Deux-Mers. If you are travelling from the north along the Autoroute A 10 (*l'Aquitaine*), the best place to start the tour is at Blaye (off the motorway at exit 28 along the D 254 and then the N 137). The town is situated beside the broad estuary of the Gironde. It is the centre of the Côtes de Blaye, a region not known for any great wines but one that produces a large volume of honest red wine as well as some white and rosé. Blaye is a charming fortified town surrounded by moats and has an imposing citadel, a fortification built by the famous seventeenth-century military engineer,

Sébastien de Vauban; within its walls is a large open park from where you get sweeping views over the river to the island fort, l'Île Pâte (also built by Vauban), and towards the distant south bank and the vineyards of the Médoc. You can stay at the Hôtel de la Citadelle, which is situated within the ramparts, and there is a Pavillon du Vin in the centre of the town where wines can be sampled and bought.

From Blaye follow the route along the D 669 through Plassac to the village of Thau, where a narrow road, the D 669E, runs close beside the river bank. Here the vineyards sweep right down to the water's edge. Continue on this road towards Bourg. Just outside the town is the Château de Tayac, once the home of the Black Prince; it stands among the vineyards overlooking the river. Bourg, which has its own appellation, is built on the banks of the Dordogne. Its Château de la Citadelle, first built in the thirteenth century and rebuilt in the eighteenth century was once the summer residence of the archbishops of Bordeaux; you can visit the building and wander through its magnificent park planted with magnolias and pistachio

A floral display enhances this farmhouse near the town of Blaye

trees. The terrace beside the old church commands fine views over the river.

The small village of Lansac is a few kilometres north-east of Bourg; during the Middle Ages, the eleventh-century monastery of La Croix-Davide here was a stopping-place for pilgrims travelling to Santiago de Compostella. A little further to the east, near the village of Prignac, are the grottoes of Pair-non-Pair, while just outside the village there is the Cave Co-opérative of Tauriac, where you can taste the local wines.

The wine road continues through the important town of St André-de Cubzac and then along the D 670 towards Libourne. The vineyards of Fronsac are cultivated in the hillsides to the north of the village and you can follow a narrow signposted wine road through the vineyards and charming small villages such as St Aignan and Saillans. Just to the west of Fronsac is the magnificent Château de la Rivière, dating from the thirteenth century, set high on the hillside above vast areas of vines; you can visit the château and its *caves* carved into the rock, where the local wine can be tasted.

Libourne, a thirteenth-century *bastide* and once a busy river port, is a bustling town with old quarters and quaysides. This is the trading centre for the wines of Fronsac, St Emilion and Pomerol. The vineyards of Pomerol, which occupy a small area just to the east of Libourne, produce some of the great French wines; you can see the town's tall church spire rising high above the vineyards for miles around. I met an eighty-two-year-old *vigneron* who owned just 1 hectare in the middle of the village. The vines from which he made his wine had been planted by his father, he said, and were over 100 years old.

Among the many important wine châteaux in this area, that of Petrus is one of the most highly acclaimed, making a superb wine from the Merlot grape. You could easily pass by without noticing it since, like many of the other châteaux here, it is a relatively modest and low-key building, quite unlike the magnificent, ostentatious examples found in the Médoc. Just across the river from Libourne are the vineyards of Graves de Vayres, and there are two châteaux in this region which are worth visiting too: Château de Vayres, with a riverside park, and Château le Grand Puch, surrounded by ancient farm buildings and vineyards.

The Route des Vins now leads up to St Emilion, an

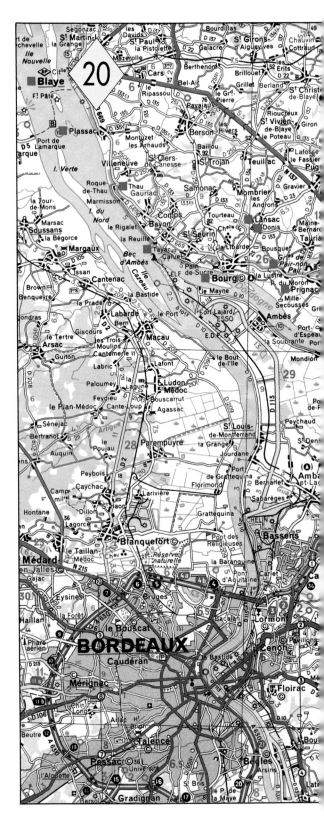

ancient wine village where the Roman poet Ausonius was supposed to have lived. Its narrow, winding cobbled streets are lined with lovely pale medieval houses built of the local limestone, with rust-coloured slate roofs. There are ruins of Dominican and Franciscan convents, and the fourteenth-century cloisters of the Collegiate church are superbly proportioned. St Emilion has a wine museum and many ancient tasting cellars, together with shops and hospitable restaurants. You could stay in the Hostellerie de Plaisance, a hotel sited on a terrace overlooking the village.

The fourteenth-century château of Monbadon (right) dominates the countryside around. The elderly woman (below) is in charge of a solitary cow

From here numerous quiet roads lead through the vineyards to small villages such as Montagne, which has a handsome Romanesque church, Lussac, Puisseguin, where there is a Maison du Vin, and Parsac, all of which have their own appellations. There are three châteaux you can visit on the way. The first, Château des Tours, is near Montagne; it dates from the fourteenth century, has a Renaissance façade and is set in an elegant park surrounded by vast areas of vineyards. The next is near the village of St Georges. Finally, a kilometre or so to the east of Puisseguin, high up on a wooded hillside, is the fourteenth-

century feudal château of Monbadon looking down over the vineyards that carpet the valley below. From here the route continues through the vineyards to the villages of St Gênes-de-Castillon and Belvès to Castillon-la-Bataille, an historic town which is the centre of the Côtes de Castillon and is the eastern limit of the vineyards of the northern Libournais. The vines continue, however, almost without a break to the start of the Bergerac Route des Vins. Alternatively, you can head south towards Sauveterre-de-Guyenne, exploring the villages and vineyards of Entre-Deux-Mers on the way.

Wine Tour Nº 21

THE MEDOC

Château Beychevelle, near St Julien, bleached by the sun

In the famous châteaux and vineyards of the Médoc you experience all the mysteries of the great wines – the aristocratic shades of colour, the myriad fragrances, all the subtleties and sensations of tastes, the fine distinctions between vintages. The Médoc is situated on a peninsula about 100 kilometres long, extending from just north of the city of Bordeaux to the Pointe de Grave, immediately opposite the seaside resort of Royan. It is bordered by the wide estuary of the Gironde to the north and by the vast pine forest of the Landes to the south.

The vineyards run for almost the entire length of the peninsula on a low-lying, gravelly hill range, in a band about 10 to 15 kilometres wide. It is divided into two areas: the Médoc to the north, as far down as St Seurin-de-Cadourne, where the lesser wines are produced, and the Haut-Médoc, stretching from St Seurin to Blanquefort. It is in the Haut-Médoc that the finest wines and the most famous place-names are to be found – St Estèphe, Pauillac, St Julien, Margaux and Cantenac.

The wines
The wines produced here are predominantly red. The finest are made mainly from the Cabernet Sauvignon and Merlot grape types, but the Cabernet Franc, Petit Verdot and Malbec are also grown. The classification method of the Médoc wines originated in 1855, when the Cru Classé was instigated by Napoleon III for the Exposition Universelle de Paris; the system is essentially the same today. The Classification ranges from Premier Grand Cru Classé through Cru Bourgeois, Cru Artisan and Cru Paysan to the basic Appellation Contrôlée *Médoc*. The way the vines are grown and the wine produced is strictly controlled, even to the method of pruning, and the best wines must come from vines that are at least ten years old. Many vines remain productive for up to eighty years, by which time they will have driven their roots down through the meagre soil to a depth of 3 metres or more. Although the quality of the wine improves as the vine ages, fewer grapes are produced, a factor which contributes to the dramatic difference in cost between a fine wine and a good one. As in all the best wine-producing regions, both the climate and the soil are such that the vine has to struggle to survive; ironically, it is usually these very conditions which create the best and most subtle wines.

The cuisine
The speciality of Bordeaux is dishes served *à la bordelaise* – in a sauce of red wine and meat stock with

tomatoes, shallots, herbs and seasoning. *Cèpes à la bordelaise*, large, brownish wild funghi with a firm meaty texture, are often served in this sauce. Lamb from the low-lying meadows around Pauillac on the Gironde Estuary is highly prized and saltwater fish and shellfish feature strongly on the local menus too. *Gravettes*, oysters found only in the Arcachon Basin a little to the south of the Médoc, have a unique, delicate flavour, reminiscent of hazelnuts.

The Route des Vins *Michelin map 71*

The Route des Vins in the Médoc is a single road which runs through the narrowish region, with smaller roads leading off to individual châteaux – indeed it is really much more a tour of the châteaux. A château in wine country can mean almost anything from a magnificent building to a modest farmhouse or even a bungalow; here they tend, very much, towards the magnificent.

There is an element of formality to observe when visiting some of these châteaux: many prefer visitors to make appointments. These can be made through the various *Maisons du Vin* in the region. There is one in Bordeaux, near the Grand Théâtre, and others in Pauillac, St Estèphe and Margaux; they provide a wealth of other useful travel information.

The signs indicating Circuit du Médoc refer to three general tourist circuits which will take you to the beaches, lagoons and forests as well as to the vineyards; if you have the time and the inclination this can be an ideal way of exploring the region. But the route suggested here concentrates on the villages, vineyards and châteaux associated with wine.

The tour starts at Bordeaux. Leave the ring road

The twelfth-century, Romanesque church in the small wine village of Moulis

At Château Batailly, a rose bush traditionally marks a row of Cabernet Sauvignon vines

around the city at Exit 7 and head for Blanquefort on a road which runs through the heart of the vineyards. Near here is Taillan, the first of the many impressive châteaux you encounter in the Médoc. It dates from the early eighteenth century, is set in lovely grounds and has an ancient double-vaulted *cave*; as well as making wine, the proprietor raises thoroughbred horses. The Château de la Dame Blanche where, according to legend, the ghost of a beautiful Moorish princess, Blanca, can be seen riding her winged horse around the castle, is here too: both the château and the town of Blanquefort are named after her.

From this point the route continues along the D 2 to Cantenac. The prestigious wine châteaux are concentrated around this very flat region where there is only a slight suggestion of rise and fall in the landscape: the highest hills you can see are on the other side of the wide, muddy Gironde River in the Côtes de Blaye. Woods and meadows dominate the landscape at this point. You can visit Château Prieuré-Lichine, the domain of the famous wine writer Alexis Lichine; he has a collection of fire-backs from all over the world decorating the courtyard.

Just beyond the Cantenac is Issan. There are two châteaux in this tiny village: the sixteenth-century moated Château d'Issan in a peaceful wooded setting along a small lane to the east of the village, and the immaculate Château Palmer, small and impressive, set beside the main road. The next village is Margaux: its château is one of the most famous in France – and deservedly so. Its Empire-style façade is framed by an avenue of plane trees. Although the château is privately owned, its *chais* can be visited: the wine made here is one of the Premiers Crus of the Médoc.

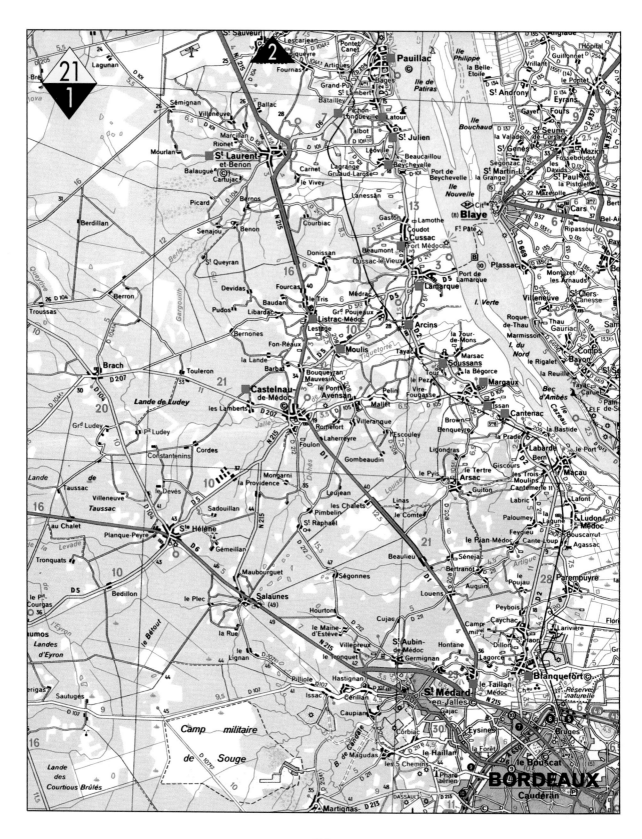

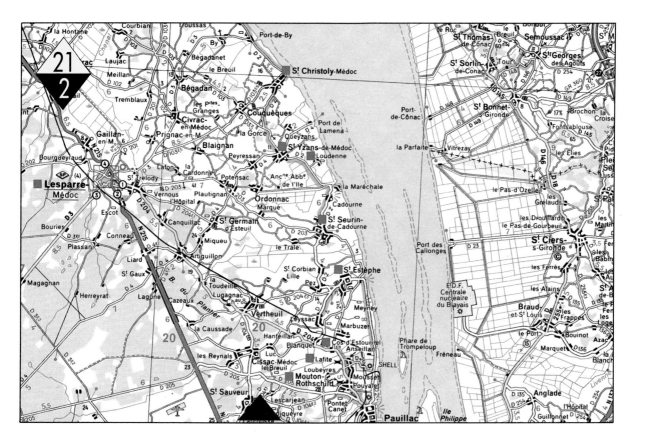

The route continues northwards through a succession of small villages: Soussans, then a detour to Moulis, which has a delightful twelfth-century Romanesque church, and Listrac, then back to Arcins, and Lamarque. Few of the villages are noteworthy – they often consist of a few rows of rather austere, single-storey terraced cottages – but they are invariably brightened up by a blaze of flowers. As an antidote to the low elevation of the houses and some châteaux, the church steeples are remarkably high. The church in Lamarque, for instance, has two enormous towers; there is an imposing château-fort here too, built in the eleventh century to resist the Viking invasion. A short distance further along the route a sign indicates a small road to the east leading to Fort Médoc, in a quiet place close to the river. It was built by Vauban during the reign of Louis XIV as part of a three-pronged defence line (with l'Isle Pâte and the Blaye citadel).

A few kilometres further on, you get to the vineyards of Château Beychevelle, looking down over the river. The name of this grand château is said to be derived from the command 'Baissez les voiles' (lower the sails) to salute the Duc d'Epernon, an admiral who lived here in the seventeeth century; the château's emblem is a ship with lowered sails. A small road beside the château goes down the river-bank, an ideal place to sit and watch the boats go by, or to watch the fishermen work their huge nets which they suspend from a gib at the end of a little pier. Many of the beautiful Médoc châteaux can be seen from the wine route. Often they are clearly signposted and you reach them along quiet lanes deep in the countryside; none is more than a few kilometres either side of the D 2.

You can't miss the village of St Julien. It has a large notice somewhat immodestly commanding passers-by to salute its celebrated vineyards; the point is reinforced by a monolithic wine bottle beside the road. Just to the north are two châteaux which you should not miss: Pichon-Longueville, an elaborate elegant building, and along a small road to the west, Château Latour, one of the Premier Crus of the Médoc.

Top: The huge, unmissable wine bottle introducing the village of St Julien. The romantic, ruined chateau of Fort Médoc (above) near the Gironde river, and (right) one of the fishing boats which ply its waters. Overleaf: Château Margaux, producing one of the world's most celebrated wines

Next, you come to Pauillac, situated beside the now very broad river. It is the largest centre on the Route des Vins and has the atmosphere of a seaside town (which it very nearly is), with its wide tree-lined promenade, a busy harbour, pavement cafés and relaxed atmosphere. In addition to Château Latour, two other Premier Crus lie within the commune of Pauillac: Château Lafite-Rothschild and Château Mouton-Rothschild. They are quite close together to the west of the D 2 north of Pauillac. You can hardly miss the ostentatious Château Cos-d'Estournel, which is right

beside the road and has ornate, oriental-style turrets and façade. This domain is within the most northerly of the great Haut-Médoc communes, St Estèphe.

The wine route continues beyond St Estèphe, at times running alongside the river, to the small villages of St Seurin-de-Cadourne and St Yzans-de-Médoc, where the Château Loudenne dominates the hills to the west of the road. The small village of St Christoly-Médoc marks the northern limit of the wine route. Although there are some vineyards further north these are mainly for the production of the more anonymous, basic Médoc wines. From here you can return towards Bordeaux by taking the D 103 E5 to Lesparre-Médoc and then the fast main road, the N 215, straight back through St Laurent-et-Benon and Castelnau-de-Médoc.

Wine Tour N° 22
THE SOUTHERN BORDELAIS

The elegant Château de Malle near Preignac

The name Graves means gravel – and gravel is what the vines of Graves grow on, over a bed of clay. In fact, this type of soil is characteristic of most of the region, but it is only the wines of Graves that take their appellation directly from the earth in which they thrive. In many ways Graves is an extension of the Médoc, but whereas the Médoc is influenced by the geological formations of the broad estuary of the river Gironde, the vineyards of Graves are cultivated on the terraces of the river Garonne.

The wines

The wines of Graves are both red and white. The whites are made from the Semillon, Sauvignon Blanc and Muscadelle grape types and the reds from the Merlot, Cabernet Franc and Cabernet Sauvignon, with a proportion of Malbec and Petit Verdot. As well as dry white wines, some of France's best sweet dessert wines – *Sauternes* and *Barsac* – are made in this region. The unique feature of these wines is that they are made from Semillon, Sauvignon and Muscadelle grapes which have developed *pourriture noble*, or 'noble rot'. This is a fungus called *Botrytis cinerea* which grows on the grapes, encouraged by the microclimate peculiar to the region – high daytime summer temperatures combined with damp, misty mornings

and evenings. Botrytis makes the grapes over-ripe; their sugar content increases, while the volume of juice decreases and becomes very concentrated. When the juice is fermented it produces a sweet wine which attains a level of alcohol of between 14 and 15 per cent. Because all the grapes do not reach the optimum degree of over-ripeness at the same time, the harvesting has to be carried out over a period of many weeks – when the grapes have reached this critical stage – thus the same vine may be gleaned many times, virtually a bunch at a time, and this makes the best of these wines very expensive.

The cuisine

The cuisine of Graves is, not surprisingly, similar to that of the Médoc and other regions of the Bordelais. A delicacy which you will find in most restaurants in the region is the large freshwater fish *alose* (shad). It has a firm white flesh with an almost buttery texture, and its flavour is quite distinctive. You will also see *esturgeon* (sturgeon), a fish which is caught in the Gironde Estuary and is often served *à la bordelaise*. *Daube bordelaise* is beef cooked with wine, onions, garlic and bacon rind, then sliced thinly; the reduced sauce is then poured over it and chilled to form a jelly. Another popular dish is *oignons à la bordelaise*, large onions

Musicians at the popular summer wine fair in the little
village of St Selve

stuffed with chopped chicken-livers and truffles then
baked in a white sauce. Steaks grilled over the glowing
embers of vine prunings are very much a speciality of
this region; the aroma of the wood imparts a wonderful
flavour to the meat.

The Route des Vins *Michelin maps 71, 75, 78 and 79*
The ring-road around Bordeaux makes a good starting
place for this Route des Vins (which is partly
signposted).

Bordeaux is a sprawling city which, over the years,
has encroached on some of the traditional vineyard
areas; indeed, many of them are now within its outer
suburbs, including one of the most prestigious claret-
makers, Château Haut-Brion. It is in Pessac, which
can be reached by leaving the ring-road at exit 14 and
driving for a short distance towards the city centre.
Samuel Pepys recorded the wonderful qualities of this
superb French wine 'Ho Bryan' in his diary. In 1855,
when the official classifications were established,
Haut-Brion was the only wine outside the Médoc to be
accorded a Premier Grand Cru Classé. Close by, and
originally part of the same estate, is the Château la
Mission-Haut-Brion, where the dates of the best
vintages of the last century are inscribed in gold on the
roof of the adjoining chapel. Also in the vicinity are
Château La Tour-Haut-Brion and Château Laville-
Haut-Brion. Drive a few kilometres to the south of
Bordeaux, on the D 111, to the village of Cadaujac, the
site of Château Bouscaut and Château Carbonnieux.
The latter, known for its white wine, was owned by the
Benedictine monks of the Abbey of Ste Croix-du-
Mont who, it is claimed, exported their wine to Turkey

as 'mineral water of Carbonnieux' in order to satisfy
that country's religious laws and its sultan, who was
very fond of their product.

A number of important vineyards and châteaux are
found close to the town of Léognan. A sign on the
D 111 indicates the Route des Graves, which guides
you around the region. Of particular note are Château
Haut-Bailly and Château La Tour-Martillac. In this
part of the Graves the vines are not cultivated
intensively and there are large areas of woods, pine
forests and meadows. A short drive from Léognan will
bring you to the village of Labrède where you can visit
Château de la Brède, the family home of the
eighteenth-century political satirist Montesquieu; it is
just outside the village in a wooded setting and is open
only at weekends and holidays. The small village of St
Selve, a few kilometres away, holds a lively, colourful
wine fair in the streets and the church square of the
first weekend of June.

Continue south on the N 113 for a short distance to
the Sauternais, where the sweet dessert wine is
produced. This wine has been famous since the
twelfth century, and Richard Lionheart is said to have
had a weakness for it. The Sauternais has its own wine
circuit which is clearly signposted from the N 113 just
south of Barsac or from the village of Preignac, a little
further south. These are two of the five communes of
the region, the others being Fargues, Sauternes and
Bommes. The route winds its way through a series of
quiet country lanes to each of these small villages in
turn. The countryside here is captivating with its

Dancers enjoying the wine, the sun and the music at St
Selve's fair

meadows and farmland, its vineyards, and the gently rolling hills with woods and pine forests. Preignac and Barsac are both busy villages situated beside the main road, and close to Preignac is the elegant Château de Malle, set in beautiful formal gardens, where visitors are welcome.

Sauternes is a small, sleepy village nestling in a hollow, surrounded by vine-clad hills. At the Maison du Vin in the square you can use the information service as well as taste and buy wines. The many châteaux in this region are clearly signposted along the way, with the rather extraordinary exception of the famous Château d'Yquem. This is because, I was told, 'There would be too many visitors'. You will be welcome though, if you do take the trouble to find it – not too difficult, since it occupies a prominent position on a hill-top near Sauternes. The lovely château is built on the site of a fortress and dates back to the twelfth century although it was heavily restored in both the sixteenth and eighteenth centuries. Thomas Jefferson visited it in 1787, and today it is the venue for the Bordeaux May Music Festival. The estate has over 160 hectares of vines, of which 120 are entitled to the appellation. Every year 2 or 3 hectares are uprooted and replanted and it is then a further six years before they are productive. The equipment used in the château's wine cellars is surprisingly modest – just three presses, a crusher and a wooden *émietteur*, enough to handle only about 4 hectares of normal vines. But because of the unique way in which Sauternes is made, the cellar needs only to deal with one day's selective harvesting at a time.

Although not on the Route des Vins circuit, the fortified Château de Roquetaillade, which dates back to the twelfth century, is worth a short detour; it is set on a hill in a park and looks just the way a medieval castle should, with battlements and towers.

The limit of the Graves region is just south of Langon (*Michelin Map 79*), a busy market town situated beside the Garonne. Here there is a Maison du Vin de Graves (there is also one at Podensac) and the well-known hotel-restaurant of Claude Darroze, making it an ideal base from which to explore the area. You can cross the river to the long-established wine town of St Macaire, also known for its sweet white dessert wines. Head back northwards on the D 10, which stays quite close to the river and passes through a succession of interesting and charming wine villages. A kilometre or so to the east, high up on the hill

This unassuming church at Verdelais is the last resting place for one of France's greatest artists, Toulouse-Lautrec

that borders the Garonne, are the delightful villages of Verdelais and Ste Croix du Mont – Henri de Toulouse-Lautrec is buried in the church at Verdelais, standing at the end of a lovely promenade shaded by plane trees. Ste Croix du Mont has the appellation Grand Vin Liquoreux de Bordeaux. Right on the edge of this village, on the hill beside the church, is a terrace with wonderful views over the Garonne Valley and the Sauternais – there is a Maison du Vin in the château nearby. This is particularly appealing countryside, threaded with tiny lanes on rounded hills.

A little further north, the small village of Loupiac also has its own appellation for dessert wines, as does its neighbour Cadillac and the village of Cérons, across the river. During the fishing season you often see signs advertizing *alose* for sale along this particular stretch of the river. Cadillac is a large fortified village with its fourteenth-century ramparts still intact. The somewhat severe Château des Ducs d'Eperon sits high

Left: The medieval, fortified Château de Roquetaillade, set in a delightful park. Above: Harvesting at Ste Croix-du-Mont near Verdelais

above the village, and houses the Maison du Vin. Every Saturday, the village centre is closed to traffic and a lively market is held in the streets and square.

From here, drive to Rions, a few kilometres to the north – it is surrounded by medieval ramparts with a fortified gate, and has an old church and narrow streets lined with crumbling stone houses. Just beyond the town is the ruined Château de Langoiran; here a small road winds up past the château to the hamlet of Haut-Langoiran, from where there are wonderful views down over the vine-clad hill to the River Gironde and the countryside of Graves. The village of Langoiran is set right beside the wide, rusty Garonne – it has a riverside promenade and is a stopping-place for the barges which ply up and down to Bordeaux.

Now you can either cross back over the river and return towards Bordeaux along the N113, or you could extend your tour to include some of the Premières Côtes de Bordeaux and Entre-Deux-Mers vineyards. This region, which lies between the Garonne and Dordogne rivers, has a signposted circuit through the countryside. Of particular interest is the majestic ruined Romanesque abbey of la Sauve Majeure, an important stop for medieval pilgrims following the Way of St James to Santiago de Compostella. Nearby Créon is an interesting fortified town, and so are la Réole and Sauveterre-de-Guyenne. But it is the unspoilt landscape and quiet country roads that make this region a real pleasure.

Wine Tour N.º 23
COGNAC

Maize flourishing in front of the small, Romanesque church at Graves

If Champagne is the king of wines, then Cognac is certainly the emperor of *eau de vie*. It is more than just a type of brandy – it is the yardstick by which all others are measured. Brandy is simply a concentrated form of wine: when wine reaches an alcohol level of about 16 to 18 per cent during the fermentation process, the yeasts that transform the sugar into alcohol are killed off. For wine to be of greater strength than this, either pure alcohol must be added – as it is with port, for example – or it must be distilled to remove some of the water. This is how brandy is made – by heating wine to boiling point, then condensing the steam which it gives off.

In the Middle Ages the major exports from the Charente region were salt and wheat; the region's white wine was often only included in a shipment to complete the load. Later, in the seventeeth century, the wine-growers of Cognac began distilling their wines, partly in competition with growers closer to the coast, who had something of a monopoly is undistilled wine, and partly so that, in their more concentrated state, they could be shipped in greater quantities. On arrival in London or Amsterdam they were diluted with water before consumption. At this time brandy (from the Dutch *brandewijn*, or burnt wine), was not the choice of the gentry but a cheap, rough wine drunk by the proletariat as an alternative to beer.

The wines
The grape types used to make the wines from which Cognac is distilled include the Saint-Emilion, a variety of Ugni Blanc, the Folle Blanche, the Colombard, the Sauvignon and the Semillon. The process of distillation is quite complex and is carried on even today on small farms in the traditional copper stills. The thin and acidic white wines of *Cognac*, which are often little more than 8 or 10 per cent alcohol, are distilled in two stages to a strength of about 70 per cent alcohol. This is too strong and, immediately after distillation, too harsh to be drunk as it is, and the fiery spirit is put into oak casks to mellow for at least two years – more for the finer Cognacs. Its warm golden colour is a result of this process and of the tannin which it draws from the oak. Caramel may be added for colour and finally distilled water is used to dilute the spirit to its final strength of 40 per cent alcohol.

As well as Cognac, this area produces *Pineau des Charentes*, which has its own appellation. This is an apéritif wine made by adding *eau de vie* to the white wine of the region; it is customarily served chilled.

Some Vin de Pays is also produced with the name of *Vin de Pays du Charentais*, and from a little further north there are *Vin Rosé de Mareuil, Vin de Pays de la Vendée* and *Vin du Haut Poitou*, which is classified VDQS.

The cuisine

The cuisine of the Cognac region benefits greatly from neighbouring Bordeaux and from Périgord to the east. Since it is close to the coast, good seafood features on most menus. In *mouclade*, mussels are prepared with egg yolks, white wine and cream, while *chaudrée* is a fish stew in which a variety of fish and shellfish are cooked in a *court-bouillon* with white wine and shallots. Charentais melons are famous, with their firm, orangey-pink flesh and sweet, honey flavour. Here they are often prepared by slicing off the top, pouring in a good measure of Pineau des Charentes and leaving to chill slightly for a few hours before serving – they are wonderful!

The Route des Vins *Michelin map 72*

The areas producing the wine from which Cognac is made are divided into six Crus: Grande Champagne, Petite Champagne, Borderies, Fins Bois, Bons Bois and Bois Ordinaires: these last, lesser Crus are grown in regions as far away as the Ile de Ré and the Ile d'Oléron off the coast at La Rochelle, while the finer and more prestigious Grande Champagne is grown on the chalky hillsides south of the river Charente, near the town of Cognac itself. The suggested tour of the Cognac region is not signposted but it is easy to follow with the use of a map and includes the most significant of the Cognac villages and countryside.

A visit to Cognac is the ideal introduction to the region. It is a rather grey, grim-looking town, its roofs blackened by a fungus which thrives on the fumes emanating from the casks of maturing brandy. These casks are stored in the old part of the town, in riverside *chais* which you can visit; there is a regional museum here too, with a section on the making of Cognac.

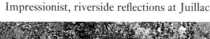

Impressionist, riverside reflections at Juillac

Nearby are the Château de Valois, where François I was born in 1494, and the twelfth-century church of Saint Léger with its impressive Romanesque façade.

From the centre of Cognac take the N 141 towards Angoulême for a short distance and then turn left on to the D 15. Cross the river to the village of St Brice, which has a lovely sixteenth-century château set in a park. Nearby, close to Châtre, is the ruined twelfth-century Abbaye de Nôtre-Dame de Châtre, an elegant old stone building standing in isolation in the middle of a wood, surrounded by meadows and vineyards. Here, you are close to the lazy waters of the Charente, in a land of lush green water-meadows and woods and rolling hills of vineyards. You get a real sense of being far away from the rush and hurry of the twentieth century, particularly when you come to a town like Bourg-sur-Charente set beside an enchanting stretch of the river and dignified by a beautiful twelfth-century church and an imposing château that dates from the sixteenth century.

Jarnac, the next town on the circuit, is considered to be the second home of Cognac; several important shippers are based here in riverside warehouses. The town has a broad, tree-lined main street and well cared-for public gardens which stretch down to the river, as well as the château of Chabannes. The peaceful little village of Triac also has a private château. From here cross the Charente and take a small road, the D 90, to the village of St Même-les-Carrières, which is a good place for a walk by the river. In Bassac the Benedictine abbey, built in the twelfth century, has an unusual four-storey Romanesque bell tower and a fortified church. There are some handsome stone houses lining the narrow streets of the town. Another peaceful riverside spot lies at the point where the small road crosses the river at St Amant-de-Graves. Nearby Graves boasts an exquisite, small Romanesque church.

Everywhere you travel in the Cognac region you will see producers' farms. These are usually contained within high, grey stone walls behind large, closed doors, giving them a rather forbidding look. However, you will always be welcomed to taste the locally made Cognac.

A thatched stockpile of logs and vine prunings at St Médard-de-Barbezieux

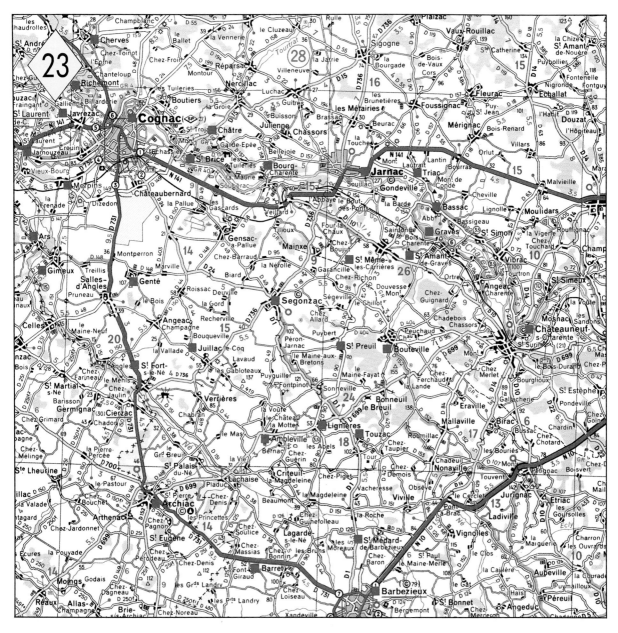

Châteauneuf-sur-Charente, further along the river, is somewhat larger than many of the other villages but quite similar in character; it has a fine twelfth-century Romanesque church. The route now turns away from the river to head back westward and begins to climb up into the chalky, domed hills where the vineyards are more densely cultivated. Between the small grey-stone village of Bouteville and its neighbour St Preuil, whose church is surrounded by vines, the road reaches the highest point of the undulating landscape, giving some fine views of the surrounding countryside. Nearby Lignières is a particularly charming village with a lovely Romanesque church and two châteaux: the moated seventeenth-century one is used as the town hall, while the other is a newer building dating from the nineteenth century.

Beyond the tiny hamlets of Touzac and St Médard-de-Barbezieux, which has a quaint, tiny church in its centre, is Barbezieux, capital of the Petite Champagne region. This mellow old town has a network of narrow

winding streets lined with old houses, a fine church and an imposing fifteenth-century château perched up above it all. There is yet another twelfth-century Romanesque church in the small village of Barret, next along the route. These churches are often quite tiny and have been so heavily restored that little of their original character remains. It is not uncommon to see fifteenth-century ribbed vaulting, a cloister that was added 200 years later and nineteenth-century marble cladding in a church dating from the Middle Ages. Beyond the town of Archiac, near St Fort-de-Né on the D731, is a fine example of the region's dolmens (megalithic tombs), their mysterious stone formation looking rather incongruous in the middle of a vineyard.

The route turns eastwards from Archiac through the villages of Ambleville and Juillac-le-Coq and its twelfth-century church, through open countryside that is a mixture of meadows, farmland, woods and vineyards. Around Segonzac, the capital of the Grande Champagne region, the rounded chalk hills are completely covered in neatly patterned vineyards,

reminiscent of the landscape in the Marne Valley where its aristocratic namesake is produced.

From here, you return towards Cognac through the small villages of Genté, Gimeux and Ars, where there is a twelfth-century church and a Renaissance château. The final part of the route leads through the villages of Merpins (stop here to visit the remains of the Roman town of Condate and the mound of a feudal castle), Jarnouzeau, Javrezac (beside the river Antenne) and Richemont (where there is a seventeenth-century château as well as an eleventh-century one).

Spring is particularly beautiful in this region; the green of the trees (above left at Jarnac) is almost dazzling. At the fortified Château de Chesnel (above) Cognac and Pineau des Charentes may be sampled

Before returning to Cognac it is worth travelling a little further to the north to visit the twelfth-century Abbaye de Fontdouce near the town of Burie on the D 73. On the way, just outside Cherves, is the fortified Château de Chesnel, the domain of the comtes de Rouffignac, where you can sample and buy both Cognac and Pineau des Charentes.

Wine Tour Nº 24

BERGERAC

The fourteenth-century château at Gageac

Cyrano de Bergerac, the legendary figure created by the nineteenth-century dramatist Edmond Rostand, was a romantic hero from a tormented past. Thus is the city of Bergerac, situated beside the Dordogne on a broad plain where the river makes its way towards the wide Gironde Estuary, inscribed in French literature. It is less famous for its wines, undeservedly so. Only 85 kilometres away from the city of Bordeaux and with the western limits of its vineyards virtually adjoining those of the Libournais, Bergerac tends to be almost ignored. But its wines are worth exploring, particularly the sweet white wine of Monbazillac. The city of Bergerac has a fascinating old quarter with narrow cobbled streets and medieval houses and courtyards and a Maison du Vin. Tobacco is an important product of the region too – indeed, you can follow a Route des Tabacs as well as the Route des Vins.

The wines

The wines of Bergerac, red, white and some rosé, are sold under the following appellations: *Bergerac* (red, white and rosé); *Côtes de Bergerac* (red and white); *Bergerac-Côtes de Saussagnac* (white); *Monbazillac* (white); *Montravel, Côtes de Montravel* and *Haut Montravel* (white); *Pécharmant* (red), and *Rosette* (white). The grape types used are principally the Cabernet Franc, Cabernet Sauvignon, Merlot, Cot (or Malbec), Semillon and Sauvignon Blanc.

Monbazillac is probably the best-known wine of the region. It is sweet and white, and can be drunk chilled as an apéritif, as an accompaniment to *foie gras* or as a dessert wine. As with the great sweet wines of neighbouring Sauternes and Barsac, Monbazillac is made from grapes affected by the Botrytis fungus.

The cuisine

The neighbouring region of Périgord has a strong influence on the cuisine of the Bergerac region. *Pâté de foie gras* studded with truffles is an expensive treat; it is perfect with a glass of golden Monbazillac wine. Walnuts are a major crop here: walnut oil is used as a dressing on salads, and you'll often see walnut bread served with the cheese. There is a superb *boulangerie*, Michel de Queker, in Ste Foy-la-Grande where you will find this as well as breads with onions, with raisins or prunes, soda bread and wholemeal bread, pastries – including croissants with ham and cheese – *croques-monsieurs* and *madames*, quiches and sweet pastries like *clafoutis*, and apple, greengage and grape tart.

The Route des Vins *Michelin map 75*

The Bergerac Route des Vins is a complete, if

meandering, circuit and is well signposted. It is also particularly well planned. If you leave by the bridge near the old quarter and cross over to the south bank of the Dordogne, you will pick up the signposts, starting on the D 933, the main road to Marmande. Very soon the Route des Vins turns left on a small country road, the D 14, towards Monbazillac. As you drive over the wide Dordogne plain you can see in the distance the large rounded hill where most of the southerly vineyards are situated. The Moulin de Malfourat, an old sailless windmill, provides a superb viewpoint over the sloping vineyards, the Dordogne Valley and the distant town of Bergerac.

There is not much of interest in Monbazillac itself, an unassuming cluster of grey stone houses around a small square. But stop at the adjacent château, an elegant and successful mixture of Renaissance and military architecture dating from the sixteenth century. It has *caves* you can visit, and a restaurant. Now you are in the heart of vineyard country. Leave the wine road for a short detour to the nearby fifteenth-century Château de Bridoire. Then continue through the small villages of Rouffignac-de-Sigoulès and Pomport on a small winding country road towards Sigoulès, which holds an annual wine fair in July. Next to it is the tiny village of Monbos with its miniature grey-stone, turreted château. Little more than a rough track leads to the village. Certainly this wine route includes the quietest and most scenic small roads wherever possible. Cycling would be an ideal form of transport here.

The countryside becomes flatter, and more open now and the vines alternate with meadows and woods. The small road continues to the hamlet of Thénac; you can taste the local wines at Château Thénac. A sequence of minute villages follows: la Bastide, Monestier and Gageac-et-Rouillac, where there is an attractive fourteenth-century château. Saussignac, the next village, is rather larger, with an imposing château. Now you head back towards the River Dordogne to the busy market town of Ste Foy-la-Grande, an ancient *bastide*. Here the route crosses the river to Port Ste-Foy, where it turns left on to the D 32 E 2 towards Vélines in the region of Montravel. The village has a lovely Romanesque church and mellow, old, grey stone houses.

From here the wine road continues to Moncaret and Lamothe-Montravel, where there is the large Cave Co-opérative of Montravel. The small village of St Michel-de-Montaigne is the next place of interest on the route; there is an old Romanesque church here and a château which you can visit and where you can buy the wines made in the surrounding vineyards. The circuit continues along a small scenic road through woods and meadows towards Montpeyroux, which also has a fine old church and a château, the Manoir de Mathecoulon. You are in the Côtes de Bergerac region now – the western limit of the Bergerac vineyards and close to the wine-producing area of St Emilion. Next is the *bastide* town of Villefranche-de-Lonchat with a nice old church, a pretty square shaded by plane trees, and a Cave Co-opérative. The lake of Gurson, a peaceful spot where there is a restaurant under the trees, is nearby; it has camping, picnic and boating facilities, and is overlooked by the ruined Château de Gurson.

From here the Route des Vins continues back towards Ste Foy-la-Grande through some small, unremarkable villages. After passing St Méard-de-

The sixteenth-century Château of Monbazillac. It has *caves* worth visiting and a good restaurant

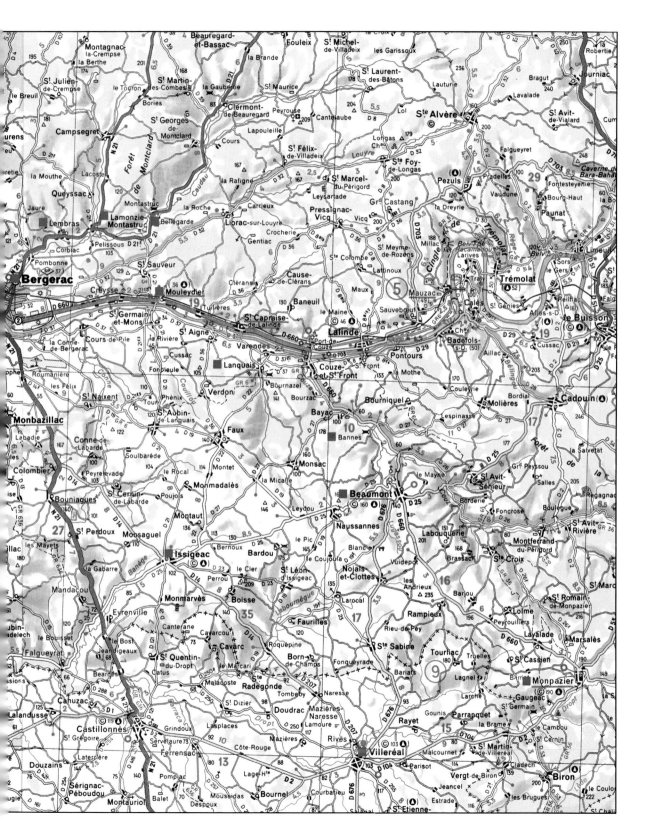

Gurçon on the main road (the D 708), the wine road turns left on to a small, country road leading to the hamlet of Ponchapt. Towards the town of le Fleix, as the road descends to the river, there are occasional views through the trees of the valley below. From here it returns to Bergerac along the D 32.

The regions of Pécharmant and Rosette lie to the north and east of Bergerac and, although not part of the signposted wine route, are well worth exploring. Take the main road, the N 21, towards Périgueux from the centre of Bergerac. After the village of Lembras

you will find the D 21 to the right leading to the little village of Lamonzie-Montastruc, which boasts the Château de Bellegarde and the Manoir de Grateloup.

To the south-east of the riverside village of Mouley-dier is Lanquais, where you can visit the very fine fifteenth-century château. There is another château in Bannes, and the medieval town of Issigeac is of interest too with a sixteenth-century church and a bishops' palace, le Château des Evêques, built a century later, as well as some picturesque old timber-framed houses.

If you want to extend your visit to Bergerac further,

you can follow the Circuit des Bastides, a shortish tour which takes you to many of the ancient *bastide* towns in the region, such as Beaumont, Villeréal, Eymet and, perhaps the greatest jewel, Montpazier, which is no great distance from the thriving vineyards of Monbazillac.

To the south-west of Bergerac is the small wine-growing region of the Côtes de Duras, where excellent red and white wines are made; if you have the time it is worth a short detour. The town of Duras, almost due south of Ste Foy-la-Grande, has a château housing an

The bridge across the Dordogne at Ste Foy-la-Grande (left). The Circuit des Bastides leads through many, old bastide towns of which Montpazier (top) is the brightest jewel. The completely symmetrical rows of vineyards at Monbazillac (above) are nearby

intriguing museum of regional agricultural implements and domestic bric-à-brac, including ancient wine presses and bottles. The countryside is tranquil and the people welcoming, and you can drive through the small villages in the vineyards, such as St Sernin and St Théobald.

Wine Tour Nº 25

ARMAGNAC

The ancient fortified village of Larressingle (above)
and (right) an abundance of sunflowers near Beaumont

Bordered by the vast pine forests of the Landes to the west, the valleys of the Lot and Garonne to the north and the majestic mountains of the Pyrenees to the south, the landscape of Armagnac includes a little of all these features. But its famous wine is unique. This is a region with a past, and a rich architectural and cultural heritage: there are ancient abbeys and churches, *bastides* and impressive châteaux built by the Gascons who ruled the area for well over 1,000 years.

The wines

If Cognac has a serious rival when the time comes for coffee and cigars, it can only be *Armagnac*. The two producing regions are relatively close geographically, yet there is a considerable difference between their wines. Armagnac has a more assertive, earthier quality than Cognac and needs a longer time in the cask to acquire finesse. The distillation process is slightly different: instead of the two-stage process used in Cognac, the thin, quite weak, white wine of the Armagnac region is brought up to a level of 50 to 55 per cent alcohol in one stage. The local oak from which the casks are made is a darker and more resinous wood than the Limousin oak used for the Cognac casks, giving the Armagnac a darker, stronger colour in a

shorter space of time. Its more rustic character, however, means that it needs longer to attain the subtlety and smoothness of its rival. The wine is distilled immediately after fermentation, at the end of September or early October, and by law all distillation stops on 30 April. On 1 April the following year that brandy is designated Compte 1, the minimum age at which it can be sold as Armagnac. Napoleon, or Extra Armagnac, must be at least Compte 5.

The wine-growing region of Armagnac is divided into three areas: Bas-Armagnac, Haut-Armagnac and Ténarèze. Bas-Armagnac is the smaller, more westerly region and the most prestigious. Ténarèze is in the centre and Haut-Armagnac extends north to the department of Lot-et-Garonne and south to the Hautes Pyrénées. As with Cognac, the final product is usually the result of blending, from different regions and different vintages. The grape types used are the Folle Blanche, or Picpoul, the Colombard and the St Emilion (Ugni Blanc). It is possible to get Armagnac made from one particular grape type. Unlike Cognac, the production of which is quite centralized, well organized and well promoted, Armagnac tends to be produced by individuals, making and selling their product in a smaller and more fragmented way. This

221

Floc and Armagnac advertized on a roadside barrel

may to some extent explain why Cognac has more impact on the world's wine-lists.

An apéritif or dessert wine is also made locally by combining the local white wine with the distilled spirit; called *Floc de Gascogne*, it is advertized extensively in the region. In addition, some sound and palatable Vin de Pays is produced called *Côtes de Gascogne, Côtes du Condomois, Côtes de Montestruc* and *Côtes de Bruhlois*. There is also an interesting white wine made only from the Colombard grape called Vin de Pays des Côtes de Gascogne.

The cuisine

A large part of the Armagnac region lies within the department of Gers, France's foremost producer of *foie gras* (specially fattened goose or duck liver). Local menus often feature duck and geese dishes. A slice from a whole *foie gras* is a wonderful way to start a meal; the delicacy is also served as a *galantine* or in thin slivers served on a *salade composée* along with perhaps some *jambon de canard* (smoked breast of duck thinly sliced and served like a Bayonne ham). André Daguin of the Hôtel de France in Auch combines a piece of *foie gras* with fresh scampi and cooks them *en papillotes*. *Confit d'oie* and *confit de canard*, pieces of goose and duck pre-cooked and preserved in their own fat, then grilled or baked until the skin is golden and crisp, are also popular here. *Magret de canard* (fillet of duck breast) is another regional speciality which is served in a variety of ways – often cooked rare, or prepared with a sauce made with cherries in Armagnac. Armagnac also features in some of the region's desserts: a delicious *tarte aux pommes* in which the apples have been soaked in the brandy, for instance.

The Route des Vins *Michelin maps 79 and 82*

Although there are signs indicating Circuit d'Armagnac, these refer to a number of quite separate circuits and so are rather difficult to follow. The route suggested here combines the best of all these circuits, including the most significant towns and aspects of the countryside.

The most logical starting point is the town of Condom. It is an easy drive from the A 61 autoroute between Bordeaux and Toulouse. On the way, along the D 930, you drive through the vineyards of the Côtes de Buzet, one of the lesser-known wines of the south-west, but well worth sampling. A few kilometres on is the very pretty medieval town of Nérac, on the northern fringe of the Armagnac region. A Gothic humpback bridge spans the River Baïse, the narrow streets by the riverside are lined with old stone houses and there is one remaining wing of a sixteenth-century château and an ancient church.

Condom is one of several towns which proclaim themselves to be the capital of Armagnac. It is certainly the capital of the Ténarèze and, being an important river port, has been a centre for the manufacture and distribution of the brandy for centuries. Its Gothic cathedral of St Pierre has an unusually large cloister with exceptional ribbed vaulting. There is a small Armagnac museum in the adjacent town hall. Follow the circuit in an anti-clockwise direction to the little fortified village of Larressingle, set in the middle of quiet rolling land patterned with vineyards. Its walls enclose a smaller cluster of old stone houses, a ruined château and a church, the whole place no larger than a modest château. An information kiosk sells local produce and

Old houses and arcades in the bastide town of Fourcès

the village's own brand of Armagnac. Just to the south of Condom is the Château de Cassaigne, where you are welcome to see the castle and taste the Armagnac. There is also an example of one of the copper mobile stills (*alembics ambulants*) that until quite recently were towed from village to village to distill the local wine. In a park close to Cassaigne, at the end of an avenue of trees, is the mellow stone Cistercian Abbaye de Flaran, which has a fourteenth-century cloister and contains ancient *chais* where the wine used to be stored. At Valence-sur-Baïse, a *bastide* with an arcaded square, there is an unusual church framed by two large belfries.

Continuing westward on the D 15 you come to the ruined château of Beaumont. Montréal, a fortified town built in the thirteenth century, is next along the route: this has the typical Armagnac central square surrounded by arcaded houses lining narrow streets built on a grid pattern. A kilometre or so to the north of Montréal is one of the most picturesque of all the *bastides*. The ramparts of Fourcès are surrounded by a moat full of water lilies, there is a small bridge leading through the fortified gateway into a little square shaded by plane trees and overlooked by old houses and arcades, and the pretty church is situated by the bridge just outside the village. Beyond the hill town of Castelnau-d'Auzan is the thermal resort of Barbotan-les-Thermes. Unlike many spa towns, this is a lively place with pavement cafés and colourful shops; a curious fortified gate acts as entrance to the town. Nearby is the lake of Uby, where you can go boating and fishing. The next town is Cazaubon, in the middle of some of the best vineyards of the Bas-Armagnac. A little further to the west is Labastide-d'Armagnac, rivalling Forcès for prettiness. Here stands a church, ancient arcaded houses and narrow streets. Among the Côtes de la Jeunesse vineyards, a few kilometres south of the village, is the museum of the Vignerons d'Armagnac; it is clearly signposted from the D 626. Near the road to the south of Labastide, surrounded by vineyards, is an ancient chapel called Nôtre-Dame des Cyclistes, where there is a small collection of relics and souvenirs on display. In the hamlet of Castex-d'Armagnac, a little further south of Labastide, is the Château Castex-d'Armagnac, its impressive *chais* lined with ancient casks. The domain of the Samalens brothers, important producers who make visitors very welcome, is quite close by in Laujuzan.

The small town of Eauze also claims to be the

Mouthwatering food displayed at Eauze market

capital of Armagnac; it has a Maison d'Armagnac and many mouth-watering food and wine shops. Market day is Thursday and in Eauze it is extremely lively. Centred in the small church square, it spills along the narrow streets towards an open space shaded by plane trees, under which some of the most delectable produce you can imagine is displayed. The Armagnac dealers used to bring their samples and trade here, but modern marketing methods now seem to have done away with this old-fashioned pleasure.

The next town on the wine route is Nogaro with its large Romanesque church of St Austinde. There is a forest at Aignan, a few kilometres further south, signposted from the village church down a narrow lane. The nearby village of Lupiac sits in the middle of beautiful scenic countryside. Going north, you get panoramic views over the rolling hills on each side of the road, which is dotted with old stone windmills. Set back in the woods is the Château de Castelmaure, the birthplace of Charles de Batz who is best known as the Gaston hero d'Artagnan, immortalized by Alexandre Dumas in *The Three Musketeers*; he is much honoured still, with varying degrees of dignity – from a statue in Auch to labels and posters advertizing Armagnac. Vic-Fézensac, the next large town, has a covered arena for the many *Courses Landaises* which it hosts throughout the year. It is also the place to stock up with the regional food specialities, such as *confits*, *foie gras* and fruits preserved in Armagnac; you will find a tempting assortment of such things at Chez Jeannot, a shop with irresistible displays.

Auch, the largest town of the region, is built on the banks of the River Gers. The Cathédrale de Sainte Marie, one of the last great Gothic cathedrals, is clearly visible from quite a distance; you can approach

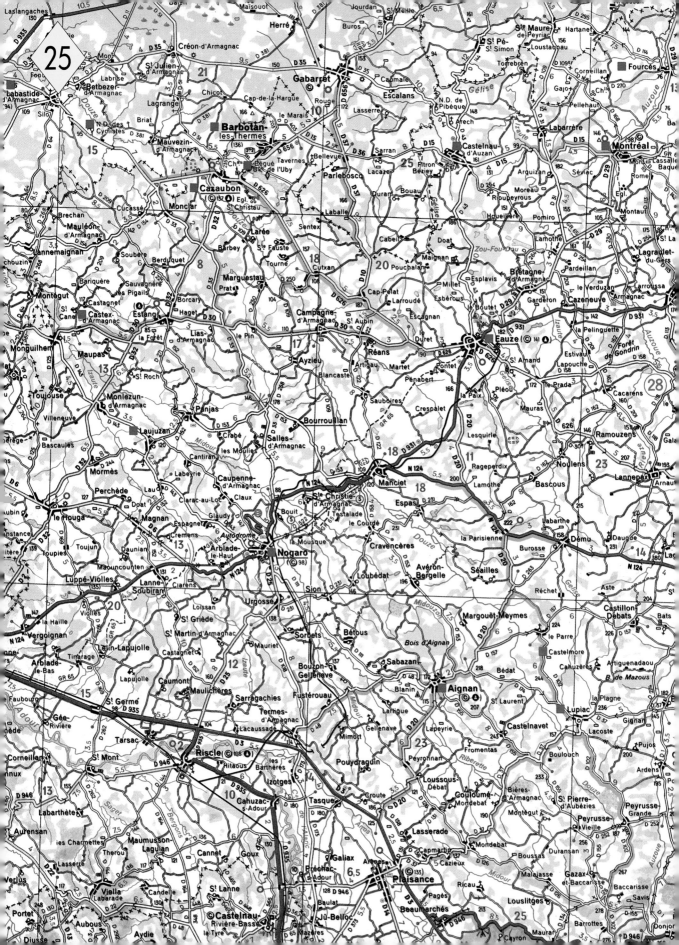

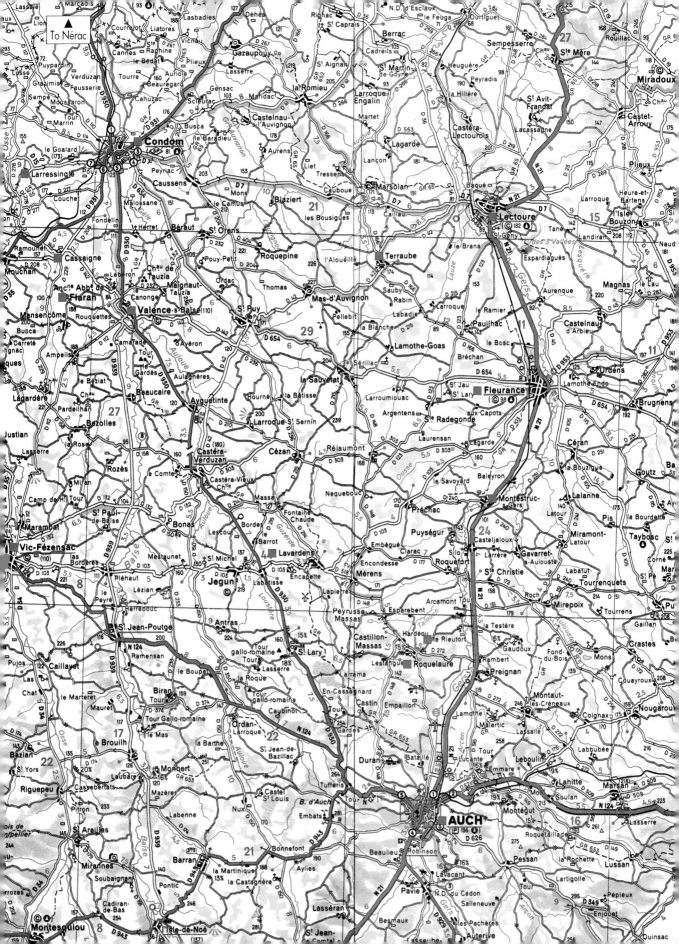

The countryside in Armagnac is gentle and peaceful. Dusty roads meander through woods and fields (as in Castex-d'Armagnac, right) where only sunflowers give a splash of vivid colour. The houses (above) are often beige with brown beams and have a hospitable look

it from the river via magnificent stone stairs. Inside, the Renaissance choir-stalls are very fine and incorporate over 1,500 individual figures and sculptures carved in heart oak; the work took over forty years to complete. The stained glass windows, in reds and purples, are the cathedral's most famous feature and date from the early sixteenth century. Outside, a large square is lined with elegant buildings and pavement cafés and the Hôtel de France, the restaurant of André Daguin, one of the region's great chefs, is around the corner.

Just to the north-west of Auch is the village of Roquelaure from whose hilltop setting you get breathtaking views of the surrounding landscape. Nearby is the Château de Rieutort, set in the midst of woods and one-time home of the Comte du Barry, whose wife became the mistress of Louis XV. In Lavardens the old stone houses are tiered up the hillside to an imposing château and old church.

Continuing northwards along the main road, the N 21, you pass the towns of Montestruc-sur-Gers, where there is a Cave Co-opérative, Fleurance and Lectoure. Fleurance has a strange, arcaded hall in the centre of its square; there is an unusual circular covered market here too. Lectoure is set on a hilltop high above the River Gers, encircled by its medieval ramparts. On the route back towards Condom don't miss the spectacular fortified town of Terraube; its enormous château looks as if it is about to topple over the edge of the hill.

Wine Tour Nº 26
MADIRAN/TURSAN

The countryside here is exceptionally rich and fertile

A few kilometres to the south of the Armagnac country are two small wine-producing areas which are not at all well known: the wines are seldom seen outside the region and this alone gives them a certain interest. But they do merit attention in their own right and the quiet, rural landscape in which the vines are grown is a constant delight. It is not in any way spectacular; its charm lies in a total lack of pretention in an area which has made virtually no concessions to tourism. The gateway to this region is the prettily named Aire-sur-l'Adour, a lively market town set beside the broad brown River Adour. It has the impressive twelfth-century cathedral of Sainte Quitterie du Mas with a Roman crypt containing the remains of the patron saint of Gascony, and makes an ideal base from which to explore the region.

The wines
The wines of *Tursan* are classified as VDQS and red and white are made as well as rosé. The white wine is made principally from the Baroque grape and the red and rosé from the Cabernet Franc and Cabernet Sauvignon.

The wines of *Madiran* are classified as Appellation Contrôlée and are exclusively red, made from the Tannat grape. An Appellation Contrôlée white wine is also produced in this region; called *Pacherenc du Vic Bilh*, it is made from the Pacherenc grape, also known as the Ruffiac. VDQS wines are those of the *Côtes de Saint Mont*. These are red, white or rosé, made from Tannat, Cabernet Franc and Cabernet Sauvignon grapes for red and from Gros Manseng, Ruffiac and Clairette for white.

The cuisine
The cuisine here reflects the diversity of the neighbouring regions of the Landes, the Gers and the Basque country. *Foie gras, confits* and *magrets* are made from geese and ducks, and there is an abundance of wild game. *Salmis de palombe* is a delicious stew of wood-pigeon simmered in a rich, red wine sauce, sometimes with the addition of *cèpes*, and *civet de lièvre* is similar, but made with hare. Another popular dish is *poulet basque*, chicken cooked with white wine, tomatoes, peppers, *lardons* and mushrooms. *Jambon de Bayonne* is a raw, cured ham served in paper-thin slices as an *hors d'oeuvre*, either on its own, with melon, or as part of a *salade composée* with *foie gras*. In *piperade*, the Basque speciality, eggs are scrambled lightly over stewed peppers, onions, garlic, tomatoes and ham. For dessert, you will find *gâteau basque*, a deliciously light, eggy cake baked to a golden crust.

The Route des Vins *Michelin map 82*

The region of Tursan lies to the east of the main road, the N 134, and just to the south of Aire-sur-l'Adour. The route through the countryside is clearly sign-posted as the Circuit du Tursan et de la Chalosse and just after leaving Aire towards Pau you will see a large sign pointing to the wine route, on the D 2.

The vineyards are, by and large, quite small individual plots scattered through the countryside, some little larger than a modest suburban back garden; consequently, most of the wine is made in the Cave Co-opérative in Geaune, the main town of the region. The rest of the countryside is planted with a variety of crops ranging from rape seed to wheat and barley, and there is a considerable amount of grazing land, relieved by woodland and copses.

The few tourists who explore this region tend to be rather conspicuous. When I visited a farm to ask permission to photograph a flock of geese, the owner said that she had noticed me in the village, several kilometres away, a few days earlier. The local people's experience of tourists is limited to those who stay in the *Gîtes Ruraux*, of which there are a number in the area.

Travelling in an anti-clockwise direction from Aire-sur-l'Adour, the wine road winds through quiet lanes to the hamlets of Duhort-Bachen, where a few arcaded houses surround a pretty village green dotted with shady plane trees, and on to Renung, just a cluster of small houses and a church. Then it crosses a flat plain and the River Adour to Cazères-sur-l'Adour.

Here the wine route follows the main road, the N 124, for a short distance to Grenade-sur-l'Adour, a larger town that has an arena for *Courses Landaises*, the bloodless bull-fights peculiar to the Landes. The larger towns, including Aire-sur-l'Adour, tend to hold well-publicized bull-fights in the summer with professional matadors, but some of the small communities have makeshift arenas and often provide a more enjoyable and informal spectacle than the bigger centres. The Syndicat d'Initiative in Aire-sur-l'Adour has information on when these village events take place. The bulls are not subjected to physical cruelty, although you could argue that it is cruel to make them so bewildered. The bull is released from its pen, partially tethered by a rope; the performer stands some 15 metres away and leaps around, gesticulating, until the bull is incensed enough to charge. The skill lies in leaving it as late as possible before twisting out of the bull's path, sometimes even somersaulting spectacularly over its back. The applause given to a particularly courageous performer is matched when a bull gets its own back, which happens fairly frequently, especially when some of the local lads have a go as well.

From here the route leads back into the depths of rural Tursan countryside to the genteel thermal resort of Eugénie-les-Bains, which is now more famous as the birthplace of *nouvelle cuisine* in the restaurant Les Prés d'Eugénie than as a spa town. Michel Guérard's restaurant and hotel, in an elegant building set in a small park, has become a place of pilgrimage for the gourmets of the world. A large sign on the outskirts of the village proclaims it to be the *'Premier Village Minceur de France'*.

The next village, St Loubouer, is one of the main centres of Tursan wine production, with a correspondingly high concentration of vineyards. It has some old stone houses, an ancient stone church and a

Many farmers (like this woman from Geaune) concentrate on producing foie gras, confits and magrets

curious isolated tower-cum-gatehouse. From here the road climbs up on to higher terrain, where there are lovely views over the surrounding countryside and the snow-capped peaks of the Pyrenees are often visible in the distance. The views from Vielle-Tursan are staggering too, up on its hilltop terrace beside the church. The next villages are Sarraziet and Montsoué; the latter has a small *Courses Landaises* arena.

There is little to remark in most of the small villages through which the circuit passes; they are often nothing more than a cluster of houses and a small church. And many of the old farmhouses, despite their rather faded and derelict charm, are functional rather than picturesque. But the remoteness and peace of this countryside is very special.

Hagetmau is a largish town with a number of hotels and restaurants as well as the Roman crypt of Saint Girons; a street festival is held here at the beginning of August. The next village on the Route des Vins, Samadet, has a museum with a collection of ancient regional pottery and a nearby shop sells reproductions of some of the pieces. From here the route leads to Geaune, the centre of the Tursan wine production. Just on its edge is the Cave Co-opérative where you can taste and buy the local wines. The town has an arcaded square, a large Romanesque church and a

small *Maison du Vin*; it hosts an annual agricultural fair at the end of July.

The Madiran wine circuit is not far away: continue on the N 134 south of Aire-sur l'Adour as far as the village of Garlin. Here the wine circuit is clearly signposted on to the D 16 towards the villages of Castelpugon and Diusse. The landscape of Madiran is subtly different from that of adjacent Tursan, and you always seem to be crossing a river, climbing a hill or plunging down into a valley. There is a mixture of meadows, woods and fields of grain and a variety of other crops. You will see many maize stores, wire and wooden cages some 2 metres deep and often up to 60 metres long – quite a sight when filled with newly harvested yellow maize. In the main the villages are quite small and there are many individual producers who invite visitors to taste and buy their wines. In the hamlet of Diusse, for example, there is *cave* attached to a fine château surrounded by vineyards, and nearby is one of the Caves Co-opératives of Crouseilles.

From Diusse the wine road runs along the top of a ridge providing fine views over the landscape to both east and west. Beyond Cadillon, from where you can see the distant Pyrenees, is Africau-Bordes, actually an amalgamation of two villages. There is a quite spectacular château of golden stone perched on the hillside

Bloodless bullfights are common in this part of France, and Grenade-sur-l'Adour (above) has an arena for the sport. Right: A somnolent farmhouse in a sheltered valley in Madiran

The views from the village of Vielle-Tursan (top) are magnificent; the Pyrenees are visible in the distance. Above: Despite its faded appearance, this Madiran farmhouse is very much part of a working farm. Right: The Château d'Africau-Bordes. This stunning château has a *cave* with a fine selection of Madiran wines available

here, and you can visit its *cave*, where a fine selection of Madiran wines of different vintages is available. The larger town of Lembeye is the southernmost point of the Madiran wine route, with a fortified gateway and a large square. The nearby hamlet of Corbère-Abères

has a *cave* which you can visit and so has Crouseilles to the north; it has an old château as well.

The village which shares its name with the wine, Madiran, is very pretty, with a fine church set in a small square surrounded by stone houses; it also has an ancient covered market. The nearby hamlet of Aydie houses the domain of Château Aydie, a well-respected producer who makes both the Madiran red and the Pacherenc de Vic Bilh. To the north-east, close to the main road, the D 935, is Castelnau-Rivière-Basse. From a terrace beside the quaint, crumbling, church

here there is a magnificent view over the countryside to the east. The village of St Mont, the northernmost point of the Madiran region, consists of a few ancient houses and a church dominated by the large Cave Coopérative of the Union de Producteurs de Plaimont. In a roadside *caveau* run by the Crouseille Cave Coopérative, at Cahuzac-sur-Adour (on the D 935) you can buy local products such as *confits* and *foie gras*, as well as a wide selection of local wines including some from the small production areas further to the south – Irouléguy near St Etienne de Baïgorry, St Jean-Pied-

de-Port in the Pyrenees, Jurançon near the town of Pau, and Béarn in the region around the town of Orthez.

These distinctive wines, which are often staggeringly cheap, and the countryside which produces them, are also worth exploring if you have the time to extend your tour a little further south. Indeed, the tiny, fragmented vineyards of Irouléguy, high up on the mountainside, reach almost to the Spanish border and justify the hike necessary to reach them, both for their wines and their views.

SOUTH–WEST FRANCE
Wine-buying Guide

THE NORTHERN BORDELAIS

This part of the region produces a great volume of wine, most of which is not well known. The wines here are relatively unaffected by the investment market that has caused prices for the top wines to spiral, and so, apart from the top wines of St Emilion and Pomerol, most fetch modest prices.

Appellations Contrôlées

St-Emilion This appellation has its own classification system for red wines:

St-Emilion, Premier Grand Cru Classé – the top 12 chateaux
St-Emilion, Grand Cru Classé – about 70 chateaux
St-Emilion, Grand Cru – fixed annually by official tasting panels
St-Emilion

Here the Merlot is the dominant red grape variety and makes generally softer wines than in the Médoc. The wines of a good year from the better château need five to ten years' ageing,

Ancient wine press

but the lesser wines are drinkable after two or three years.

The village itself, surrounded by the vineyards, is one of the most beautiful wine villages in France. Fortunately, many growers have had their homes converted into *caves* for browsing and buying.

Around St-Emilion are satellite appellations that append the name of St-Emilion. They are all red wines of a lesser standing than St-Emilion itself: Lussac-St-Emilion, Montagne-St-Emilion, Puisseguin-St-Emilion, Saint-Georges-St-Emilion.

Since 1973 all the wines of Parsac-St-Emilion have been sold as Montagne-St-Emilion.

Pomerol A small appellation north-east of Libourne producing rich, sturdy red wines. The estates are all quite small by Bordeaux standards and there is no official classification system. However, Château Pétrus is acknowledged as being by far the best and is therefore the most expensive Bordeaux wine. Again, the Merlot is the predominant grape variety here.

Lalande-de-Pomerol A satellite appellation to Pomerol making similar but less rich red wines.

Néac A tiny appellation next to Lalande-de-Pomerol making similar red wines.

Fronsac An appellation, producing soft, rich red wines similar to Pomerol, that has somehow always missed the limelight enjoyed by Pomerol and St-Emilion. A second appellation, Canon Fronsac, exists for similar red wines in the same delimited area.

Côtes de Blaye, Premières Côtes de Blaye Some dry to sweet white wines but mostly red of a rustic and soft nature. The best vineyards for the red are by the River Gironde. The

Premières Côtes de Blaye is from the same district but is required to have an extra half degree of alcohol.

Bourg and Côtes de Bourg A much smaller appellation area adjacent, and very similar, to Blaye.

Côtes de Castillon Red wines from just west of St-Emilion. This appellation is technically a Bordeaux Supérieur and produces good value wines.

Graves de Vayres A small appellation, not to be confused with Graves, making red, dry white, and demi-sec white wine all to be drunk young.

Entre-deux-Mers A large appellation area that used to produce sweet white wines but now is only allowed to produce drier styles. It should be drunk young and is a good value apéritif. Red wines produced in this area are designated Bordeaux or Bordeaux Supérieur.

Premières Côtes de Bordeaux Some red and Clairet wines but the white, ranging from dry to sweet, is best known. Most of the wines are inexpensive and good value.

Sainte-Foy-Bordeaux The extreme eastern appellation of Bordeaux, bordering Bergerac, making red and dry to sweet white wines.

Côtes de Bordeaux Saint-Macaire Sweet or semi-sweet white wine normally drunk young.

Addresses

This is a small selection of châteaux you can visit without an appointment. All are so well signposted that a full address is not necessary.

Château de Bousquet
Bourg (off D 23)

Château Segonzac
Blaye (off D 9)

Château de la Dauphine
Fronsac (behind the town)

Château Petit Village
Catusseau

Château Larmande
(Town centre, St Emilion)

Château Moulin St Georges
St-Emilion (on entry to town on
D 122)

Château Fombrauge
St Christophe-des-Bardes
(D 17 from St-Emilion)

THE MEDOC

This vineyard district commands worldwide attention from both wine lovers and the investment market. Most of the greater châteaux are not geared up to welcome tourist visitors, especially those without an appointment, and will anyway have tied up arrangements for selling their wine through brokers and *négociants*.

During the normal holiday months, May to September, the two preceding vintages will be undergoing their early maturation in oak casks. Most properties will allow visitors to sample wines from the cask but bear in mind that they will be nowhere near ready for drinking, and the *maître de chais* may be pressed for time. Therefore, you might like to have these guidelines:

● have some knowledge of the past three or four vintages and be able to discuss them in French;
● do not visit between 12 and 2 pm unless you have been asked to
● do not smoke in the *chais*. Never pour wine left in your sampling glass back into the cask
● be courteous, shake hands and comment briefly on the wines you have tasted without wasting the *maître de chais'* time

The châteaux that do sell directly are well aware of the tourist market and charge accordingly. It might be better to buy wines from the Vinothèque shop at the end of the Allées de Tourny opposite the theatre.

The appellations

The generic wines are sold as Médoc and Haut Médoc, both of which only cover red wines.

The Haut Médoc is subdivided into communes which all have their own appellations: Listrac, Moulis, Margaux, St-Julien, Pauillac and St-Estèphe.

Château Prieuré-Lichine

Within these commune appellations there are châteaux rated on the classification scale of Grand Cru (a scale set out in 1855 with five divisions), Cru Bourgeois, Cru Artisan and Cru Paysan.

The 1855 Grand Cru Classification

This classification was formed by the Bordeaux Chamber of Commerce on the instructions of Napoleon III for the *Exposition Universelle de Paris*. It was based on the price fetched per *tonneau* of wine in 1855.

Since the original classification, some châteaux have fallen into disrepute, while others have gained in stature, making the system rather inaccurate. Nevertheless, it still persists.

In 1855 four châteaux were rated Premier Grand Cru Classé: Château Lafite-Rothschild and Château Latour in Pauillac, Château Margaux in Margaux and Château Haut Brion in Graves.

Although Graves is not normally considered as part of the Médoc, Haut Brion is nevertheless universally recognized and classified as a Premier Grand Cru.

In 1973 a presidential decree elevated Château Mouton-Rothschild (in Pauillac) to a Premier Grand Cru so there are now five. There are also 14 Deuxième Grand Cru châteaux, 14 Troisièmes Crus, ten Quatrièmes Crus and 18 Cinquièmes Crus.

Addresses

There are many châteaux in this region but these are some where visitors are usually received kindly. They are all well signposted.

The Wine Museum
Château Mouton Rothschild
Pauillac

Château Latour
Pauillac

Château Prieuré Lichine
Cantenac

Château Margaux
Margaux

Château Lascombes
Margaux (owned by Bass Charrington)

Châteaux Beychevelle
Beychevelle

Château Léoville Lascasses
St Julien

Château Cos d'Estournel
St Estèphe

THE SOUTHERN BORDELAIS

This area starts within the suburbs of Bordeaux itself and stretches south-eastwards. The best Graves estates of Château Haut Brion, La Mission Haut Brion and La Tour Haut Brion are, quite surprisingly, in the built-up area of Pessac.

Appellations Contrôlées

Graves This appellation produces red and dry to demi-sec white wines. The quality ranges from a Premier Grand Cru, Château Haut Brion, through a succession of Grand Cru Classé châteaux, down to the basic commune wine, Graves. An appellation of *Graves Supérieures* exists for commune white wine, ranging from dry to sweet, with an extra degree of alcohol.

Sauternes This appellation produces only sweet white wine made from grapes infected by the Botrytis fungus. This rich, luscious alcoholic wine is the most perfect accompaniment for puddings of *foie gras*. In some years the ripeness and effect of the Botrytis is better than others and makes richer, more concentrated wines that will last and improve over time.

Barsac Again, a sweet white wine from Botrytis-infected grapes but marginally lighter than Sauternes. All Barsac is entitled to be called Sauternes but not *vice versa*.

Cérons This appellation, adjacent to Barsac, also makes sweet white wines from grapes infected by the Botrytis fungus, but makes dry wines as well.

The wines are less rich than Barsac or Sauternes and do not last as long.

Loupiac and Cadillac Opposite Cérons on the right bank of the Garonne, these two adjacent appellations make semi-sweet to sweet white wines of which Loupiac is the richer.

Sainte-Croix-du-Mont Sweet white wines are produced here next to Loupiac. Some wine is made dry to be sold as Bordeaux sec, but most has a lemony lusciousness. The wines are well made and provide a cheaper, less intense alternative to Sauternes or Barsac.

Addresses

This is a small selection of châteaux you can visit without an appointment. All are so well signposted that a full address is not necessary.

Château Olivier,
Léognan

Château La Louvière
Léognan

Château d'Yquem
Sauternes

Château Gilette
Barsac (office at Rue de l'Horloge across river in Cadillac)

Château Coutet
Barsac

Château Clousot
Barsac
(behind Château Coutet. Some old vintages usually available)

Château Fayau
Cadillac

BORDEAUX

General Bordeaux Appellations

Bordeaux is the biggest AC region in France, with a massive production and several large generic appellations covering lower quality wines.

Bordeaux Red, dry or sweet white, and rosé wines from any part of the Bordeaux region. The dry white wines must state *sec* on the label. These wines are more likely to be

blends made by *négociants* than to come from a single estate.

Bordeaux Clairet An appellation to cover wines that are light red/dark rosé. The English word Claret is a corruption of this name. This is the original style of Bordeaux red wine but now is only really found on estates where they produce it for home consumption.

Bordeaux Mousseux The sparkling *méthode champenoise* wine that can be dry to *demi-sec*.

Bordeaux Rosé Dry rosé wine, not common.

Bordeaux Supérieur Red, dry to sweet white, and rosé wine that is the same as generic Bordeaux except that it has an extra degree of alcohol, and comes only from the more noble grape varieties.

COGNAC

This is a much-copied name, often used to describe grape brandy. In fact it is the spirit from this delimited region. Within the Cognac district there are six sub-districts: Grande Champagne, Petite Champagne, Borderies, Fins Bois, Bon Bois and Bois Ordinaires, in order of quality. The quality of the spirit depends on the chalk content of the soil.

Commercial Cognac houses blend spirits from all or just a few of the districts to make their house styles. Three-star is the least quality designation, requiring the spirit to be aged for a minimum of two years in Limousin oak barrels. VSOP (Very Special Old Pale) must have a

A church overlooks vineyards
in Loupiac

minimum of three years' ageing but
in practice both three star and VSOP
are invariably aged longer. Five years
is now the maximum age allowed to
be stated on a label, however old the
blend of spirits is. Most houses
produce a de-luxe blend that contains
a proportion of old, long-aged spirits
but the packaging undoubtedly adds
to the expense. Vintage Cognacs do
exist and you may be able to buy
them from a merchant in the UK
with old stocks, but they are now
outlawed in France so do not expect
to see any there.

On the other side of the coin there
are many small growers and
producers (*fermiers*) who make a less
blended, perhaps finer Cognac that
enthusiasts often prefer. Do not
expect to see very much at these
smaller firms, but you will probably
find it interesting to taste the drink
and hear their philosophies on
cognac. When tasting, smell the spirit
with your nose an inch from the
glass. Don't stick your nose right into
the glass or the fumes will
anaesthetize your sense of smell.

To get a balanced view of Cognac,
try to spend some time with
producers of alternative cognacs such
as M. Voisin of Léopold Gourmel.

Pineau des Charentes This is a Vin
Doux Naturel, used as an apéritif and
fortified to about 18°. It has not
caught on abroad but is well worth a
try.

Vin de Pays

Vin de Pays Charentais Red, dry
white and rosé wines of which the
whites are the best, from the
départements of Charente and
Charente-Maritime.

Addresses

M. Voisin
Léopold Gourmel
16106 Cognac Cedex

BERGERAC

The vineyards start immediately to
the east of Bordeaux and are rather
overshadowed by it. Most of the
wines are fairly ordinary ones in the
Bordeaux style, but there are

appellations within the generic
Bergerac AC that make interesting
wines.

Appellations Contrôlées

Bergerac This generic appellation
covers the red and less interesting
rosé wines. A separate AC, Bergerac
Sec, exists for the dry white wine
made primarily from the Sauvignon
grapes. The sweet whites are called
moëlleux.

Côtes de Bergerac Superior red wines
with an extra degree of alcohol
produced in the same area as
Bergerac.

Côtes de Bergerac-Côtes de Saussignac
A dry white wine from five
communes around Saussignac.

Pécharmant This is a better red wine
produced in the north-eastern part of
Bergerac, with one degree more
alcohol than straight Bergerac.

Monbazillac An appellation within
Bergerac that produces sweet white
wine. Although these wines are made
with Botrytis-infected grapes, similar

to nearby Sauternes, they do not achieve the richness of Sauternes. The wine can be drunk young or with up to four years' ageing and is very good value. In good years it can be kept longer.

Rosette A semi-sweet white wine from north of Bergerac. It is not very common, and most is drunk locally.

Montravel An appellation technically within the *enclave* of Bordeaux but actually in the *département* of Dordogne. Dry, *demi-sec* and sweet white wines are made under the name Montravel and the reds are sold as Bergerac. Côtes de Montravel-Haut-Montravel also exists within Montravel.

Côtes de Duras Red and dry and sweet white wines made in western Bergerac. The wines resemble Bordeaux wines and can be quite attractive as well as good value.

Côtes de Buzet This appellation makes red, dry white and rosé wines of quite good quality. Most of the production is from the Cave Co-opérative at Buzet-sur-Baise where they have a prestige red wine called Cuvée Napoléon aged in new oak casks. The rosé production is tiny.

VDQS

Côtes du Marmandais Although only VDQS status, these red and dry white wines are well made and good value. The reds are the best.

Addresses

UNIDOR (Union des Co-opératives Vinicole de la Dordogne) 24100 St-Laurent-des-Vignes

Monbazillac/Bergerac: Château Poulvère Monbazillac 24240 Sigoulès

ARMAGNAC

Prior to 1905 the best of Armagnac's production was sold off to be blended with Cognac to give more colour and depth of bouquet to Cognac blends. This, and the fact that Armagnac has always been sold in a fragmented

fashion by growers and producers rather than by commercial marketing concerns, means that Armagnac has not made the international impact that Cognac has.

Now however, the commercialization of Armagnac is growing apace and perhaps its success in the upper quality levels may be attributed to the fact that, unlike Cognac, it may be sold with a vintage date. Old vintage Armagnacs are not as rare as you might expect.

Old casks in Château Castex-d'Armagnac

There are many individual growers of note, particularly in the Bas-Armagnac, that are well worth visiting. The aroma within an Armagnac maturing *chais* is quite heady. The single distillation, as opposed to Cognac's double one, preserves the flavouring elements other than alcohol in the spirit and results in a more aromatic, pungent, rustic bouquet.

Vin de Pays

Vin de Pays Condomois Red, dry white and a rare rosé. All should be drunk young and locally.

Côtes de Gascogne Good red, dry white and rosé wines.

Côtes de Montestruc Very similar to Côtes de Gascogne.

Addresses

Francis Darroze SA Route de St Justin 40120 Roquefort

MADIRAN/TURSAN

(AND OTHER WINES IN SOUTH-WEST FRANCE)
Appellations Contrôlées

Madiran Red wine only from the Tannat, Fer, Cabernet Sauvignon and Cabernet Franc grapes. This wine compares with Cahors for a rich, deeply coloured, long-lasting wine. It must spend 20 months in oak casks before bottling. The production comes both from a co-operative and from growers.

Béarn Red, rosé and some dry white wines from quite a wide area. These are best drunk locally.

Côtes du Frontonnais Red and rosé wines only from a small area north of Toulouse.

Gaillac Red, rosé, and white wines varying from dry to *demi-sec*, mostly from Caves Co-opératives. The whites are often marketed as *perlé*, with a small amount of bubbles. A *doux* and *mousseux* also exist, as does a separate AC, Gaillac Premières Côtes.

Pacherenc du Vic Bihl White wine from the same region as Madiran. Ranges from dry to medium-sweet and is made from the Ruffiac, Gros Manseng, Petit Manseng and Courbu grapes. The production is very small from vines trained high at 2 metres (6 feet) off the ground.

Jurançon These white wines were all sweet before the war but now Jurançon Sec is mostly made. The wine has a haunting apricot and cinnamon bouquet and can be quite delicious.

Irouléguy Red, white and rosé wines from a small vineyard district hear the Spanish border. The reds are the best, with a full earthy fruit flavour.

VDQS

Tursan Red, dry white and rosé wines produced around Geaune and Aire-sur-l'Adour. The red wine is solid with plenty of tannin, the rosés simple and fruity, and the white full-

bodied and made from the Baroque grape.

Côtes de Saint-Mont, Vins d'Entraygues et du Fel, Vins d'Estaing Red, white and rosé wines.

Vins de Lavilledieu, Vins de Marcillac Red and rosé wines only.

Vin de Pays

Vin de Pays de la Gironde Red and white wines only.

Coteaux de Glanes, Coteaux et Terrasses de Montauban Red and rosé wines only.

Vin de Pays de la Dordogne, Vin de Pays des Landes, Agenais, Comte Tolosan, Côtes de Montestruc, Côtes du Brulois, Côtes du Tarn, Gorges et Côtes de Millau, Saint-Sardon Red, white and rosé wines.

Addresses

Domaine Laplace
Aydie
64330 Garlin

Château de Payros
Corbères Abères
64350 Lembeye

The following is a selection of reliable Caves Co-opératives which are so well signposted that a full address is not necessary.

Cave Co-opérative
Madiran

Cave Co-opérative
Aire sur l'Adour

Cave Co-opérative
St Jean-Pied-de-Port

Cave Co-opérative de Gau Jurançon
(south of Jurançon)

Calendar of Events

Wine fairs are an important and very enjoyable part of the year's festivities in France, and almost any type of celebration in the wine regions, such as harvest festivals, agricultural fairs – even saints' day – will hold some interest for the wine-lover. The nature and atmosphere of such events varies considerably, ranging from simple village gatherings taking place at the weekend to major commercial wine fairs held in vast exhibition halls and lasting for a week. There are also other quite formal occasions with street processions, ceremonies and church services.

These festivals all have one thing in common: the opportunity to taste, and buy, the regional wines. Even at a small village affair there will usually be at least 10 or 12 producers with their own stands, displaying their range of wines and freely offering a glass to anyone who asks. The villagers tend to treat these occasions as a chance for a free day's drinking and make no pretence at serious tasting; first and foremost it is a day to have fun. In addition to wines, local producers also display cheeses, hams, bread and pastries and pâtés, and there are often local craftsmen demonstrating their skills.

During the day there is usually a procession of assorted tractors, farm carts and other vehicles decorated with flowers and wine barrels. Many of the villagers, dressed in regional costume, give displays of folk dancing. Quite often a small village attracts thousands of people from many miles around, closing its streets to traffic and designating a large field as a car park. I visited one such fair in a small village in the Bergerac region, Sigoulès. The local restaurant placed all its chairs and tables out along the main street for a splendid lunchtime feast on Sunday – a delightful and lively occasion. In the small square one stall was selling oysters, another fresh bread and cheeses; trestle tables and chairs were provided under the shady plane trees to complete the setting for a perfect picnic. In the evening the square was given over to a *bal,* with a band playing and the villagers dancing into the early hours of the morning. There are often also fringe events taking place, such as a cycle race, a football or *pétanque* match or a regional sport such as a *Course Landaise.*

Many of the fairs take place during the summer months, but by no means all of them. Many regions celebrate the new vintage in November, and at Easter-time there are wine fairs throughout France. For the really major events, such as the Trois Glorieuses in Beaune and the Fêtes de Biou in Arbois, it is advisable to book accommodation well in advance.

The following is a chronological list of wine-related events, both grand and humble, arranged region by region. This information is issued annually by Food and Wine from France, in London, but many of these events occur at roughly the same time each year. To be absolutely safe, write in advance to the nearest regional tourist information centre or check with your hotelier who will almost certainly be aware of any celebrations.

NORTH–WEST FRANCE

January

1st weekend – Wine fair in Angers (Anjou)

Sunday nearest the 22nd – Angers Festival (Maine-et-Loire)

Sunday nearest the 22nd – Festival of St Vincent at the Château de Goulaine (Loire Atlantique)

Sunday nearest the 22nd – Festival of St Vincent in Pouilly-sur-Loire (Nièvre)

Last Saturday – Wine festival in Vouvray (Indre-et-Loire)

End of the month – Festival of St Vincent in various towns in the Loire: Angers, Nantes, Vouvray, Tours, Chinon

February

Wine festival in Jaunay Clan (Vienne)

Wine festival in Loudun (Vienne)

1st weekend – Wine festival in Bourgueil and St Nicolas-de-Bourgueil (Indre-et-Loire)

2nd Saturday – Wine fair in Tours-Fondettes (Indre-et-Loire)

2nd weekend – Wine fair in Saumur (Maine-et-Loire)

Last Saturday – Wine fair in Azay-le-Rideau (Indre-et-Loire)

Last Saturday – Wine fair in Montlouis (Indre-et-Loire)

Last weekend – Wine fair in Chalonnes (Maine-et-Loire)

March

2nd Saturday – Wine fair in Chinon (Indre-et-Loire)

Middle of the month – Muscadet wine fair in Vallet (Loire-Atlantique)

3rd weekend – Wine fair in St Amand Montrond (Cher)

4th Sunday – Wine fair in Machecoul (Loire Atlantique)

1st weekend – Wine festival in Loreaux Bottereau (Loire Atlantique)

2nd Saturday – Wine festival in Vallet (Loire Atlantique)

End of the month – Wine fair in Thonas (Deux Sèvres)

April

1st weekend – Wine fair in Reuilly (Indre-et-Loire)

Beginning of the month – Wine fair in Châteaumeillant (Cher)

Easter – Wine fair in Amboise (Indre-et-Loire)

Easter – Wine fair in St Georges-sur-Cher (Loir-et-Cher)

Easter – Wine fair in Bourgueil and St Nicolas-de-Bourgueil (Loir-et-Cher)

2nd Saturday after Easter – Wine fair in Onzain (Indre-et-Loire)

May

1st – Touraine wine fair in Panzoult (Indre-et-Loire)

3rd Saturday after Easter – Wine fair in Onzain (Loir-et-Cher)

3rd weekend – Wine fair in Valençay (Indre-et-Loire)

Ascension – Wine fair in Clisson (Loire Atlantique)

Ascension – Wine fair in Cravant-les-Coteaux (Indre-et-Loire)

Easter – Wine fair in Sancerre (Cher)

Easter – Wine fair in Meusnes (Loir-et-Cher)

June

Wine festival in Vertou (Loire Atlantique)

July

1st Saturday – Touraine wine fair in Thésée (Loir-et-Cher)

1st Sunday – Rillandée de Brissac in Brissac (Maine-et-Loire)

14th – Millésimés Wine fair in St Aubin-de-Luigné (Maine-et-Loire)

Last Sunday – Giennois wine fair in Bonny-sur-Loire (Loiret)

August

1st Sunday – Wine fair in Montsoreau (Maine-et-Loire)

15th – Wine fair in Pouilly (Cher)

15th – Wine fair in Montlouis (Indre-et-Loire)

15th – Wine fair in Pouilly-sur-Loire (Nièvre)

15th – Wine fair in Amboise (Indre-et-Loire)

15th – Wine fair in Vouvray (Indre-et-Loire)

3rd weekend – Wine fair in Thorée-la-Rochette (Loir-et-Cher)

Last weekend – Wine fair in Quincy (Cher)

Last weekend – Wine fair in Sancerre (Cher)

September

3rd weekend – Wine fair in Thouars (Deux-Sèvres)

October

Middle of the month – Wine fair in Pont Crétien, Chabenet (Indre)

November

Middle of the month – Wine fair in Nantes (Loire Atlantique)

Last Sunday – Flower festival in Bouillé-Loretz (Deux-Sèvres)

December

Fair in Ancenis (Loire-Atlantique)

NORTH–EAST FRANCE

March

1st week – Wine competition at the Porte de Versailles in Paris

2nd Sunday – Presentation of new wines in Eguisheim (Haut-Rhin)

April/May

Porte de Versailles in Paris – Wine competition at the Porte de Versailles

May

1st – Wine fair in Molsheim (Bas-Rhin)

Ascension – Wine fair in Guebwiller (Haut-Rhin)

June

3rd weekend – Petit Vin Blanc Festival in Nogent-sur-Marne (Marne) – alternate years, next 1987

11th – Kugelhopf (cake) fair in Ribeauvillé (Bas-Rhin)

Saturday nearest 24th – Festival of St John in Cumières (Marne)

Saturday nearest 24th – Festival of St John in Epernay (Marne)

Saturday nearest 24th – Festival of St John in Hautvillers (Marne)

Saturday nearest 24th – Festival of St John in Rheims (Marne)

July

Middle of the month – Wine fair in Barr (Bas-Rhin)

3rd weekend – fair in Ribeauvillé (Haut-Rhin)

3rd weekend – Riesling festival in Riquewihr (Haut-Rhin)

Saturday after 14th – Fête des Guinguettes d'Europe in Husseren-les-Châteaux (Haut-Rhin)

End of the month – Wine festival in Wellolsheim (Haut-Rhin)

Last weekend – Wine festival in Mittelbergheim (Bas-Rhin)

August

1st Sunday – Fair of the almond trees in Mittelwihr (Haut-Rhin)

1st weekend – Alsace wine festival in Bennwihr (Haut-Rhin)

1st weekend – Wine festival, Au Pays du Brans, in Turkheim (Haut-Rhin)

1st fortnight – Regional fair of Alsace wines in Colmar (Haut-Rhin)

1st fortnight – Wine festival in Dambach-la-Ville (Bas-Rhin)

Middle of the month – Wine mini fair in Obernai (Bas-Rhin)

3rd weekend – Festival of arts and crafts of Riesling wines in Scherwiller (Bas-Rhin)

Last Sunday – Vintage festival in Eguisheim (Haut-Rhin)

Last Sunday – Champagne festival of the Aube vineyards in the Aube district once every three years, next 1987

September

1st Sunday – Fête des ménétriers in Ribeauvillé (Haut-Rhin)

Beginning of the month – Wine festival in Wolxheim (Bas-Rhin)

13th/14th – Val de St Grégoire festival in Zimmerbach (Haut-Rhin)

2nd Sunday – Festival of St Vincent in Ambonnay (Marne)

2nd Sunday – Champage wine fair in Bar-sur-Aube (Aube)

3rd week – Harvest festival in Bagneux (Seine-et-Marne)

3rd week – Festival and wine fair in Charly-sur-Marne (Aisne)

Last weekend – Harvest festival in Seltz (Bas-Rhin)

Last weekend – Harvest festival in Valff (Bas-Rhin)

First weeks of October

Harvest festivals in various villages of Alsace: Barr, Hunawihr, Itterswiller, Katzenthal, Niedermorschwihr, Obernai, Rosheim.

October

1st Saturday – Harvest festival in Paris/Montmârtre

1st weekend – Harvest festival in Barr (Bas-Rhin)

1st Sunday – Harvest festival in Suresnes (Seine-et-Marne)

1st fortnight – Harvest festival in Hunawihr (Haut-Rhin)

1st fortnight – Harvest festival in Katzenthal (Haut-Rhin)

2nd weekend – Grand Festival of the grape in Molsheim (Bas-Rhin)

3rd weekend – Harvest festival in Marlenheim (Bas-Rhin)

3rd weekend – Harvest festival in Obernai (Bas-Rhin)

3rd week – Wine competition at the Porte de Versailles in Paris

CENTRAL AND EASTERN FRANCE

January

Sunday nearest 22nd – Festival of St Vincent in Gevrey-Chambertin (Côte d'Or)

22nd – Festival of St Vincent in Champlitte (Haute-Saône)

Sunday nearest 22nd – Wine show in Château d'Aine Aze (Saône-et-Loire)

Sunday nearest 22nd – Wine show in Mâcon (Saône-et-Loire)

Sunday nearest 22nd – Festival of St Vincent in Coulanges-la-Vineuse (Yonne)

March

Saturday before Palm Sunday – Wine fair in Lugny (Saône-et-Loire)

April

End of the month – Wine auction in Nuits-St-Georges (Côte d'Or)

End of April/beginning of May

Election of queen of the wines of the Mâconnais in Château d'Aine (Saône-et-Loire)

May

3rd week – Mâcon fair and French wines competition in Mâcon (Saône-et-Loire)

July

3rd Sunday – Wine festival in Arbois (Jura)

August

15th – Vin de Table fair in Chagny (Saône-et-Loire)

Last weekend – Wine festival in St Pourcin-sur-Sioule/Allier (Auvergne)

September

Savoie fair in Chambéry (Savoie)

1st Sunday – Fêtes de Biou wine festival in Arbois (Jura)

9th–10th – International festival of wines in Dijon (Côte d'Or)

Middle of the month – Wine festival in St Jean-de-Vaux (Saône-et-Loire)

October

Last Saturday – Fête Raclet, exhibition and sale of Beaujolais Primeur in Romanèche-Thorins (Saône-et-Loire)

End of the month – Presentation of Beaujolais Primeurs in Lacenas (Rhône)

November

Beginning of the month – Sale and exhibition of Beaujolais Crus in Fleurie (Rhône)

1st fortnight – Gastronomic fair in Dijon (Côte d'Or)

2nd weekend – Sauvignon festival in St Bris-le-Vineux (Yonne)

Middle of the month – Exhibition and competition of Crus Juliénas in Juliénas (Rhône)

End of the month – Exhibition and competition of Brouilly and Côtes de Brouilly in Cercie (Rhône)

3rd weekend – *Les Trois Glorieuses* wine fair of the Côte d'Or in Beaune. Saturday: Château Clos de Vougeot; Sunday: auction in the market then dinner in the Hospices de Beaune; Monday: Paulée de Meursault.

Last Saturday – Wine fair in Chablis (Yonne)

December

1st weekend – Competition and exhibition of the 11 Crus Appellations of Beaujolais in Villefranche (Rhône)

Middle of the month – Baptême Parisien of the Beaujolais Nouveau in Villefranche (Rhône)

Middle of the month – Sale of the Hospice de Beaujeu wines in Beaujeu (Rhône)

SOUTHERN FRANCE

January

Beginning of the month – Wine competition of the Aude in Carcassonne (Aude)

Weekend in middle of month – Competition for tasting new wines in Orange (Vaucluse)

Sunday nearest 22nd – Wine market in Ampuis (Rhône)

February

Beginning of the month – Fête du Raisin in Valbonne (Alpes Maritimes)

March

Weekend a fortnight before Easter – Wine exhibition in Vinsobres (Drôme)

April

Côtes du Rhône Gardoise Wine Fair in Villeneuve-lès-Avignon (Gard)

Middle of the month – Var and Provence wine festival in Brignoles (Var)

End of the month – Spring wine fair in Narbonne (Aude)

25th – Festival of St Mark in Châteauneuf-du-Pape (Vaucluse)

Last Sunday – Festival of St Vincent in Tavel (Gard)

May

Festival of Côtes du Rhône wines in Vacqueyras (Vaucluse)

Ascension – Vins de Pays festival in Roquemaure (Gard)

June

June – Cherry festival in Caromb (Vaucluse)

Middle of the month – Côtes de Provence wine festival in Le Thoronet (Var)

Middle of the month – Côtes de Provence wine festival in St Raphaël (Var)

July

Beginning of the month – festival of beer and sauerkraut in Lacapelle-Marival (Lot)

1st fortnight – Wine festival in Trausse Minervois (Aude)

2nd fortnight – Wine and local products festival in Minerve (Hérault)

3rd week – Wine fair in Buisson (Rhône)

July and August

Permanent wine exhibition in the amphitheatre grotto in Orange (Vaucluse)

August

Summer feast in Caromb (Vaucluse)

Wine festival in Baixas (Pyrénées Orientales)

Muscat festival in Rivesaltes (Pyrénées Orientales)

1st Sunday – vine festival in Nice (Alpes Maritimes)

1st fortnight – Wine festival in Lézignan (Aude)

1st fortnight – Great wine festival in Saissac (Aude)

2nd weekend – Wine fair in St Antonin (Var)

Weekend of 15th – Great wine festival in Stade Sigean (Aude)

Weekend of 15th – Feria de Béziers (Wine fountain) in Béziers (Hérault)

2nd weekend – Wine and vine festival in Fréjus (Var)

2nd fortnight – Wine festival in Lagrasse (Aude)

2nd fortnight – Wine and local products festival in Minerve (Hérault)

Middle of the month – Wine festival in Estagel (Pyrénées Orientales)

Middle of the month – Wine fairs in Séguret (Vaucluse)

4th weekend – Vine festival in Le Plan de La Tour (Var)

4th weekend – Wine and vine festival in Ste Maxime (Var)

September

Harvest festival in La Cadière d'Azur (Var)

Festival of St Maurice in Caromb (Vaucluse)

1st weekend – Harvest festival in Grimaud (Var)

1st weekend – Wine festival in St Péray (Ardèche)

1st fortnight – Wine festival in Bram (Aude)

Middle of the month – Harvest festival in St Tropez (Var)

3rd weekend – Harvest festival in Bormes-les-Mimosas (Var)

3rd weekend – Announcement of the harvest in Châteauneuf-du-Pape (Vaucluse)

3rd weekend – Harvest festival in Tain l'Hermitage (Drôme)

3rd weekend – Harvest festival in Taradeau (Var)

End of the month – Corrida des vendanges in Arles (Bouches-du-Rhône)

Last Sunday – Corrida des vendanges in Nîmes (Gard)

October

2nd fortnight – International wine and vine fair in Montpellier (Hérault)

Middle of the month – Ball and festival for the wine harvest in Flottes (Lot)

3rd Sunday – New wine fair in Béziers (Hérault)

November

Beginning of the month – Côtes du Rhône competition in Vaison-la-Romaine (Vaucluse)

Middle of the month – Festival of the new wine in Lacapelle-Cahors (Lot)

December

1st Sunday – Wine fair in Cornas (Ardèche)

SOUTH–WEST FRANCE

January

18th – Festival of St Vincent in various villages in the Médoc and Graves areas (Gironde)

3rd Sunday – Festival of St Vincent in St Estèphe (Gironde)

April

2nd fortnight – spring wine festival in Gaillac (Tarn)

May

Spring wine festival in Bordeaux

Spring wine festival in Fronsac (Gironde)

Spring wine festival in Guyenne (Gironde)

Spring wine festival in Loupiac (Gironde)

Spring wine festival in Pomerol (Gironde)

Spring wine festival in St Emilion (Gironde)

Week of Ascension – Amageais Fair at Eauze (Gers)

21st – Wine festival in Montagne St-Emilion (Gironde)

End May/beginning June

Wine festival in Pomerol (Gironde)

June

1st weekend – Flower festival in Pauillac (Gironde)

19th – Wine festival at Ste Croix-du-Mont (Gironde)

19th – Flower festival in various villages in the Médoc and Graves areas (Gironde)

3rd week – Flower festival in Loupiac (Gironde)

July

14th – Goat cheese fair at Plaisance (Gers)

Weekend nearest 14th – Wine fair in Sigoulès (Dordogne)

End of the month – Beer festival in Thiviers (Dordogne)

August

Second week – Regional products fair in Riscle (Gers)

Middle of the month – Wine festival in Gaillac (Tarn)

Middle of the month – Wine and cheese fair in St Aulaye (Dordogne)

September

First days of the month – Chasselas festival in Moissac (Tarn-et-Garonne)

1st Sunday – Folklore festival of the vines in Burie (Charente-Maritime)

2nd Sunday – Wine-growers' festival in Cazeneuve (Gers)

12th – Wine festival in Bordeaux (Gironde)

12th – Wine festival in Fronsac (Gironde)

18th – Ban des vendanges (announcement of the harvest) in various villages in the Médoc and Graves areas (Gironde)

19th – Announcement of the harvest in St Emilion (Gironde)

Middle of the month – Harvest festival in Amarans (Tarn)

Middle of the month – Harvest festival in Tauriac (Tarn)

4th Sunday – Announcement of the harvest in St Emilion (Gironde)

Last Sunday – Harvest festival in Albas (Lot)

October

1st Sunday – Harvest festival in Pouillon (Landes)

1st Sunday – Harvest festival in Semussac (Charente Maritime)

2nd Sunday – Harvest festival in Berneuil (Charente Maritime)

2nd Sunday – Harvest festival in Clavette (Charente Maritime)

2nd Sunday – Wine harvest festival in les Réaux (Charente Maritime)

2nd Sunday – Harvest festival in Rouffiac (Charente Maritime)

3rd Sunday – Wine harvest festival in Breuillet (Charente Maritime)

3rd Sunday – Wine harvest fair in St Porchaire (Charente Maritime)

Last Sunday – Harvest festival in Cassaigne (Gers)

Last Sunday – Festival of La Gerlande in Fronsac (Gironde)

Last Sunday – Wine harvest ball in Fronton (Haute-Garonne)

Last Sunday – Harvest festival at St Rome-de-Cernon (Aveyron)

30th/31st – Harvest festival in Beauvais-sur-Matha (Charente Maritime)

November

Harvest festival in Chaniers (Charente Maritime)

2nd fortnight – New wine festival in Gaillac (Tarn)

20th – Autumn festival in Guyenne (Gironde)

General Wine-buying Guide

There are many ways of buying wine in the wine regions of France. Some growers, particularly the smaller ones, have *Vente Dégustation* (taste and buy) signs on the roadside and actively encourage passing trade. Other larger estates, often those producing the best wines of the district, have fixed arrangements or exclusivities with brokers (*négociants*) so that buying from them is impossible or, at best, limited to a few bottles. In between there exists every sort of opportunity to purchase and even if you cannot buy direct from the very best estates, you will find that most towns, even smallish ones, have a wine shop that offers a good selection of wines from the surrounding district and they should be able to give you helpful advice.

Appointments

Appointments are not always necessary, but in most cases the courtesy of a letter prior to your departure giving the approximate date of your visit, followed by a telephone call when you reach the district, is advisable. The bigger establishments, particularly those which export abroad, will be well geared up to receiving visitors, and your guide is likely to speak English. However, at the smaller *vignerons* someone may literally have to be called in from a field to deal with you.

This raises the problem of language. It is obviously helpful to have a working knowledge of French, and most *vignerons* will make the effort to try and understand you if you make the effort to speak their language.

Wines

The range of wines available varies from property to property, from just one speciality to a great many fine wines. Some establishments make more than one type or colour of wine, or may even produce more than one *cuvée* of the same wine. There may be more than one vintage of a wine available, especially if some has not sold from previous, poorer years. Remember, when a *vigneron* is selling, every year is fantastic! So try and have a clear idea of what you are after before you enter the premises.

Vintages

Most of the vintages available for purchase will be very young. Some wines are of course best drunk young or even '*de l'année*' (in the year in which they are made)

and so this presents no problem. But you may wish to purchase some wines for laying down. The French attitude to ageing and maturing wine is a particular one. They tend to drink wines much younger than the rest of us, and youthful tannin is not regarded as a drawback. In France it would be considered quite normal to drink a 1983 vintage red Bordeaux Supérieur, i.e. a more humble classification, in 1985. Ask a *vigneron* about the keeping qualities of a wine, and then perhaps leave it a year or so longer than he suggests. However, do beware: some wines have a very fruity, fresh style when young, and then a very different, more mellow style when mature. You have to decide how you like your wine.

A vintage guide can be useful so long as you only use it as general information. Sometimes properties produce excellent wines in indifferent or poor years, and the reverse is also true. Allow your palate to be your guide.

Prices

It is impossible to give guidance on the prices of wines in each appellation because they change all the time (usually in an upward direction). Most *vignerons* selling wine direct will have a printed tarif card, so while tasting you will be able to assess value for money. Others have prices chalked on a blackboard or a similar informal system, but some publish no prices and doubtless weigh you up and quote a price accordingly. Haggling is not advisable if you are only buying a small quantity, say under 100 bottles. The French do not normally give receipts, but you may need one when returning through Customs.

Those larger concerns which have UK or American agents may be less anxious to sell you any bottles direct from their cellars, so do not press if they are reluctant, but take the name and address of their agent.

Tasting

The larger, more prestigious, companies should be able to give you a tour of their cellars followed by a tasting. The more humble establishments should at least be able to offer you a tasting. The more communicative and appreciative you are, the more responsive your hosts will be.

Express an interest in the region, and perhaps non-commitally mention other people you have visited.

Some *vignerons* get on well with their neighbours and won't mind your being reasonably complimentary about them, others have a jealous attitude, so don't be over-enthusiastic about the local competition. You may hear some amusing opinions expressed about neighbours. People from other wine districts are usually regarded as 'foreigners'.

Usually, if your guide is the *patron*, or is actively involved in the wine-making, he will taste with you. Tasting is not an exercise in getting the wine from the glass to your throat as quickly as possible and then deciding in retrospect whether or not you liked it. Hold the glass by the stem or base and first of all look at the wine, even if there is not much light in the cellar. This allows you to judge its clarity and colour (if it is a sample drawn from a cask don't worry if it is not very clear). Then smell it with several short sniffs and try to identify the individual aromas. Finally *taste* it; allow the wine to swirl around so that it reaches the entire inside of your mouth. Try and pick out the individual components of the taste, particularly the fruit, the acidity, and the tannin (in reds and rosés only). When you have finished swirling and analyzing, spit the wine out. It is not advisable to swallow when tasting, since you may have several samples to taste in a day, as well as having to drive. No-one is offended by spitting out the wine. In some cellars spitting on the floor is quite acceptable, in others receptacles are provided. In the cellars of Château Guiraud in Sauternes there is a long porcelain wall urinal for spitting into. To avoid embarrassment, it is best to follow the directions and example of your host.

If you find some of the wines in the range different, outstanding or atypical do ask why and discuss these wines with your host. Most wine-makers are delighted to talk about their wines, and the more interest you show and the more you enthuse, the happier and more hospitable they become. If you succeed in establishing a good rapport you may be fortunate enough to taste some older vintages, which most *vignerons* tuck away for themselves. However, do not be surprised if they are not offered to you for sale, or if they are, then only in small quantities, and at high prices.

A little note of thanks when you return, especially if you have re-tasted the wines and can comment on their suitability to your climate, is always well received, and ensures a more friendly welcome another year.

Travelling with wines
Assuming that you will be travelling by car, remember that wines do not like extremes of temperature. If wines are left in the boot of a parked car in sunshine, they can seep past their corks as the temperature rises and thus be ruined. Direct sunlight shining through the glazed rear of hatchbacks on to uncovered bottles of wine creates even higher temperatures and can ruin wine. In winter, severe frost can freeze wines left in a car overnight, causing them to push their corks out. Try to keep the wines as near as possible to the temperature of the cellar from which they come.

If you purchase more bottles than the duty-free limit applicable in your country of origin you will be required to pay the duty and tax on the number of bottles by which you exceed the limit.

Glossary of Wine Terms

Acetic A wine with a vinegary smell, sharp and harsh on the palate.

Acidity A necessary element in a wine, giving it crispness and freshness; a natural content of grape juice. Too little acidity causes a wine to taste flat; too much makes it harsh and tart.

Aftertaste The flavour a wine leaves on the palate after it has been swallowed. A wine in which this quality predominates is said to have a good finish.

Alcohol The essential substance which is created by the fermentation of grape juice; some or most of the juice's sugar content is converted to alcohol. A wine with a high alcohol content has body and substance as well as the ability to keep and improve with age, a wine with a low alcohol level is thin and weak. Alcohol is, of course, the cause of intoxication. Most wines have a level of alcohol of between 10 and 15 degrees, although some inexpensive Vins de Pays and Vins de Table have a lower level than this. The enzymes which cause fermentation are killed off at higher levels, causing the process to cease. Wines which have a higher alcohol content, such as apéritifs, port and sherry, are made by adding *eau de vie*, distilled wine.

Apéritif A wine which is drunk before a meal to stimulate the appetite and taste-buds. It is often a fortified wine, usually served chilled, such as sherry or vermouth. A popular apéritif in France is Kir, a mixture or Bourgogne Aligoté, a crisp dry white wine, and Cassis, a liqueur made from blackcurrants.

Assemblage The technique of blending different wines from the same region.

Aroma This describes the way a wine smells. A more familiar wine term is *bouquet*. Wine experts have an extensive vocabulary to describe this elusive quality, usually with reference to other things such as fruits, flowers and spices.

Astringent A bitter, acrid taste which can be caused by an excess of both tannin and acidity. If present in a young wine it can diminish or disappear with age.

Austere Not necessarily a fault in a wine. The term describes a quality of taste which may be lacking in softness or mellowness, with a less immediate and obvious appeal.

Balance The relationship between the basic elements of a wine – acidity, body, alcohol and tannin – which combine to create the final effect on the palate.

Beefy A full-bodied red wine which has a strong presence in the mouth; chewy is used in a similar context.

Beeswings The translucent flakes of sediment found in old wines such as port.

Bite Often used to describe the taste of a wine which has a predominant acidity, not necessarily unacceptable in a full-bodied wine.

Bitter Taste usually caused by an excess of tannin, often present in new wines.

Blackcurrants Used to describe both aroma and taste.

Blanc de Blancs A white wine made exclusively from white grapes.

Bland A wine with little character and a flat, uninspired taste.

Body The way in which a wine's presence is sensed in the mouth. A full-bodied wine is the result of a high alcohol level and good balance.

Bottle age The period of time that a wine spends in the bottle, as opposed to its vintage. Some wines are aged in the cask for several years before bottling, others are bottled immediately.

Bouquet Perhaps the most difficult quality of a wine to define but, loosely, its smell. (See Aroma)

Brut Bone-dry, a wine in which all the sugar has been converted into alcohol.

Carbonic maceration A technique in which the grapes are macerated prior to fermentation in order to reduce the period of time before the wine is ready for consumption.

Capsule The small sleeve which is fitted over the cork. With fine wines these are often still made of lead foil but plastic is now widely used, and is more difficult to remove.

Caramel A bouquet which has a sweet and/or burnt quality.

Cave A cellar with a stable temperature in which wine is stored, either in casks or bottles, prior to shipping or sale.

Caveau A place, open to the public, where wines can be tasted and bought.

Cave Co-opérative A place where the grapes from a number of individual growers are vinified and marketed.

Cedar A bouquet which has elements of sweetness and spice.

Cépage The grape variety.

Chais A wine storage place, above ground.

Chambrer Allowing a bottle of wine to come slowly up to room temperature after it is taken from the cellar.

Chaptalisation The technique of adding sugar to the fermenting must when the natural sugar level of the grape is too low to create the desired level of alcohol. This is sometimes caused by unsuitable weather conditions prior to the harvest.

Chewy (see Beefy).

Clean A wine that is fresh in both taste and *bouquet*, with no undesirable elements to mar one's enjoyment.

Corsé A term used to describe a full-bodied, robust wine with a high degree of alcohol.

Coupage The technique of blending wines of different origins.

Crémant Half-sparkling, 'creaming'.

Cru Vintage.

Cuvée Blend.

Decanting The process of pouring the contents of a wine bottle carefully into another container (decanter) in order to leave any sediment behind, usually only necessary with wines of a good age.

Dégorgement The technique of removing the sediment from the bottle by releasing a small amount of wine after the secondary fermentation needed to create sparkling wines, as in the case of Champagne.

Demi-sec Sweet (of Champagne).

Depth This can relate both to the colour of a wine and to its overall character.

Development The progress and changes that take place in a wine during the ageing process.

Distillation The process of heating wine, or other fermented juices, and condensing the vapour which is given off, to produce a spirit with a high degree of alcohol.

Dry A wine which has little or no residual sugar after fermentation.

Earthy A term often used to describe the taste and aroma of, usually, a full-bodied red wine.

Eau de vie A generic term given to distilled liquors. Brandy is an *eau de vie* made from wine. *Eau de vie* can also be made from other fruits, such as cherries (Kirsch), apples (Calvados) and plums (Slivowitz).

Fading The loss of colour, bouquet and taste of a wine as it is affected by ageing.

Fat Often used to describe a wine with qualities of body, alcohol and sweetness.

Finesse A term used to describe a fine wine with subtle qualities of taste and bouquet.

Finish The aftertaste of a wine. A wine with a good finish lingers on the palate long after being swallowed.

Firm A wine that is well made and well balanced, with a definable character.

Flabby The opposite of firm, usually caused by a lack of acidity and/or tannin.

Flat A thin wine with little or no bouquet and an uninspired taste.

Fortified A wine which has had *eau de vie* added to it to increase its alcohol content. Most apéritif wines are made in this way, as are port, sherry, Madeira and many dessert wines.

Fresh Usually used to describe young wines with a pleasing bouquet and taste.

Fruity A wine in which the quality of the grape is still evident in both the bouquet and taste.

Full-bodied A wine which has a high alcohol content combined with a good balance of tannin and acidity.

Hard A term used to describe a wine which has a predominant quality of tannin in its taste. Often used in reference to young wines.

Heavy One (unfavourable) stage further than full-bodied, when the taste and alcohol of a wine are excessive and cloying.

Lean A not unfavourable term for a wine, in the same vein as firm and austere.

Liquoreux A sweet wine with a high alcohol content.

Maderized A wine that has aged too much and is going brown through oxidization.

Marc The grape skins left behind in the press after the juice has been extracted. These can be distilled to make cheap brandy, *eau de vie de marc.*

Méthode Champenoise A technique for producing sparkling wines in which a secondary fermentation takes place after bottling, causing a natural sparkle in the wine.

Millésimé The wine produced from a specific vineyard in a good year.

Moëlleux A term used to describe a smooth, well rounded, luscious wine.

Mousseux A sparkling wine.

Must The fermenting grapes after they have been crushed.

Négociant A broker or wine merchant who is also involved in the control or the production of wine he sells through the growers who supply him – either with grapes or newly made wine.

Oak The wood favoured for casks, used as an element in the ageing process and to impart both colour and tannin to wines and spirits like brandy.

Oenology The study and science of wines.

Oxidization The effect on wine of ageing or exposure to the air, through an unsound cork for example. It causes a red wine to take on a brownish tint.

Pasteurization A technique in which the wine is heated in order to destroy the active bacteria remaining after fermentation is complete.

Pétillant A wine which has a very small amount of effervescence.

Phylloxera An aphid which destroys vines. In the middle of the nineteenth century it wiped out vast areas of Europe's vineyards. The problem was only resolved by grafting new vines on to American root stocks which were resistant to the disease.

Pourriture noble 'Noble rot', a mould which forms on ripe grapes creating a highly concentrated sugary juice from which sweet, highly alcoholic wines such as Sauternes are made.

Ullage The proportion of wine or spirit which is lost through a wooden cask by evaporation. Known poetically as 'the angels' share'.

Sec Slightly sweet (of Champagne).

Severe A wine which lacks softness, often caused by high acidity and/or tannin.

Sharp This usually relates to an excess of acidity in both the bouquet and the taste of a wine.

Spritzig A German word describing wines which have a slight tingle on the palate.

Stalky A word used to describe the taste of a wine. It often relates to an excess of tannin caused by leaving the skins and stalks of the grapes together with the juice too long during fermentation.

Supple A favourite term used to suggest a well-balanced wine.

Sweet A wine that contains a quantity of sugar. This can be the result of a high level of sugar in the grapes before fermentation, as in the case of Sauternes, or by the addition of *eau de vie* to the must before fermentation is complete, leaving residual sugar, as in the case of port.

Tannin A basic element of wine, vital to the taste. It is derived from the skins and stalks of the grapes.

Tart A term used to describe an acidic wine.

Thin Wine which lacks body and is low in alcohol.

Vin de garde A wine to keep, one that ages well.

Viticulture The science of vine cultivation.

Vinification The process of converting grapes into wine.

Vintage wine Wine made from the grapes of one year only.

Woody A wine that has been kept for too long in the cask.

Bold numbers indicate photographs

ACKNOWLEDGEMENTS

I have had invaluable assistance and encouragement from a number of people in the course of making this book and I would like to thank them all. In particular, Colin Webb, who found a way of turning what was initially only an idea and an ambition into a reality, and for this more than mere thanks are due.

I would also especially like to thank Graham Chidgey and Lorne Mackillop for compiling the wine buying guides which appear at the end of each region. Graham has been in the wine trade for 30 years and his work takes him on regular monthly visits to France where he is one of the leading independant buyers of Claret and Burgundy. His excellent book *Wines of Burgundy* was first published in 1977 and reprinted in 1984. Lorne has been a wine merchant for 10 years and in 1984 became the youngest Master of Wine in this country. He is currently on the Education committee of the Institute of Masters of Wine. I am most grateful to both of them for their meticulous work and for the expert knowledge which they have shared with me, and to Graham in particular for explaining the art of professional wine tasting.

Anne Dobell, Mary Trewby and Gillian Denton are also owed a debt of thanks for their editing skills and thoroughness in dealing with my text – and checking my French spelling. I must also thank Bernard Higton for being very indulgent with my preferences when it came to picture selection, and Vivien Bowler for bringing it all together so smoothly.

I would also like to thank John Miller for his skills with the black and white prints and Julien Busselle and Tim Myers for their long hours helping to sort, edit and file thousands of colour transparencies. And many thanks are owed to Pat Busselle for looking after everything during my absence.

Food and Wine from France, in London, were extremely helpful with information concerning wine fairs and harvesting dates, and the regional offices of the Comité Interprofessionnel des Vins and the Syndicat d'Initiative provided me with an abundance of useful information on each of their respective wine areas.

Finally, thanks to all the kind and helpful *vignerons* I met who so freely gave me friendship and hospitality and helped to make it all so enjoyable.

THE Michelin maps in this book will help you explore the wine regions of France. But since they are only extracts, just think where a whole map could take you.

Amusez-vous bien.

Michelin publish 73 maps, 24 tourist guides and one hotel and restaurant guide (the famous red one).

And this is only for France.

MAKE SURE IT'S A MICHELIN